The Contemporary Church
and the Early Church

The Evangelical Theological Society Monograph Series

VOLUME 4
Did Jesus Teach Salvation By Works?
The Role of Works in Salvation in the Synoptic Gospels
—Alan P. Stanley

VOLUME 5
Has God Said?
Scripture, the Word of God, and the Crisis of Theological Authority
—John Douglas Morrison

VOLUME 6
The Light of Discovery:
Studies in Honor of Edwin M. Yamauchi
—John D. Wineland, editor

VOLUME 7
The Lord Is the Spirit:
The Authority of the Holy Spirit in Contemporary Theology and Church Practice
—John A. Studebaker Jr.

VOLUME 8
The Sinner in Luke
—Dwayne H. Adams

The Contemporary Church and the Early Church

Case Studies in Ressourcement

Edited by
Paul A. Hartog

◉PICKWICK *Publications* · Eugene, Oregon

THE CONTEMPORARY CHURCH AND THE EARLY CHURCH
Case Studies in *Ressourcement*

Evangelical Theological Society Monograph Series 9

Copyright © 2010 Wipf and Stock Publishers. All rights reserved. Except for brief quotations in critical articles or reviews, no part of this book may be reproduced in any manner without prior written permission from the publisher. Write: Permissions, Wipf and Stock Publishers, 199 W. 8th Ave., Suite 3, Eugene, OR 97401.

Pickwick Publications
An Imprint of Wipf and Stock Publishers
199 W 8th Ave., Suite 3
Eugene, OR 97401

ISBN 13: 978-1-60608-899-9

Scripture quotations taken from the New American Standard Bible®, Copyright © 1960, 1962, 1963, 1968, 1971, 1972, 1973, 1975, 1977, 1995 by The Lockman Foundation. Used by permission. (www.Lockman.org)

Cataloging-in-publication data:

The contemporary church and the early church : case studies in ressourcement / edited by Paul A. Hartog

    Evangelical Theological Society Monograph Series 9

    xii + 250 p. ; 23 cm. Includes bibliographical references.

    ISBN 13: 978-1-60608-899-9

    1. Church history—Primitive and early church, ca. 30–600. 2. Church. I. Hartog, Paul A. II. Title. III. Series.

BR165 C9 2010

Manufactured in the U.S.A.

*I dedicate this compilation to my three children.
May they become discerning heirs of the tradition.*

Contents

Acknowledgments / ix

Abbreviations / x

List of Contributors / xi

1. The Complexity and Variety of Contemporary Church—Early Church Engagements
   —Paul A. Hartog / 1

2. Learning from Patristic Evangelism and Discipleship
   —Edward Smither / 27

3. Learning from Patristic Community Formation
   —Rex D. Butler / 50

4. Learning from Patristic Use of the Rule of Faith
   —Bryan M. Litfin / 76

5. Learning from Patristic Responses to Cultural Opposition
   —W. Brian Shelton / 100

6. Learning from Patristic Preaching of Social Ethics
   —Brian J. Matz / 131

7. Learning from Patristic Christology
   —Francis X. Gumerlock / 155

8. Evangelicals and the Quest for the Historical Church—A Lutheran Response
   —Glen L. Thompson / 180

9. Evangelicals and the Tensions of *Ressourcement*—A Baptist Response
   —Paul A. Hartog / 201

Bibliography / 229

Acknowledgments

❖ THE WRITING of books often "takes a community." I wish to thank Matt LaPine who, while serving as a research assistant, formatted the footnotes and bibliography. Martha Hartog proofed various drafts with a careful eye and ready pen. Amy Kramer manifested exemplary patience in the inter-library loan department. Tony Byrne, George Houghton, and David Ponter traced down a few intractable materials for me. I also thank Christian Amondson, Charlie Collier, Diane Farley, Patrick Harrison, and Chris Spinks of Wipf and Stock Publishers for their support. Finally, I am grateful for the Patristics and Medieval History Section of the Evangelical Theological Society, which provides an academic context conducive to valuable discussion, refinement, and debate. Most of the essays in this volume were the subject of discussion at the society's annual meeting in 2008. May readers of these contributions and responses feel as if they were at that forum in person, gleaning from both the noteworthy agreements and significant disagreements among the panelists.

Abbreviations

ACCS	Ancient Christian Commentary on Scripture
ACW	Ancient Christian Writers
ANF	*Ante-Nicene Fathers*
CCSL	Corpus Christianorum: Series latina
ECF	The Early Church Fathers
EEC	*Encyclopedia of Early Christianity*, edited by Everett Ferguson (2nd ed.; New York: Garland, 1997)
EECh	*Encyclopedia of the Early Church*, edited by Angelo Di Berardino, translated by Adrian Walford (2 vols.; New York: Oxford, 1992)
ETS	Evangelical Theological Society
FC	Fathers of the Church
LCL	Loeb Classical Library
NPNF1/2	*Nicene and Post-Nicene Fathers*, Series 1/2
OECT	Oxford Early Christian Texts
OrChrAn	Orientalia christiana analecta
PG	Patrologia graeca
PL	Patrologia latina
RAC	*Reallexikon für Antike und Christentum*, edited by Theodor Klauser et al. (22 vols.; Stuttgart: Hiersemann, 1950–)
WSA	The Works of Saint Augustine: A Translation for the 21st Century

Contributors

Rex D. Butler, Associate Professor of Church History and Patristics, New Orleans Baptist Theological Seminary (PhD, Southwestern Baptist Theological Seminary)

Francis X. Gumerlock, Professor of Historical, Biblical, and Systematic Theology, Providence Theological Seminary (PhD, Saint Louis University)

Paul A. Hartog, Associate Professor of New Testament and Early Christian Studies, Faith Baptist Theological Seminary (PhD, Loyola University Chicago)

Bryan M. Litfin, Associate Professor of Theology, Moody Bible Institute (PhD, University of Virginia)

Brian J. Matz, Assistant Professor of Historical Theology, Carroll College (PhD, Saint Louis University; PhD, Katholieke Universiteit Leuven)

W. Brian Shelton, Associate Professor of Systematic and Historical Theology, Toccoa Falls College (PhD, Saint Louis University)

Edward Smither, Associate Professor of Church History and Intercultural Studies, Liberty Baptist Theological Seminary of Liberty University (PhD, University of Wales-Lampeter)

Glen L. Thompson, Professor of History, Wisconsin Lutheran College (PhD, Columbia University)

1

The Complexity and Variety of Contemporary Church —Early Church Engagements

Paul A. Hartog

❊ I HAVE watched with both anticipation and trepidation as a keen interest in the early church has recently blossomed among those who are self-acclaimed "evangelicals."[1] It is a source of personal satisfaction to recognize that the importance of one's academic *raison d'être* has been validated in wider circles. On an ecclesiastical level, this *ressourcement* "can be welcome news to many believers who wonder about the seemingly empty content and ahistoricalism of their worship services."[2] "The sons and daughters of modernity are rediscovering the neglected beauty of classical Christian teaching," declares Thomas Oden. "It is a moment of joy, of beholding anew what had been nearly forgotten, of hugging a lost child."[3] D. H. Williams exclaims, "A nerve within contemporary evangelicalism has been hit, and its effects are ushering in enormous potential change."[4]

---

1. Throughout my essays, I use "evangelical" broadly of those historical movements rooted in the Reformation that have emphasized personal conversation through faith in Christ as proclaimed in the gospel (the "evangel"). For an introduction to this and other uses of the term "evangelical," see Olson, *Pocket History of Evangelical Theology*, 7–13.

2. Williams, *Evangelicals and Tradition*, 12.

3. Thomas Oden in 2003, as quoted in Armstrong, "Future Lies in the Past," 23.

4. Williams, *Evangelicals and Tradition*, 15.

The Contemporary Church and the Early Chruch
The Status Quaestionis

At the same time, I must confess that I have my personal apprehensions. Some of the more "populist" conversations have been structured and led by those who are not patristic scholars by training. Moreover, "outside" observers sometimes form a monolithic view of "*the*" evangelical engagement with the church fathers.[5] The February 2008 issue of *Christianity Today* included an engaging article on "the recent upsurge of evangelical interest in patristics."[6] The piece explained, "One of the most promising developments among evangelical protestants is the recent 'discovery' of the rich biblical, spiritual, and theological treasures to be found within the early church."[7] I would maintain that such language of "*the*" recent discovery of the patristic period subtly (though unintentionally) masks the complexity and variety found among evangelicals revisiting the early church. It is also noteworthy that an entire section of this *Christianity Today* piece highlighted evangelicals "jumping ship" and joining the Roman Catholic and Eastern Orthodox communions.[8] In addition, the illustrations for the article—filled with candles, crucifixes, and Eucharistic vestments—perhaps confirmed a surface-level *ressourcement* in the minds of some.

Many trace evangelical *ressourcement* to 1977, when a group of forty-five evangelical leaders and scholars framed the "Chicago Call," a document bidding a return to the "historic" roots of Christianity. There were, of course, earlier rumblings and signs of things to come.[9] For example, in 1971, Geoffrey Bromiley published "The Promise of Patristic Study" in a volume entitled *Toward a Theology for the Future*.[10] Nevertheless,

---

5. For an explanation of the label "church fathers," see Litfin, *Getting to Know the Fathers*, 18–19.

6. Armstrong, "Future Lies in the Past," 22–29.

7. As quoted from the "Call for Papers" of the 2007 Wheaton Theology Conference. Selected proceedings were eventually published in Husbands and Greenman, *Ancient Faith for the Church's Future*.

8. Armstrong, "Future Lies in the Past," 27–28. See also Campbell, *New Faithful*; and Harper, *True Light*.

9. "Chicago Call of 1977." See Poe, "E. Glenn Hinson"; Hinson, "Some Things I've Learned"; and Shelton, "Resounding the Chicago Call."

10. Bromiley, "Promise of Patristic Studies." This piece, still worth reading, begins by

the "Chicago Call" garnered much publicity as it described the "pressing need to reflect upon the substance of the biblical and historic faith and to recover the fullness of this heritage."[11] Within a decade, about half a dozen of the leading signatories of the "Chicago Call" had left evangelicalism, including Peter Gillquist (to the Antiochian Orthodox Church) and Thomas Howard (to Roman Catholicism).[12] The topic of evangelicals converting to Roman Catholicism became a touchy subject in 2007, due to the well-publicized (re-)conversion of Francis Beckwith, who was serving as president of the Evangelical Theological Society.[13] In the public explanation of his journey back to Rome, Beckwith highlighted, among other things, his study of the church fathers.[14]

In August of 2007, after presenting a paper at the Fifteenth International Conference on Patristics Studies, I was approached by a young student from Regent's Park College, a "Baptist by heritage" constituent member of Oxford University. When this student discovered that I was a Baptist laboring in patristics, he seemed genuinely surprised. He went on to describe how he, a former Mennonite, had converted to Roman Catholicism after his academic study of Augustine. And he wondered why I also had not crossed the Tiber. This discussion was still running through my mind the next morning, as I was conversing with Everett Ferguson, a "free church" patriarch of patristic scholarship.[15] This true gentleman of early church studies, past president of the North American Patristics Society and previous editor of the *Journal of Early Christian Studies*, insisted (just as he did publicly at an Evangelical Theological Society session in 2000), that the church fathers are "more

---

stating, "Patristics is one of the most neglected areas in evangelical theology" (125). It ends by declaring, "Patristic study is in no sense an alternative to biblical study. It is nevertheless an important and salutary supplement both for the sake of biblical study and also for its own sake" (151).

11. "Chicago Call of 1977."

12. Armstrong, "Future Lies in the Past," 27. See Gillquist, *Becoming Orthodox*; and Howard, *Lead, Kindly Light*.

13. Of course, the road to conversion is a two-way street. See Mendoza, "Why Do Catholics Become Evangelicals?"

14. Hodges, "Prominent Evangelical Returns to Catholic Roots." One also thinks of the reception of J. Budziszewski into the Roman Catholic Church on Easter Sunday, 2004.

15. See Ferguson, "'Congregationalism' of the Early Church," in Williams, *Free Church*.

ours than theirs." I myself am not ready to divide up the inheritance of the fathers mathematically among their ecclesiastical descendants, but I am convinced that one can appreciate both the necessary corrective of the Reformation and the necessary foundation of the patristic period.[16]

When I was a graduate student at Loyola University Chicago, a Roman Catholic professor generalized, "Evangelicals know their Bibles, while Catholics know their history." John Henry Cardinal Newman already threw down the gauntlet when he claimed, "To be deep in history is to cease to be a Protestant."[17] Michael Haykin, a professor of church history and Reformed spirituality, counters, "Our forbears at the time of the Reformation well knew the benefit of studying the patristic era."[18] Recent studies have examined how the magisterial Reformers frequently cited the church fathers. One thinks, for example, of Peter Fraenkel's *Testimonia Patrum: The Function of Patristic Argument in the Theology of Philip Melanchthon* and Anthony Lane's *John Calvin: Student of the Church Fathers*.[19] Consider the optimistic approach of the Anglican John Jewel (1522–1571):

> But what say we of the fathers, Augustine, Ambrose, Hierome [Jerome], Cyprian, &c.? What shall we think of them, or what account may we make of them? They be interpreters of the word of God. They were learned men, and learned fathers; the instruments of the mercy of God, and vessels full of grace. We despise them not, we read them, we reverence them, and give thanks unto God for them. They are witnesses unto the truth, they were worthy pillars and ornaments in the church of God. Yet may they

---

16. Thomas Oden notes that "Protestants have a right to the Fathers. Athanasius is not owned by Copts, nor is Augustine owned by North Africans. These minds are the common possession of the whole church." Cited in Armstrong, "Future Lies in the Past," 29. "No one communion can represent itself as a privileged extension of the early church." Williams, *Evangelicals and Tradition*, 14.

17. D. H. Williams responds, "I hope I am able to prove Newman wrong by showing that the necessity of appropriating doctrinal history in the preservation of Christian orthodoxy is no less true for the Protestant free church than it is for any other species of Protestantism. To be 'deep in history' for evangelical Protestantism need not be and should not be oxymoronic." Williams, *Retrieving the Tradition*, 12.

18. Haykin, "Why Study the Fathers?"

19. Fraenkel, *Testimonia Patrum*; Lane, *John Calvin*. See also Backus, *Reception of the Church Fathers in the West*.

not be compared with the word of God. We may not build upon them: we may not make them the foundation and warrant of our conscience: we may not put our trust in them. Our trust is in the name of the Lord.[20]

The Puritan divine William Perkins, in his study *The Reformed Catholic*, claimed that the Reformation was a return to the early church.[21] The General Baptist "Orthodox Creed" of 1678 declared that the ancient creeds "ought thoroughly to be received and believed," since they "prevent heresy" and contain "all things in a brief manner that are necessary to be known, fundamentally, in order to our salvation."[22] After citing various early church fathers, the Pietest leader Philipp Jakob Spener argued that "it is the same Holy Spirit who is bestowed on us by God, who once effected all things in the early Christian, and he is neither less able nor less active today to accomplish the work of sanctification in us."[23] John Wesley, the father of Methodism, called the early church "that true, genuine Christianity, directing us to the strongest evidence of the Christian doctrine."[24]

As previously mentioned, the illustrations of the *Christianity Today* piece highlighted candles, crucifixes, and Eucharistic vestments. For many people, returning to the early church means adopting such liturgical accouterments in a form of "ancient-seeming worship."[25] The *Christianity Today* article noted that "younger evangelicals" are flocking to monasteries, observing the daily office and divine hours, abiding by the Christian calendar, and practicing Celtic spirituality.[26] "Break out the candles and

---

20. Cited in White, "Why Bother with History?" The spelling of "pillars" in this piece was originally "pillers."

21. See Webber, *Ancient-Future Faith*, 25.

22. The "Orthodox Creed" of 1678, Article 38. A contemporary Baptist, Stephen Wellum, describes the early church councils as "no doubt subservient to Scripture, but which we neglect and ignore to our peril." Wellum, "Standing on the Shoulders of Giants," 3. The entire volume of the *Southern Baptist Journal of Theology* that contains this Wellum essay was dedicated to "Learning from the Church Fathers."

23. Spener, *Pia Desideria*, 85.

24. As cited in Williams, *Evangelicals and Tradition*, 10.

25. Moore, "Listen Closely," 25.

26. See the critical analysis in Bradley, *Celtic Christianity*. Bradley concluded "that Celtic Christianity is less an actual phenomenon defined in historical and geographical

incense. Pray using the *lectio divina*. Tap all the riches of Christian tradition you can find."[27] One should note that crucifixes (representations of Christ attached to the cross) came into use in the fifth century.[28] The current notion of Lent was formed when the Easter fast was extended to forty days sometime between AD 300 and 325.[29] Advent would come later, as it had to await the acceptance of Christmas.[30] Pachomius, a fourth-century Egyptian, is often credited with the establishment of "cenobite" monasticism. As Everett Ferguson reminded me in our conversation at Oxford, when some speak of returning to "the early church," they unwittingly mean the church of the fourth and fifth centuries. This state of affairs seemed mildly to disappoint Professor Ferguson, whose lifetime of scholarship has especially focused upon the second and third centuries. But such tensions do highlight the complexity of going back to "the" early church.

Furthermore, Chris Armstrong's article in *Christianity Today* seemed to gloss over the various contemporary church–early church engagements currently taking place.[31] And I am not alone in this critical analysis. Trevin Wax declares, "It's true that this 'blast from the past' is taking place in evangelical life . . . I am glad to see the evangelical movement looking *backwards* for a change. It is deeply humbling to see the vastness of the Christian tradition and our speckled and shining history and then to discover we are part of something bigger than ourselves."[32] Yet Wax also protests, "[Chris] Armstrong's article points out the return to liturgy and tradition, but he leaves out the *variety* of ways that evangelicals are connecting with the past."[33] Wax insists, "I can't be pigeon-holed."[34]

---

terms than an artificial construct created out of wishful thinking, romantic nostalgia and the projection of all kinds of dreams about what should or might be" (vii).

27. Armstrong, "Future Lies in the Past," 26.
28. Snyder, *Ante Pacem*, 165.
29. See Sahas, "Lent."
30. The exact origins of Advent cannot be determined with certainty. The Council of Tours in 567 recognized Advent as a period of fasting before Christmas.
31. To be fair, one understands the natural limitations of magazine journalism.
32. Wax, "Evangelicalism's Blast from the Past."
33. Ibid.
34. Ibid.

The Complexity and Variety of Contemporary Church—Early Church Engagements

Professional historians recognize that broad brushes can never replicate the finer details of reality. The particularities of history make any monolithic understanding of "the" recent discovery of the early church not only naïve but also impossible. The patristic period spans about a half millennium of doctrinal and ecclesiastical developments. All historians concede that the sixth-century churches differed in various ways from the second-century churches, and even contemporaneous churches manifested regionally-formed and personality-driven disparities. Simplistic summaries of what "the early church" believed and practiced lack the necessary diachronic, regional, and other qualifications. One does not have to examine Peter Abelard's *Sic et Non* in order to understand that the fathers do not provide a uniform stance in theology and practice. While searching for the *vox Patrum*, one discovers that they do not sing in complete unison.[35] "The old temptation to concoct a single mind of the fathers, who are then made to speak in a convenient chorus, is implausible on historical grounds—as any straightforward reading will show—and it is also unhelpful in the practice of Christian life and learning."[36] In addition, one must also acknowledge the role of various "outside forces" (whether social, political, philosophical, or cultural) upon the development of patristic theology.[37]

In a further complication, evangelicalism itself is a multi-faceted historical movement with a manifold pedigree, manifesting divergent denominational, theological, and cultural emphases.[38] This variety has caused D. G. Hart to refer to the "wax nose" of evangelicalism, such that it can be twisted this way and that.[39] At times, the label "evangelical" seems

---

35. Robin Darling Young, a Roman Catholic scholar, refers to "the illusion that the fathers of the Church spoke with one voice or that they should have the last word—a nostalgic delusion that the fathers themselves would vehemently have rejected." Young, "Texts Have Consequences," 41.

36. Ibid.

37. "Sociologists tell us that the theology of every generation is conditioned by the culture through which it passes—and of course they are right. But whereas the sociologists are professedly indifferent to whether such a state of affairs is right or wrong, . . . theology cannot remain indifferent." Torrance, *Theology in Reconciliation*, 273.

38. See Dayton and Johnston, *Variety of American Evangelicalism*.

39. Hart, *Deconstructing Evangelicalism*, 16–17.

to be so supple as to be devoid of content.[40] Those *soi-disant* evangelicals seeking to engage ancient Christianity bring along with them divergent theological pre-commitments, purposes, approaches, and motivations.

What is "evangelicalism?"[41] Perhaps the most famous attempt to characterize the "evangelical" movement is the so-called Bebbington Quadrilateral, based upon David Bebbington's list of four standard characteristics.[42] The first emphasis is "biblicism," or a commitment to the authority of the Scripture. The second trait is "crucicentrism," or a soteriological focus on the atoning work of Jesus Christ on the cross. Third comes "conversionism," the belief that individuals need to be personally converted. The final quality is "activism," or the stress placed upon evangelism, missions, and other gospel ministry and service.[43]

Because of its complex history, "evangelicalism" is a large umbrella covering various subsets. There are Lutheran, Anabaptist, Reformed, Baptist, Wesleyan and Holiness, "historic" Fundamentalist, and Pentecostal and Charismatic forms.[44] In order to understand contemporary *American* evangelicalism in particular, one must understand the influences of the early church, the Reformation, the Great Awakenings, and the modernist-fundamentalist controversies. The "orthodox" theology of American evangelicalism is rooted in the Christology and Trinitarianism hammered out during the patristic period. Its soteriological emphasis upon salvation "by grace through faith" and its doctrine of

---

40. "Evangelicalism needs to be relinquished as a religious identity because it does not exist." Ibid., 16. "In truth, there is no such thing as evangelicalism." Hatch, "Response," 97. Cf. Dayton, "Some Doubts."

41. The word "evangelical" is used in differing senses in different contexts; for example, as a synonym for "Lutheran" in certain German-speaking environments (*evangelische*).

42. Bebbington, *Evangelicalism in Modern Britain*. Of course, Bebbington has faced some valid criticism. Scholars have especially questioned his thesis that evangelicalism proper began in the eighteenth century, as a result of the Enlightenment. See Haykin and Stewart, *Emergence of Evangelicalism*. Throughout my essays, I am using "evangelicalism" of those who are gospel-centered, emphasize personal conversion, and espouse biblical authority (which would include the Reformers themselves). Cf. J. I. Packer's "six belief-and-behavior principles" that characterize evangelicalism in Packer, "Stunted Ecclesiology?," 121–22.

43. In the words of Charles Spurgeon: "Brethren, do something; do something; do something." Spurgeon, *Lectures to My Students*, 217.

44. This list, of course, is representative and not comprehensive.

sola scriptura were refined in the Reformation.[45] Its experiential view of "conversionism" was largely influenced by the Great Awakenings. And the modernist-fundamentalist debates and their aftermath brought the question of biblical authority again to the fore.

Varieties of Engagement

Because of the complexity of these two terrains (contemporary evangelicalism and the patristic heritage), there is no single bridge that connects them. Evangelicals who engage the patristic past include proponents of a "Mere Christianity" wishing to be centered in the Great Tradition, advocates of worship renewal adopting liturgies from late antiquity, "restorationists" seeking to recreate the earliest house churches, "emerging" representatives claiming to free themselves from Enlightenment constructs, cultural critics applying "pre-Constantinian" insights to a "post-Christian" milieu, and apologists defending the notion of "orthodoxy" against popular and scholarly challenges.

Let us briefly examine, in a descriptive fashion, some of the varieties of contemporary church–early church engagements, along with the tensions that sometimes surface between these various endeavors. We should also acknowledge that there are overlaps between these models, so that some individuals may implement more than one paradigm. In addition, this litany is obviously not exhaustive.[46]

First, proponents of "Mere Christianity" have called for a purposeful return to the church fathers for the sake of "common consensus." In 1943, during the height of World War II, C. S. Lewis presented a series of radio lectures that were eventually published as *Mere Christianity*.[47] He wanted to present the basics of Christianity to his contemporary

---

45. The slogan *sola Scriptura*, states Anthony Lane, is the forthright concession and necessary reminder "that the church can err." Lane, "*Sola Scriptura*?," 324. While the church fathers "loved the scriptures immensely," since "Scripture was in the very air they breathed" and "nourished their souls," the fathers were still "susceptible to error." "We should always keep a critical eye out, submitting every doctrine to the penetrating light of the Word of God." Litfin, *Getting to Know the Church Fathers*, 20–21; 27.

46. One thinks, for example, of the patristic influence upon the recent renewal of "theological interpretation" of the Bible.

47. Lewis, *Mere Christianity*.

intellectuals who had not been immersed in Christian theology. Lewis feared a theological reflection estranged from the common roots and ancient consensus of the church. He described "mere Christianity" not as some insipid interdenominational religiosity but as "something positive, self-consistent and inexhaustible. . . . In the days when I still hated Christianity, I learned to recognize, like some all too familiar smell, that almost unvarying *something* which met me . . ."[48] Lewis maintained that "The only safety is to have a standard of plain, central Christianity ('mere Christianity' as Baxter called it) which puts the controversies of the moment in their proper perspective. Such a standard can be acquired only from the old books."[49]

Thomas Oden has called for a return to "paleo-orthodoxy" or "centered orthodoxy."[50] He writes, "The agenda for theology at the end of the twentieth century, following the steady deterioration of a hundred years and the disaster of the last few decades, is to begin to prepare the postmodern Christian community for its third millennium by returning again to the careful study and respectful following of the central tradition of classical Christian exegesis."[51] "The patristic stones the modern builders rejected must now become the major blocks for rebuilding upon the Chief Cornerstone, the unique theandric person, Jesus Christ."[52] Oden's own journey from theological liberalism to classical Christianity has been well chronicled.[53] His emphasis upon "paleo-orthodoxy" has led to the *Ancient Christian Commentary on Scripture*, "which brings together in talmudic format individual pericopes with representative commentaries from the writings of the Fathers."[54]

---

48. Lewis, "Introduction," 6.

49. Ibid., 4. The name Baxter refers to Richard Baxter, the seventeenth-century Puritan minister and theologian. Lewis continued, "It is a good rule, after reading a new book, never to allow yourself another new one till you have read an old one in between. If that is too much for you, you should at least read one old one to every three new ones."

50. Oden, *After Modernity*; *Requiem*; and *Rebirth of Orthodoxy*. See also Cutsinger, *Reclaiming the Great Tradition*.

51. Oden, *After Modernity*, 34. The entire passage is italicized in the original.

52. Ibid., 106.

53. See Hall, "Back to the Fathers"; and "Introduction," 7–12.

54. Mammana, "Orthodox Twenty-Somethings," 50. As another example of internal tensions within *ressourcement*, see the exchange concerning the ACCS series in Oden,

The Complexity and Variety of Contemporary Church—Early Church Engagements

In 2007, Paternoster Press published *Remembering our Future: Explorations in Deep Church*.[55] Like "Mere Christianity," the label "Deep Church" was also utilized by C. S. Lewis, who asserted that those Christians who retained the traditional notion of "supernatural" Christianity lacked a unifying name. Lewis penned, "May I suggest 'Deep Church'; or, [if] that fails in humility, Baxter's 'mere Christians.'"[56] In a manifestation of the complexity of *ressourcement*, some advocates of a "deep ecclesiology" have critiqued those anti-creedal and a-historical manifestations found within the "emerging" conversation.[57] The emerging church, claims Andrew Jones, possesses "a predisposition towards the 'mutability' of the gospel rather than its continuity."[58]

While the discipline of contemporary theology seems to prize innovation and the ability to "reason independently," the church fathers incessantly referred to apostolic tradition. As Christopher Hall notes, "the wisest Christian thinkers also recognized they were 'bearers of tradition,' a tradition founded on Scripture, subjected to critical examination, tested in the lives of 'countless men and women,' defended against critics, and 'elaborated in myriad social and cultural settings.'"[59] The "Vincentian canon" declares that orthodoxy and catholicity must "hold fast to what has been believed everywhere, always, and by all."[60] On the other hand, it should be noted that an irony lies beneath the surface of this oft-quoted snippet, for Vincent of Lérins opposed Augustinian theology.[61]

One must recognize that differences among Trinitarian denominations are real, and sometimes (ironically) these disparities can be traced

---

"Fighting about the Fathers." Cf. Young, "Texts Have Consequences," 40–43.

55. Walker and Bretherton, *Remembering our Future*.

56. Lewis, letter to the *Church Times*, February 8, 1952.

57. Jones, "Deep Church."

58. Ibid. At the same time, one should note that various emerging church leaders have formally disparaged the "seeker-sensitive" model.

59. Hall, *Reading Scripture with the Church Fathers*. See also Hall, *Learning Theology with the Church Fathers*.

60. Vincent of Lérins, *A Commonitory* 6 (*NPNF2* 11:132). D. H. Williams further notes that the Vincentian principle stems, even if indirectly, from Augustine's *On the Usefulness of Belief* 14.30–31. See Williams, *Retrieving the Tradition*, 34 n. 50.

61. See Williams, *Retrieving the Tradition*, 34 n. 50.

to variations among the church fathers themselves. When Justin Martyr described his chiliastic (millennial) views, he explained that "I and many others are of this opinion ... but, on the other hand, I signified to you that many who belong to the pure and pious faith, and are true Christians, think otherwise."[62] The fathers held to divergent practices as well. When Polycarp of Smyrna met with Anicetus of Rome, he claimed apostolic support for his Quartodeciman practice of Easter.[63] The two bishops could not agree, but Anicetus allowed Polycarp to celebrate the Eucharist, and they parted in peace with the issue unsettled.[64] Nevertheless, Quartodecimanism was later rejected by the Council of Nicaea.[65]

D. H. Williams contrasts the "apologetic-polemical" depiction of tradition, which emphasized its unity, and the "interecclesial" perspective, which admitted diversity on certain issues.[66] For example, Irenaeus "presents the catholic [universal] faith in monolithic style" while writing against the gnostics, but "in his intra-church activities, he knows all too well of the differences that exist and result in divided opinions."[67] Furthermore, a theological reductionism may lurk within some accounts of "mere Christianity," so that some minimize the necessary corrective of the Reformation or discard all "denominational distinctives."[68]

Second, leaders of "worship renewal" have appealed to the early church. Worship renewal has called churches beyond performance-centered, music-driven, culture-accommodating, and program-controlled

---

62. Justin Martyr, *Dialogue with Trypho* 80 (*ANF* 1:239).

63. See Hartog, *Polycarp and the New Testament*, 41–43. The Quartodecimans tied their Easter celebration to the Jewish calendar, which celebrated Passover on the fourteenth of Nissan, rather than consistently celebrating Easter on Sunday.

64. Eusebius *Hist. eccl.* 5.24.

65. The Greek text of "The Letter of the Synod in Nicaea to the Egyptians" declared, "All the brethren in the East who have hitherto followed the Jewish practice will henceforth observe the custom of the Romans and of yourselves and of all of us who from ancient times have kept Easter together with you."

66. Williams, *Evangelicals and Tradition*, 23.

67. Ibid., 23. See Eusebius *Hist. eccl.* 5.24.

68. Such reductionism "implicitly trivializes the points at issue that have defined Orthodoxy, Catholicism, Lutheranism, Anglicanism, and Reformed Christianity (not to mention Puritanism, Methodism, and the several denominations to emerge from those traditions)." Hart, "Born Again Free," 27.

models to a sense of worship beginning with God's initiative of grace that inspires human response. Some have turned to the "Convergence Movement," which "seeks to blend or merge" three major streams of thought and practice: "the Charismatic, Evangelical/Reformed and Liturgical/Sacramental."[69] One of the characteristic traits of this "Convergence Movement" is "an increased appetite to know more about the early church."[70]

The "elder statesman" of the worship renewal movement was Robert Webber, who popularized the label "ancient-future faith."[71] In 1978, Webber published *Common Roots: A Call to Evangelical Maturity*, which summoned its readers to study and appropriate the early church fathers. "My argument," wrote Webber, "is that the era of the early church (AD 100–500), and particularly the second century, contains insights which evangelicals need to recover."[72] Webber is perhaps most famous for his Ancient-Future Faith Series, published by Baker Books.[73] "The burden of *Ancient-Future Faith* is to say that the road to the future runs through the past."[74] Webber became a father figure to various younger evangelicals who wanted "to immerse themselves in the past and form a culture that is connected to the past, a culture that remembers its tradition as it moves into the future."[75] According to his critics, however, Webber's

---

69. Boosahda and Sly, "Convergent Movement." See also Lovelace, "Three Streams, One River?" Richard Foster influenced the movement through his *Celebration of Discipline*. See also Willard, *Spirit of Disciplines*.

70. Boosahda and Sly, "Convergent Movement." "For many Christians, a vacuum has existed between the pages of the New Testament and the contemporary church. This has left a disconnected Body with no historic heritage. Like a boat adrift, the church can no longer explain who she is, where she came from, or why she exists."

71. For Webber's take on the "Convergence Movement," see his *Signs of Wonder*.

72. Webber, *Common Roots*, 8.

73. On Webber's view of worship, see his *Ancient-Future Worship*.

74. Webber, *Ancient-Future Faith*, 7. "How do you deliver an authentic faith into the new cultural situation of the twenty-first century? How do you carry the great wisdom of the past into a postmodern and post-Christian world? The way into the future, I argue, is not innovation or a new start for the church. Rather, the road to the future runs through the past." Webber, *Ancient-Future Evangelism*, 9–10.

75. Webber, *Younger Evangelicals*, 82.

concern for relevance sometimes slipped surreptitiously into utilitarian and pragmatic argumentation.[76]

During the last decade of his life, emerging church proponents often cited Webber's materials. But tensions could surface between the father figure and his younger offspring. For example, after Webber attended the Emergent Convention at Nashville in 2004, he bemoaned, "For the most part, the general sessions just look like an extension of the megachurch movement and the 'rah-rah' youth movement—feelings and loudness . . . the louder you can be, the more direct relationship you have with God."[77] "There's nothing here in the public face that lifts you theologically or lifts you into liturgy or anything that has historic connection or depth or substance."[78]

Webber also organized "The Call to an Ancient-Evangelical Future," a revised statement of the 1977 "Chicago Call." As a further example of tension, some of the guardians of "Mere Christianity" criticized "The Call to an Ancient-Evangelical Future," even aggressively so.[79] A piece by Russell Moore, published within *Touchstone: A Journal of Mere Christianity*, complained that the "ancient futurists" seemingly "want to borrow some of the trappings of a time when Christianity was counter-cultural, . . . while embracing primary aspects of contemporary cultural libertarianism (including feminism and pluralism)."[80] He went on, using hyperbolic language, to castigate the ancient-future movement as "keeping the ancient Christian witness at bay by mocking it with mimicry."[81]

---

76. See the critique of Hart, "Evangelical *Ressourcement*."

77. Quoted in Bader-Saye, "Emergent Matrix."

78. Bader-Saye, "Emergent Matrix."

79. A milder critique can be found in Lucas, "Call to an Ancient Evangelical Future." Lucas especially critiqued the Call's characterization of "mere" propositions and its seeming antipathy between propositional theology and narrative.

80. Moore, "Listen Closely," 25.

81. Ibid., 26. Compare the disparagement of Wilfred McClay within the same *Touchstone* issue: "I wish I didn't have the feeling, reading this document ["The Call to an Ancient-Evangelical Future"], that I was reading about the roll-out of a self-consciously 'retro' new-model car, a sort of ecclesiastical PT Cruiser, which thinks itself 'ancient' because it can play Gregorian chant on its sumptuous audio system." McClay, "What Lies Behind," 24.

The Complexity and Variety of Contemporary Church—Early Church Engagements

According to "Convergent" leaders, their movement is becoming progressively diffuse: "An increasing number of local congregations and leaders from many backgrounds are finding 'treasures old and new' in the spiritual heritage of the church universal."[82] Critics, however, have claimed that some of these eclectic treasure-seekers look more like robbers "picking and choosing" their booty, blithely adopting liturgical symbolism without the sacramental underpinnings.[83] In some cases, advocates seemingly implement the *res* while ignoring the *ratio*. They may genuflect before the consecrated host, but they have no undergirding theology that calls for such an action. Often these criticisms hang on mere stereotypes, but they do not always hang on thin air.

Third, there is a restorationist or primitivist brand of patristic engagement.[84] The seasoned Webber had come to warn against "the dangers of the evangelical proclivity toward 'primitivism' (the belief that one can discover and return to a mythical 'golden age' of the church)."[85] "I always cringe when I hear of those who are attempting to take the Church back to some earlier and hypothetically more pristine time," admits Stanley Porter.[86] "A moment's thought will tell us that such a pipe dream is sheer and ridiculous fantasy."[87] Despite such detractors, "primitivism"—in many ways a laudable impulse—is demonstratively alive and well. Restorationists demand that today's churches be replaced by "organic churches": open-participatory and relational communities of believers.

One spokesperson of the restorationist, house-church movement who has been active in patristic studies is David Bercot.[88] When Bercot

---

82. Boosahda and Sly, "Convergent Movement."

83. "Most convergence churches have a dominant base ... while expressing additional elements of worship and ministry from other streams." Boosahda and Sly, "Convergent Movement".

84. Subsequent discussion will reveal that I am *not* using the label "restorationist" as a synonym for the Stone-Campbell movement.

85. Armstrong "Future Lies in the Past," 28.

86. Porter, "Contemporary Church Music."

87. Ibid.

88. Although Bercot was not academically trained as a patristic scholar, he has been an active member of the North American Patristics Society. To his credit, Bercot does list several "common mistakes" in his *Dictionary of Early Christian Beliefs*: first, the danger of prooftexting; second, to assume that early Christian writers "were making dogmatic

first began investigating early Christianity, he was an Anglican priest and an attorney. After Bercot published *Will the Real Heretics Please Stand Up: A New Look at Today's Evangelical Church in the Light of Early Christianity* and compiled *A Dictionary of Early Christian Beliefs*, he left Anglicanism and became a leader in a restorationist movement with Anabaptist leanings.[89] Such a case is fascinating because it challenges the simplistic notion that patristic study inevitably leads one to turn to "high church" liturgy. Obviously, a model that seeks to restore the second century leads to a different end-product than one that emphasizes the fifth century. Restorationists like Bercot espouse a strong view of "the Constantinian Fall," a perspective that has been nuanced or countered by various "free church" scholars.[90] One must acknowledge the indebtedness the "free churches" have to the post-Constantinian churches and the theological refinements of late antiquity. History is complex, and a refined historiography will not allow a simplistic understanding of a rapidly precipitous "Great Apostasy" overtaking the church in the early fourth century.

Perhaps the most radically restorationist model to break upon the popular scene as of late has been *Pagan Christianity*, a book originally written by Frank Viola and later co-presented with George Barna under an imprint of Tyndale House. "We are living in the midst of a silent revolution of faith," exclaims Barna. "Millions of Christians throughout the world are leaving the old, accepted ways of 'doing church' for even older approaches."[91] "Rather than foster continued resistance to methodological innovations, it's time that the body of Christ get in touch with both the Word of God and the history of the church to arrive at a better understanding of what we can and should do—as well as what we cannot

---

theological pronouncements every time they spoke"; third, "We also must be careful not to read technical or post-Nicene meanings into theological terms used by the pre-Nicene Christians." Bercot, *Dictionary of Early Christian Beliefs*, xii–xiii.

89. Bercot, *Will the Real Heretics Please Stand Up* and *Dictionary of Early Christian Beliefs*.

90. See Bercot, *Kingdom that Turned the World Upside Down*. Cf. Williams, *Retrieving the Tradition*, 101–31; Litfin, *Getting to Know the Church Fathers*, 24–28; and Hinson, "Some Things I've Learned," 733.

91. Viola and Barna, *Pagan Christianity?*, xxv.

and should not do."[92] The thesis of the book is straightforward: "We are also making an outrageous proposal: that the church in its contemporary, institutional form has neither a biblical nor a historical right to function as it does."[93] *Pagan Christianity* argues that the use of instrumental music, pulpits, steeples, church buildings, orders of worship, ushers and collection plates, lecture-style sermons, Bible colleges and seminaries, and ordained pastors have no warrant from the New Testament and the earliest church.[94] All of these "pagan" barnacles should be scraped off the good-ship Church and should be abandoned to the ash heap of history.[95] Strictly speaking, this is not a *ressourcement* of patristics, but an examination of the period for the express purpose of casting the patristic church aside. Yet, as Trevin Wax acknowledges, a "desire for rootedness" is present in these restorationist, house-church movements as well.[96]

Primitivists sometimes succumb to idealizations and romanticizations, but these repristination lobbyists do serve a didactic purpose.[97] Younger evangelicals are seeking rootedness in church history, and some park along the Puritans, others return to the Reformers, and some

---

92. Barna in ibid., xxii.

93. Viola in ibid., xx. "When we dig deeper, we are compelled to ask: Where did the practices of the contemporary church come from? The answer is disturbing: Most of them were borrowed from pagan culture. Such a statement short-circuits the minds of many Christians when they hear it. But it is unmovable, historical fact, as this book will demonstrate." Viola in ibid., xix.

94. Concerning church buildings, Viola and Barna refer to "a love affair with brick and mortar," which is simply a case of an "edifice complex." Ibid., 9–10.

95. For example: "The message of the steeple is one that contradicts the message of the New Testament" (ibid., 33). "The building is an architectural denial of the priesthood of all believers" (2). "The Protestant order of worship is largely unscriptural, impractical, and unspiritual. It has no analog in the New Testament. Rather, it finds its roots in the culture of fallen man" (77). Although "the contemporary sermon does not have a shred of biblical merit to support its existence, it continues to be uncritically admired in the eyes of most present-day Christians" (101).

96. Wax, "Evangelicalism's Blast from the Past."

97. In an intriguing turn of events, Viola has entered into conversation with leaders of emerging churches. His articles are being published in *Next-Wave*, an emerging-friendly online journal. As an aside, one wonders, "Were publishers like Tyndale House and e-zines like *Next-Wave* used by the first-century church?" George Barna is the chairman of Good News Holdings, a multimedia firm that produces movies, television programming, and other modern media content.

find a foundation in the fathers. Yet all such broad historical categories mask multiple complexities. In this case, "the early church" undeniably witnessed sundry developments over the centuries. To declare that "the early church" followed certain practices in a particular manner (over a five-century span) is similar to asserting that "the American church" has practiced a specific pattern from the Age of Exploration until now (a comparable length of time).[98] Moreover, the restorationist models remind us that one must vigilantly discern between "extra-apostolic" additions and "anti-apostolic" accretions in any diachronic study of the patristic period.

Fourth, emerging churches engage the patristic period "in an effort to reclaim the sense of mystery found in the ritual and symbols of the faith's ancient past."[99] Emerging church proponents often wed ancient rituals with postmodern philosophy, and "this strange marriage takes place in a variety of ways."[100] They call for holistic, corporate expressions of the gospel embodied in the totality of life and in Christian communities. "Missional" leaders of the emerging church often speak of the *missio Dei* within the postmodern world. Emerging churches emphasize the "mystical," the "communal," the "relational," the "aesthetic," and the "experiential." Some have called for a "New Monasticism" and a "remonking of the church."[101] Nevertheless, not all are convinced by emerging church claims to a patristic foundation. For example, at the 2005 annual meeting of the Evangelical Theological Society, Anthony Bradley presented a paper entitled "The Emergent Church: Ancient Roots of a Modern Movement, Yeah Right!" Joe Hellerman critiques those who

---

98. From the first European missionaries near the year 1500 to the present day.

99. Associated Press, "Young Christians Ditch Glitz." I recognize that the diverse "emerging" and "emergent" "conversations" and "threads" represent complex phenomena in and of themselves. It is nearly impossible to give a history and description of the emerging church that is fully nuanced to everyone's satisfaction. For an introduction to the "conversation," see Sweet, *Church in Emerging Culture*; Webber, *Listening to the Beliefs of Emerging Churches*. Zondervan published both McLaren, *Generous Orthodoxy*; and Carson, *Becoming Conversant with the Emerging Church* (a critical assessment).

100. Wax, "Evangelicalism's Blast from the Past."

101. See Charlton, "Waiting for St. Benedict." See also Sloan, *Flirting with Monasticism*; McLaren, *Finding Our Way Again*. Cf. the critique of Haykin, "Recovering Ancient Practices," 62–67.

want the "relational solidarity" of the early churches without their "robust boundaries."[102] Colleen Carroll Campbell warns, "Some relish the trappings of traditional worship without subscribing to the conventional morality and theology typically associated with it."[103] The nagging question of authority remains.

Some emerging church leaders claim to reach behind the European Enlightenment by embracing the language of mystery and paradox. These younger evangelicals are longing to "embody" an "authentic" Christianity in a "holistic" manner. At times, however, they seem caught upon the horns of various false dilemmas. For example, some argue that "traditional" churches are too "hung up" on words and propositions; therefore, one should turn to the "embodied authenticity" of early Christianity. "And so," explains Chris Armstrong, "rejecting both rigid propositional definitions of the faith and the pragmatic promises of the church-growth movement, these Christians are seeking a way of living the faith that can be for them an anchor and a bulwark against the culture."[104] Nevertheless, although patristic church leaders emphasized an authentic embodiment of Christianity as a way of life, they also fought keenly over various doctrinal issues. Emerging church supporters may plead, "Stop endlessly debating and advertising Christianity, and just embody it."[105] But the early church provides no asylum for those seeking shelter from theological conflict or the importance of theological delineations.

As David Mills has keenly argued, "dogma" is necessary for unity, and all other substitutes (whether a common ethical standard, a common religious experience, a common ecclesiastical process, or a common institution) will ultimately fail.[106] "The paranoia among anti-fundamentalists is so strong," muses D. H. Williams, that any form of Christianity which "advocates doctrinal standards tends to be rejected as incongruent with personal freedom in Christ."[107] But one simply cannot overlook

---

102. Hellerman, "Ancient-Future Community," 3.

103. As cited in Mammana, "Orthodox Twenty-Somethings," 51.

104. Armstrong, "Future Lies in the Past," 29.

105. Ibid., 26.

106. Mills, "Necessary Doctrines," 106–19.

107. Williams, *Tradition, Scripture, and Interpretation*, 18. In a footnote, Williams explains that "fundamentalism" is "a problematic term because its alleged associations are

the christological and Trinitarian debates of the early centuries. If one is astounded by the politicization and power-mongering of contemporary church business meetings, what would one think of the so-called "Robber Council" of Ephesus in 449?[108] The formation of the ecumenical creeds was a sometimes messy affair. But through the fires of theological conflict came such treasures as the christological definition hammered out at Chalcedon, an important expression of orthodox faith.[109]

Fifth, cultural critics investigate the early church for parallels between the pre-Christian milieu and the post-Christian environment. Influential works include the 1989 manifesto *Resident Aliens: Life in the Christian Colony* and Rodney Clapp's *A Peculiar People: The Church as Culture in a Post-Christian Society*.[110] These prophets warn that too many Christians are captive to the culture. As the sun appears to set upon Western Christendom, these critics turn to various counter-cultural prophets, including the Anabaptists of the sixteenth century.[111] But they also highlight the marginalized early Christians living in the hostile Roman Empire. Like many restorationists, some cultural critics reflect "a built-in nostalgia for the pre-Constantinian Church."[112] Others, however, call for the formation of an alternative Christian culture by pointing to the culture-building processes found in the later patristic period.

---

too broad, unless we are using it in reference to a particular history or an identifiable group." Ibid., 18 n. 8. Historic "fundamentalism" refers to a consistently anti-liberal evangelicalism that arose in "militant defense of the fundamentals" in the early 1900s.

108. "The club-wielding Egyptian monks who accompanied Dioscorus showed their anger at Flavian by so beating him up that he died later of the wounds inflicted. The atmosphere was so strong that the papal delegates feared to read the *Tome* of Leo to the assembly." Ferguson, *From Christ to Pre-Reformation*, 264.

109. "Chalcedon again is a guide to all future work. The false paths which had been followed are here blocked off, for example, by the famous adverbs. There is no claim that the last word has been said. But these erroneous ways will yield no positive benefit and hence there is no sense in wasting time on them" (Bromiley, "Promise of Patristic Studies," 137).

110. Hauerwas and Willimon, *Resident Aliens*; Clapp, *Peculiar People*. See also Hauerwas, *After Christendom*; Carter, *Rethinking Christ and Culture*.

111. Cf. the works of Stuart Murray, who is the chair of the UK Anabaptist Network (Murray, *Post-Christendom* and *Church after Christendom*).

112. Mammana, "Orthodox Twenty-Somethings," 51.

The Complexity and Variety of Contemporary Church—Early Church Engagements

Cultural critics accost not only the contemporary culture surrounding churches, but also the contemporary churches saturated with the culture. Some caution against "contemporary pastoral ministries so compatible with culture that they camouflage God's story or empty it of its cosmic and redemptive meaning."[113] To these prophets, the megachurch model is "a version of 'Christianity' that would seem surrealistic, or even somewhat traumatizing, to just about anyone but a modern American suburbanite who is already inured to the frenzied and hectic environment of an airport or shopping mall."[114] The church is not "a pragmatic set of programs and organizations to be manipulated by managers into a cash machine for the needs of modern Westerners," but "the powerful, untamable, Spirit-driven, Mysterious Body of which Paul spoke."[115] Churches are not to be enslaved by the tyranny of despotic "relevance," nor to be tossed to and fro by every wind of methodology.

An interest in the ancient church is especially booming among young people, or "young fogeys."[116] Many young people sense that the contemporary church has bowed the knee to the idols of consumerism, blind patriotism, sentimentalism, hyper-individualism, privatism, relativism, pragmatism, and materialism. Chris Armstrong notes, "Many 20- and 30-something evangelicals are uneasy and alienated in mall-like church environments; high-energy, entertainment-oriented worship; and boomer-era ministry strategies and structures modeled on the business world. Increasingly, they are asking just how these culturally camouflaged churches can help them rise above the values of the consumerist world around them."[117] Such young people yearn for calls to spiritual discipline, commitment, sacrifice, and selfless service.

Why study the fathers as one seeks to be freed from cultural captivity? Michael Haykin responds that an examination of the fathers, "like

---

113. Webber, "Call to an Ancient-Evangelical Future." It seems that the "call" cannot be boxed into one model of *ressourcement*.

114. Hart, "Evangelical *Ressourcement*," 38. Hart continues, "The church fathers would flee such a place to find a true sanctuary for the worship of God Almighty."

115. Armstrong, "Future Lies in the Past," 29.

116. The label "young fogeys" has been coined by Thomas Oden to refer to those young thinkers returning to the classical tradition.

117. Armstrong, "Future Lies in the Past," 28.

any historical study, liberates us from the present."¹¹⁸ One must learn to listen attentively "and actually hear voices from the past with different assumptions entirely about the world and time and human culture."¹¹⁹ The fathers free us from "the *Zeitgeist* of the twenty-first century."¹²⁰ The task of re-appropriation reminds us that "the study of ancient Christianity is not merely an antiquarian pursuit but can provide the church with the resources it needs to be relevant in its postmodern context"¹²¹

Sixth, contemporary apologists have also engaged the early church.¹²² Many of these apologists are New Testament scholars who jump over the disciplinary fence and foray into the field of patristics.¹²³ In this regard, one is reminded of J. B. Lightfoot's explanation, over a century ago, of his time spent in the Apostolic Fathers: "I have been reproached by my friends for allowing myself to be diverted from the more congenial task of commenting on S. Paul's Epistles; but the importance of the position seemed to me to justify the expenditure of much time and labour in 're-pairing a breach' not indeed in 'the House of the Lord' itself, but in the immediately outlying buildings."¹²⁴

Sometimes popular challenges force this necessary reassignment. For example, the questions raised by the *Da Vinci Code* phenomenon required answers gleaned not only from New Testament scholarship but also from patristic studies.¹²⁵ At other times, the ranks of worthy opponents are lined with professional scholars. Foundational questions such as the formation of the canon and the nature of unity and diversity in early Christianity inevitably require a journey into the second, third, and fourth centuries. The long shadow of Walter Bauer's *Orthodoxy and Heresy* still falls upon the field of early Christian studies.¹²⁶ Modified views, such

---

118. Haykin, "Why Study the Fathers?"

119. Oden, *Word of Life*, 219–20.

120. Haykin, "Why Study the Fathers?" Haykin has "*Zeitgesit*" [sic] in the original.

121. Harmon, "'All of Church History as the History of Us All,'" 573–74.

122. See Wellum, "Standing on the Shoulders," 3.

123. On the problematic "intellectual divide" between these two disciplines, see Williams, *Retrieving the Tradition*, 84.

124. Lightfoot, *Apostolic Fathers* II.1, 15.

125. Brown, *Da Vinci Code*.

126. First published as Bauer, *Rechtgläubigkeit und Ketzerei im ältesten Christentum*.

as those of Helmut Koester, Gerd Lüdemann, and Bart Ehrman, have required new responses.[127]

Moreover, doctrinal apologists who defend the Trinity and the deity of Christ must be conversant with the patristic period as well. "This is the era in which the formulation of Christian doctrine, canonization, and the interpretation of the Bible took place, making it 'ground zero' for the way in which all subsequent ages of the church have defined themselves."[128] Much of our understanding of "theological orthodoxy" has undeniably "come through the portals of the early church."[129] Williams explains, "One cannot move simply from the Bible to the chief doctrines of the Christian faith without passing through those critical stages of development that link the past and present together and which make our present interpretation of the Bible intelligible."[130] The patristic period was "*the critical period for the very formation of the New Testament, for the propounding of the doctrines of Christ and the Trinity, for the confessions of redemption and eternal hope—in short, for the development of what it is to think and live as an orthodox Christian.*"[131]

A Discussion Forum

Bridging the early church and the contemporary church is a difficult but necessary endeavor, and there seems to be no one-size-fits-all solution.[132] Patristic *ressourcement* is a difficult task because it involves humbling oneself as a stranger in a strange land. "The past is a foreign country: they do things differently there," quipped L. P. Hartley.[133] On the other

---

Bauer argued that what later become known as heresies were early and powerful movements that enjoyed widespread acceptance in a context of diverse Christianities. Over time, the influence of Rome marginalized such Christian movements through political and social pressure. Many now think of them as heresies simply because the victors write the histories.

127. See Trebilco, "Christian Communities in Western Asia Minor."
128. Williams, *Evangelicals and Tradition*, 25.
129. Williams, *Tradition, Scripture, and Interpretation*, 7.
130. Williams, *Retrieving the Tradition*, 29.
131. Ibid., 27; italics original.
132. As rightly noted by Armstrong in "Future Lies in the Past," 29.
133. This is the opening sentence of L. P. Hartley's novel *The Go-Between* (1953).

hand, the task is necessary and even urgent. The variety and complexity of engagements should not discourage us from sitting at the feet of our patristic forbears. A renewed study of the church's patristic heritage is absolutely necessary, if Christians are to have any sense of historic rootedness. Just as personal identity is linked to memory, so ecclesial identity is linked to corporate *memoria*, or tradition.[134]

Joel Scandrett warns against various pitfalls that neophytes must avoid as they enter patristic studies. First, "Anachronism": "Naively interpreting the tradition in light of contemporary assumptions." Second, "Romanticized Traditionalism": "Being unwilling to see the flaws in the early church's traditions." Third, "Eclecticism": "Selectively appropriating ancient practices without regard to their original purposes or contexts."[135] Scandrett cautions that retrieval "is not a simple matter, but requires an understanding of the intellectual context in which that tradition developed."[136] Gillis Harp criticizes the "fanciful and selective invocation of the Church of the ancient Fathers," which seeks "to recover some exceedingly vague and romantic model of the early Church."[137] Chris Armstrong refers to a "naïve romanticism" that has plagued many programs of *ressourcement*. At the same time, he acknowledges that "All signs point to the maturing of the ancient-future church," signs that the movement has "moved from naïveté to maturity." At the very least, a responsible retrieval must be founded upon a critical awareness and a comprehensive understanding of the historical and cultural contexts of early Christianity.

The complexity and variety of *ressourcement* is inescapable, but so is its necessity. This present, public forum (at the 2008 ETS annual meeting) modestly allows a panel of patristic scholars to explain various lessons they believe can be learned from the early church. Before the forum, the participants were told that the introductory essay would "lay out the land" and "clear the ground," but it would not tell them how to farm the soil. Specific topics in this symposium include evangelism and

---

134. See Wilken, *Remembering the Christian Past*.

135. Summaries in Armstrong, "Future Lies in the Past," 24. Joel Scandrett refers to "uncritically romanticized traditionalism." Scandrett, "Trouble with Tradition," 2.

136. Scandrett, abstract of "Trouble with Tradition."

137. Harp, "Antiquity & Absence," 29.

discipleship, community formation and maintenance, use of the "rule of faith," the preaching of social ethics, responses to cultural opposition, and christological development.

As an academic roundtable of contributors, the authors and respondents will not agree on the particulars of scholarly *ressourcement*, of course. But they certainly agree on the importance of informed engagement, as well as appropriations they deem to be both cogently reasoned and historically conscientious.[138] Two responses follow the six topical essays. Glen Thompson, a confessional Lutheran historian, has written the first rejoinder, and I have prepared the second from a Baptist "free church" perspective.[139] These response essays allow divergent viewpoints, sometimes tied to confessional commitments, to come to the foreground. This responsive approach will also enable readers to note differences among the various forum participants (even pronounced differences at times) and to learn from our dissimilarities.[140]

The term "Father" is pregnant with meaning as an illustration of both the importance and nature of patristic *ressourcement*. Vincent of Lérins explained, "Therefore, whatever has been sown by the fidelity of the Fathers in this husbandry of God's Church, the same ought to be cultivated and taken care of by the industry of their children, the same ought to flourish and ripen, the same ought to advance and go forward to perfection."[141] Across cultures, children are taught to respect their parents, and descendants are told to honor their ancestors. Children come to realize that they are not exactly like their parents, yet they also recognize that their very existence is contingent upon those parents. Even as children may respect yet diverge from their natural parents, ecclesial descendants may creatively honor their forbears without adopting them

---

138. Cf. Hall, "Introduction," 12: "Yes, the conclusions and emphases of the contributors may well vary, but at heart there is the fundamental consensus that we neglect our theological forebearers [sic] to our own peril."

139. I currently serve as chairperson of the ETS Patristics and Medieval History Section. Glen Thompson preceded me in this position.

140. Let the reader take note: I do not agree with all of the contributors' specific views. *Caveat emptor.*

141. Vincent of Lérins *A Commonitory* 57 (*NPNF2* 11:148).

wholesale.[142] Martin Luther stated, "Whenever we see that the opinions of the fathers are not in agreement with Scripture, we respectfully bear with them and acknowledge them as our forefathers; but we do not on their account give up the authority of Scripture. . . . For although both, truth and friends, are dear to us, preference must be given to truth. . . . Human beings can err, but the Word of God is the very wisdom of God and the absolutely infallible truth."[143]

We must not idolize the fathers with feet of clay, but to ignore the fathers through historical "self-imposed amnesia" is to commit ecclesiastical patricide.[144] In some ways, ignorance is more intolerable than suspicion or opposition.[145] A preponderant ignorance cuts us off from "our theological family of origin."[146] In the words of Scandrett, neglecting the patristic heritage is "perilous," adoring it is "idolatrous," but embracing it is "wondrous."[147] In our recovery of memory, we are called to be neither naïve eulogists nor careless undertakers. We will not bury our fathers through forgetfulness, but we will not recklessly idealize them either. Instead, in the words of Chris Armstrong, we are called to "mix critique with appreciation and even reverence" as we "return to the historical sources."[148] *Ad fontes*!

142. See Wellum, "Standing on the Shoulders," 3.
143. English translation in Pelikan, *Luther's Works* 1:122.
144. See Wilken, *Remembering the Christian Past*.
145. See Williams, *Evangelicals and Tradition*, 17.
146. Scandrett, "Trouble with Tradition," 2.
147. Ibid., 16.
148. Armstrong, "Future Lies in the Past," 29.

2

Learning from Patristic Evangelism and Discipleship

Edward Smither

> Make disciples of all the nations . . . Go into all the world and preach the gospel to all creation . . . As the Father has sent Me, I also send you . . . Repentance for forgiveness of sins would be proclaimed in His [Jesus'] name to all the nations . . . You will be my witnesses in Jerusalem, and in all Judea and Samaria, and even to the remotest part of the earth.[1]

❊ Each Gospel writer (including Luke in Acts) remembered these commands and promises as the last words spoken by the Lord to his disciples. The mandate was to proclaim Christ—his person and his work (especially his death, burial, and resurrection)—and to persuade the nations to become followers of his teachings and example.[2] More than mere parting words, these evangelical values were also at the center of Jesus's earthly ministry. After three years of apprenticing with the Lord, the Twelve and the broader community of disciples[3] had also

---

1. Matthew 28:19; Mark 16:15; John 20:21; Luke 24:47; Acts 1:8 (NASB).

2. In this paper, I will work from the broad definition of evangelism as proclaiming the person and work of Christ. That said, space does not permit an exhaustive commentary on the essence of the message *(kerygma)* proclaimed by the Apostles. This has been discussed more thoroughly by Dodd, *Apostolic Preaching and Its Developments*, 7–35; and Green, *Evangelism in the Early Church*, 76–115.

3. For a discussion on the relationship between the Twelve, the Seventy, and the

seized these convictions, as early Christian history testifies. At the end of the second century, Tertullian (c. AD 160–220) would boast to the Roman authorities in Carthage: "We are but of yesterday, and we have filled every place among you—cities, islands, fortresses, towns, marketplaces, the very camp, tribes, companies, palace, senate, forum—we have left nothing to you but the temples of your gods."[4]

Though Tertullian was given to exaggeration, Governor Pliny of Bithynia (in northern Asia Minor) was certainly not. In a letter to Emperor Trajan in AD 112, he indicated that Christians were present in the towns and cities, and could be found on every level of society in his province.[5] The reality of the gospel traversing class lines—itself an indication of a mature church movement that was transforming culture—was acutely observed when the noblewoman Perpetua faced martyrdom alongside her servant Felicitas in Carthage in 203. In all, by the time of Constantine's rise to power in the early fourth century, there were six million Christians in the Roman Empire alone—ten percent of the population—and the gospel had also spread eastward to places like Edessa (Osroehene), Armenia, and Persia.[6]

Though extensive studies on the geographical expansion of Christianity in the patristic period have been published, including the social conditions in which the gospel spread and the reasons for its success, my goal in the present chapter is simply to explore a few themes related to evangelism and discipleship in the first five centuries.[7] In the first

---

broader discipleship community, see Meier, *Marginal Jew* 3:21; and Smither, *Augustine as Mentor*, 6.

4. Tertullian *Apology* 37.4 (*ANF* 3:45).

5. Pliny *Letter* 10.96; also Latourette, *History of the Expansion of Christianity*, 141.

6. Stark, *Rise of Christianity*, 6. Edessa, which joined the Roman Empire around 216, had already been evangelized by the end of the second century.

7. While Latourette's work continues to be a helpful source, a more recent work showing the eastward spread of the gospel is Irvin and Sunquist, *History of the World Christian Movement*. More general works on the history and theology of mission that focus some attention on the patristic period include: Neill, *History of Christian Missions*, 13–52; Bevans and Schroeder, *Constants in Context*, 74–136; and Bosch, *Transforming Mission*, 41–44; 181–238. See also Harnack, *Mission and Expansion of Christianity*, 19–35; Green, *Evangelism in the Early Church*, 29–49; Schnabel, *Early Christian Mission*, 1556–61; and Kreider, "'They Alone Know,'" 167–76.

part of the chapter, I will argue that Christians—including "full-time," "part-time," and anonymous evangelists—were integrated members of society who shared their faith from that position. Given this reality, I will discuss one aspect of evangelism—communicating testimonies or faith stories, which will include accounts of conversion stories delivered orally, the testimonies of martyrs, and those who witnessed through telling the faith stories of others. In the second part of the chapter, I will discuss two approaches to spiritual formation—catechesis and monastic communities—from which I will propose some prevailing patristic discipleship values. With careful attention to the world of the early church, I will conclude with some suggestions concerning what the modern church might recover from early Christian evangelism and discipleship.

A Socially Integrated Witness

The pre-Constantinian Christian movement in the Roman Empire experienced sporadic and varying degrees of discrimination and persecution from the greater pagan society and, at times, even from the imperial authorities. Branded as members of a new and illegitimate religion, the Christians were regarded as traitors in a Roman society that considered piety toward the traditional deities as the mark of a good citizen.[8] Though some Christian communities met in homes during the pre-Constantinian era and others possibly gathered under the creative guise of a funerary association, one should not assume that Christians were segregated or marginalized from the greater society. As noted, Pliny's observation about Christians in second-century Bithynia and Tertullian's claims about second- and third-century Carthage indicate otherwise. Valerian's and Diocletian's pogroms against the church, which included purges of the senate, confiscating property from the wealthy, and even arresting royal family members, also show that Christians were quite integrated into daily Roman life.[9] This evidence supports the view of the anonymous author of the second-century *Epistle to Diognetus* who wrote: "For

---

8. See Lane Fox, *Pagans and Christians*, 43, 66; Sordi, *Christians and the Roman Empire*, 83, 125; and Frend, *Martyrdom and Persecution*, 106, 110.

9. Sordi, *Christians and the Roman Empire*, 114; Eusebius *Hist. eccl.* 8.1; also Kreider, "'They Alone Know,'" 171. Valerian's edicts came in 257–58 while Diocletian's were given between 303–5.

Christians are no different from other people in terms of their country, language or customs. Nowhere do they inhabit cities of their own, or live life out of the ordinary ... They inhabit both Greek and barbarian cities according to the lot assigned to each ... they participate in all things as citizens ..." The writer continues: "They live in their respective countries, but only as resident aliens; they participate in all things as citizens, and they endure all things as foreigners. They marry like everyone else and have children, but they do not expose them once they are born. They share their meals but not their sexual partners. They are found in the flesh but do not live according to the flesh. They live on earth but participate in the life of heaven."[10]

The argument continues in much the same way, with the author essentially stating that Christians are "in the world but not of the world." Though their allegiance is to heaven, they are very much integrated in the present world.

In the ministry of Cyprian (195–258) in Carthage, this integrated witness included courageous service. Following on the heels of Decius' persecution in 250–51, an even greater enemy—plague—struck the city. While many were leaving Carthage for more healthy environments, Cyprian urged the Christians to stay in the city and to minister to their pagan neighbors by providing food, water, and basic nursing, and by visiting them.[11] Hence, for Cyprian, Christian witness required a certain social engagement.

The letter to Diognetus and the account of Cyprian's actions are representative of an apparent "spirit"[12] of patristic evangelism—that Christians testified *to* their eternal hope *from* their position as fully committed citizens in the "earthly city."[13] In order to support this claim

---

10. *Epistle to Diognetus* 5.1–6 (Schnabel, *Early Christian Mission* 2:1566).

11. Cyprian *Mortality* 8, 15; Pontius *Life of Cyprian* 9; Kreider, "'They Alone Know,'" 173–74.

12. It would be ungainly to offer prooftexts on evangelism from the fathers. However, in following Robert Wilken's general stream of thought on patristic theology, I suggest that a case can be made for this broadly observed guiding principle of patristic evangelism. See Wilken, *Spirit of Early Christian Thought*.

13. Bevans and Schroeder, *Constants in Context*, 85–86.

"Full-time" and "Part-time" Evangelists[14]

Despite Kreider's recent assertion that "the earliest Christians did not engage in public preaching; it was too dangerous,"[15] there is evidence that there were official, full-time evangelists who proclaimed the gospel publicly.[16] The *Didache*, perhaps a late first-century or early second-century text, refers to a group of prophet-like evangelists who served as traveling, itinerant preachers.[17] Eusebius of Caesarea (c. 260–341), referring to the post-apostolic period, spoke of those who "... preached the Gospel more and more widely and scattered the saving seeds of the kingdom of heaven far and near throughout the whole world... Then starting out upon long journeys they performed the office of evangelists, being filled with the desire to preach Christ to those who had not yet heard the word of faith, and to deliver to them the divine Gospels."[18] In the third century, Origen (c. 185–254) also made reference to full-time evangelists who "made it their business to itinerate not only through cities, but even villages and country houses, that they might make converts to God."[19]

Although official evangelists existed, others also proclaimed the Gospel, though it was not their primary vocation. Perhaps the most obvious were certain bishops—those already set apart to pastor established churches—who also engaged in evangelism.[20] Ignatius of Antioch (d. 110)

---

14. Though each evangelist mentioned in this discussion performed the basics of evangelism—proclaiming the person and work of Christ—it should be noted that their contexts, methods, and approaches varied greatly.

15. Kreider, "'They Alone Know,'" 169.

16. Though my intent is not to quibble over what constituted a public place, it remains clear that the nature of evangelistic preaching was quite open and public. See Green, *Evangelism in the Early Church*, 234–42.

17. *Didache* 11–13 (Schnabel, *Early Christian Mission* 2:1527).

18. Eusebius *Hist. eccl.* 3.37.1–2 (*NPNF2* 1:169). Eusebius also recounted Pantaenus' second-century Indian mission in *Hist. eccl.* 5.10.1–4.

19. Origen *Against Celsus* 3.9 (Schnabel, *Early Christian Mission* 2:1528).

20. In early Christianity, the bishop generally emerged as a church organizer and leader after a community had been evangelized and some semblance of a church was founded. Hence, bishops did not function primarily as evangelists.

exhorted his fellow bishop Polycarp (d. 156) to "press on in your course and exhort all men that they may be saved."[21] Irenaeus (c. 115–200), known for defending the church against Gnosticism in the late second century, made it a point to learn the local dialect of southern Gaul in order to preach in the pagan villages around Lyon.[22] Consecrated bishop of Pontus in 240, Gregory Thaumaturgus (c. 213–70) is most remembered for evangelizing his home province in Asia Minor.[23] Finally, evangelism was an important aspect of the ministries of Martin of Tours (c. 316–97) and Patrick of Ireland (c. 387–461) in the fourth and fifth centuries.

Other "part-time" evangelists included Pantaenus (d. 200) and Origen, who functioned primarily as teachers. Gregory Thaumaturgus (previously mentioned) came to faith through Origen's teaching before accepting the mission to Pontus.[24] Finally, one scholar highlights the apologetic and evangelistic activities of Justin Martyr (c. 100–165) and Minucius Felix (c. second–third centuries), whom he describes as philosopher-evangelists.[25]

Anonymous Evangelists

It seems quite natural that these bishops, teachers, and philosophers—all students of Scripture and its related disciplines—would be spokespersons for the Christian faith. However, laymen—including businessmen and merchants, colonists, and soldiers—also played a significant role in early church evangelism. Though his intention was to mock the church, the pagan Celsus confirms that unsophisticated, uneducated Christian tradesmen were active in sharing the gospel.[26] Similarly, Justin's *First Apology* highlights the integrity of Christian businessmen in an otherwise dishonest marketplace.[27]

---

21. Ignatius *Polycarp* 1 (Green, *Evangelism in the Early Church*, 239).

22. Green, *Evangelism in the Early Church*, 240.

23. Ibid., 268.

24. Gregory Thaumaturgus *Panegyric to Origen* 5 (Bevans and Schroeder, *Constants in Context*, 82–84).

25. Green, *Evangelism in the Early Church*, 240–42.

26. Origen *Against Celsus* 3.55 (Schnabel, *Early Christian Mission* 2:1526).

27. Justin *First Apology* 16 (Schnabel, *Early Christian Mission* 2:1526).

Learning from Patristic Evangelism and Discipleship

These laymen participated in a largely anonymous and otherwise volunteer missionary movement—one of the most remarkable qualities of early church evangelism. Harnack asserts that "the great mission of Christianity was in reality accomplished by means of informal missionaries."[28] Stephen Neill adds, "Every Christian was a witness . . . nothing is more notable than the anonymity of these early missionaries."[29] Indeed, it is not insignificant that the two largest communions in the early Western church—Rome and Carthage—had undocumented origins.[30]

North African Christianity, in particular, provides an intriguing case study for anonymous mission work. Before Augustine (354–430) made his mark in patristic theology in the fourth and fifth centuries and prior to Cyprian's innovation in organizing the Carthage church and providing oversight to the bishops during mid-third-century African church councils, the African church had already grown significantly. Though Tertullian's claim that Christians were the majority in Carthage is doubtful, the Council of Carthage of 220, presided over by Agrippinus and attended by seventy bishops from a single African province (Proconsular Africa), testifies to a developed African church by the early third century. It should be noted that the Council of 220 occurred just forty years after the first literary reference to Christianity in Africa—the account of the martyrs of Scilli who were condemned at Carthage in 180. The fact that a majority of these twelve martyrs (seven men and five women) had Punic-Berber names signifies that the church had penetrated the African interior, which provides further evidence that Christianity was present in North Africa well before 180. Also, the catacombs of Hadrumetum (modern Sousse, Tunisia), which contain at least 15,000 graves of second- to fourth-century Christians, have mid-second-century origins.[31] Though Carthage was probably the first African city touched by the gospel, the French archaeologist Paul Monceaux discovered Christian

---

28. Harnack, *Mission and Expansion of Christianity*, 368.
29. Neill, *History of Christian Missions*, 24.
30. Schnabel, *Early Christian Mission* 2:1492.
31. Decret, *L'histoire du christianisme*, 20.

graves in Jewish cemeteries in Cyrene (Ben Ghazi, Libya), which date to the early second century.[32]

Hence, North African Christianity had early beginnings (at least early second-century or even late first-century) that were strikingly anonymous. Decret concludes that "the opening pages of Christianity in North Africa did not begin with a golden legend or a holy apostle who arrived to convert the unbelievers."[33] Rather, North Africa was probably first evangelized by Christian merchants, colonists, and even soldiers. Like the bishops, teachers, and others mentioned, the early African Christians were integrated into the daily life of their social context and seemed accustomed to witnessing freely about their Christian faith.[34]

Forms of Public Testimony

The early Christians believed Jesus's message and were committed to imitating his life and example. Schnabel remarks, "They confessed Jesus not only as Messiah but also as Kyrios: his behavior was the model and standard for their own behavior"; that is, the gospel was lived out and proclaimed in word and deed.[35] For believers integrated into local society, verbal witness was best authenticated through upright and moral lives. On his journey to Rome in the early second century, Ignatius instructed the Ephesian believers: "Pray continually for the rest of humankind as well, that they may find God, for there is in them hope for repentance. Therefore, allow them to be instructed by you, at least by your deeds. In response to their anger, be gentle; in response to their boasts, be humble; in response to their slander, offer prayers; in response to their errors, be steadfast in the faith; in response to their cruelty, be civilized."[36]

In *A Plea for the Christians*, addressed to Marcus Aurelius and Lucius Aurelius Commodus around 177, Athenagoras defended such Christian

---

32. Latourette, *History of the Expansion of Christianity*, 92.

33. Decret, *L'histoire du christianisme*, 18. English translation is my own.

34. Schnabel, *Early Christian Mission* 2:1548.

35. Ibid., 2:1544, 1548. For a discussion on the tension between Jesus's message and example, see Smither, *Augustine as Mentor*, 6–13; also, Burridge, *Imitating Jesus*, has offered an innovative look at ethics by emphasizing Jesus's example.

36. Ignatius *Ephesians* 10.1–2 (Holmes, *Apostolic Fathers*, 191).

conduct: "But among us you will find uneducated persons, and artisans, and old women, who, if they are unable in words to prove the benefit of our doctrine, yet by their deeds exhibit the benefit arising from their persuasion of its truth: they do not rehearse speeches, but exhibit good works; when struck, they do not strike again; when robbed, they do not go to law; they give to those that ask of them, and love their neighbors as themselves."[37]

At the turn of the fifth century, John Chrysostom (c. 347–407) urged his flock in Constantinople: "Let us overcome by our manner of living rather than by our words alone . . . For though we give ten thousand precepts of philosophy in words, if we do not exhibit a life better than theirs, the gain is nothing . . . Let us win them therefore by our life."[38]

One prevalent aspect of evangelism in this period that combined the gospel message and authentic living was an articulated testimony. Let us consider a few different approaches to this strategy, including recorded oral accounts and written narratives.

Recorded Testimonies

One of the earliest recorded testimonies was Luke's narration of Paul telling his conversion story to a hostile mob in Jerusalem.[39] In his speech, Paul attempts to identify with his Jewish audience by speaking to them in Hebrew, by highlighting his own Jewish background, and by admitting his own initial hostility toward Christians.[40] Afterward, he recounts his dramatic conversion story—largely a retelling of the events of Acts 9—and then continues with a straightforward account of his post-conversion life prior to being shouted down by the crowd.[41]

In the first eight chapters of his transcript of his *Dialogue with Trypho* (c. 155), Justin recounts his journey to faith. The philosopher-evangelist also endeavored to connect with his audience—philosophically minded readers or listeners—by narrating his experiences in various schools of

37. Athenagoras *Plea for the Christians* 11 (*ANF* 2:134).
38. John Chrysostom *Homilies on First Corinthians* 3.9 (*NPNF*1 12:15).
39. Acts 21:37—22:22.
40. Acts 21:40—22:5.
41. Acts 22:6-22.

Greek philosophy.[42] His conversion story comes to a climax when he meets an aged man by the seashore who challenges Justin's belief about Plato and introduces him to the Hebrew prophets and the Messiah.[43] Only after believing in Christ does Justin realize that he has become a true philosopher.[44]

In the eighth book of his *Confessions* (c. 397), Augustine shares one of the most stirring conversion accounts in the early church period. The final stage of his conversion experience includes several intriguing features. First, he vividly relates the psychological and emotional battle that went on within him in the garden near Milan.[45] He writes: "When I was making up my mind to serve the Lord my God . . . I was the one who wanted to follow that course, and I was the one who wanted not to."[46] Secondly, up until the very end of the garden experience, Augustine was in the company of his friend Alypius; so, the spiritual struggle was not an individual one.[47] In fact, immediately after confessing Christ, Augustine went inside and told his mother what happened.[48] Finally, from the famous "pick it up and read" *(tolle lege)* narrative, we learn that Scripture—in this case Paul's letters—played a central role leading up to and encompassing the moment of Augustine's conversion experience.[49]

Martyrdom

Most commentators on early Christianity assert that the morality, purity, and suffering of the early Christians served as a compelling witness to the pagan society around them.[50] Despite the unhealthy infatuation of some

---

42. Justin *Dialogue with Trypho* 2.

43. Ibid., 3–7.

44. Ibid., 8; also Wilken, *Spirit of Early Christian Thought*, 4–8.

45. Augustine *Confessions* 8.8.19—12.29.

46. Ibid., 8.10.22. All *Confessions* translations are from Boulding, *St. Augustine's Confessions*.

47. Ibid., 8.8.19; 8.11.27; 8.12.29.

48. Ibid., 8.12.30.

49. Ibid., 8.12.29.

50. Green, *Evangelism in the Early Church*, 261–62; Kreider, "'They Alone Know,'" 171; Stark, *Rise of Christianity*, 163–89; Guy, *Introducing Early Christianity*, 76–81.

Learning from Patristic Evangelism and Discipleship

Christians toward dying for the faith and a resulting cult of the martyrs, martyrdom was itself a form of public testimony in the early church.[51] Also, the written *Martyrdoms* and *Passions* of Polycarp, the Scillitans, Perpetua and Felicitas, and Cyprian record their verbal declarations of faith.[52]

Interpreting the outcome of this suffering witness, Tertullian proclaimed that "the blood of Christians is seed [for the church]."[53] In his polemic to Scapula, he added, "For all who witness the noble patience of its martyrs, as struck with misgivings, are inflamed with desire to examine into the matter in question; and as soon as they come to know the truth, they straightway enroll themselves its disciples."[54] Though Tertullian's claims are probably inflated, they nevertheless find general support in the early Christian period. The Synoptic Gospel writers showed that Jesus's crucifixion led to the conversion of an observing centurion.[55] Polycarp's holiness and integrity throughout his detention apparently had an impact on the police who arrested him.[56] In his *Second Apology*, Justin testified that the purity and suffering of Christians had an impact on his journey to faith: "For I myself, too, when I was delighting in the doctrines of Plato, and heard the Christians slandered, and saw them fearless of death, and of all other-things which are counted fearful, perceived that it was impossible that they could be living in wickedness and pleasure."[57]

Perpetua reported in her diary that the prison guard Pudens, moved by the testimony of Perpetua and her companions as they awaited execution, treated them with kindness and then he was also converted to faith.[58]

---

51. A helpful introduction to martyrdom in early Christianity can be found in Guy, *Introducing Early Christianity*, 50–81, while Frend, *Martyrdom and Persecution*, offers a more thorough study.

52. For multiple other examples, see Musurillo, *Acts of the Christian Martyrs*.

53. Tertullian *Apology* 50.16 (*ANF* 3:55).

54. Tertullian *To Scapula* 5 (*ANF* 3:108).

55. Matt 27:54; Mark 15:39; Luke 23:47.

56. *Martyrdom of Polycarp* 7.

57. Justin *Second Apology* 12 (*ANF* 1:192).

58. *Passion of Perpetua and Felicitas* 9.21; also Kreider, "'They Alone Know,'" 171.

Telling the Faith Stories of Others

While martyrdom was a form of witness, a genre of sacred biography—including accounts of the martyrs—quickly developed.[59] Though these biographies, along with a developing feast day tradition, functioned primarily to exhort Christians toward imitating these examples of faith, non-believers in the local society were probably also familiar with these faith stories. Through his preaching, Augustine regularly reminded his audience at Hippo, which certainly included non-believers, about martyrs like Perpetua and companions, Cyprian, as well as other saints.[60]

In recounting his conversion story in *Confessions*, Augustine also narrates the faith stories of four other converts. These were testimonies that clearly encouraged him on his journey to faith that Augustine in turn uses to influence his readers toward the gospel. He begins by declaring that he will "not pass over in silence" how Simplicianus (d. 400) told him the conversion story of the philosopher and *rhetor* Marius Victorinus (b. 300).[61] Victorinus, who had been a pagan, became convinced of the gospel's veracity through reading the Scriptures. Simplicianus, who personally witnessed to Victorinus, urged him to forsake his public reputation and declare his faith in the context of the church. As a result, he enrolled as a catechumen, was baptized, and publicly confessed his faith before the church assembly.[62]

Augustine interpreted Simplicianus' intentions for telling the story by writing: "I was fired to imitate Victorinus; indeed it was to this end that your servant Simplicianus had related it."[63] Indeed, Augustine had much in common with Victorinus, as both men were interested in philosophy,

---

59. A number of martyrs' biographies have been collected in English translation in Musurillo, *Acts of the Christian Martyrs*.

60. Augustine preached around one hundred sermons commemorating the saints on their feast days. They have been nicely grouped in WSA. Three more feast day sermons (*Sermons* 283, 299A, 306E) are in the recently discovered Dolbeau sermons in WSA pt. 3, vol. 11. Eleven sermons were dedicated to Cyprian (*Sermons* 309–12; 313A–313F; and one recently discovered sermon that is now in the process of being catalogued), while three were dedicated to Perpetua and her friends (*Sermons* 280–82).

61. Augustine *Confessions* 8.2.3.

62. Ibid., 8.2.3–5.

63. Ibid., 8.5.10.

Learning from Patristic Evangelism and Discipleship

were on a similar career path, had concerns about their public reputation, and had an interest in the Christian Scriptures. Hence, Augustine was encouraged to pursue Christian faith because Victorinus had.[64]

In the middle of Simplicianus' narrative, including Augustine's take on Simplicianus' motives, Augustine pauses and offers a prayerful commentary that seems very much intended for his own readers: "Come, Lord, arouse us and call us back, kindle us and seize us, prove to us how sweet you are in your burning tenderness; let us love you and run to you. Are there not many who return to you from a deeper, blinder pit than did Victorinus, many who draw near to you and are illumined as they become children of God?[65] Could it be that Augustine was also reaching out to his philosophically minded, career-oriented readers who could relate to both Victorinus and Augustine?

In the very next passage, Augustine tells of a visit from Ponticianus, a Roman functionary, who told Augustine and Alypius about the Egyptian monk Antony (c. 251–356). While recounting Antony's call to the ascetic life, Ponticianus also related the story of two Roman officials from Trier, who after reading Athanasius' *Life of Antony*, resigned from their posts in order to pursue an ascetic lifestyle. Augustine, intrigued by the accounts, wrote: "even while he [Ponticianus] spoke, you [God] were wrenching me back toward myself . . . that I might perceive my sin and hate it."[66]

Ponticianus' account connected with Augustine for a number of reasons. First, there was probably a cultural connection because Ponticianus was an African who was telling the faith story of another African (Antony) to two other Africans (Augustine and Alypius) in Milan.[67] Second, Antony's conversion to an ascetic lifestyle—as well as the similar conversion of the officials from Trier—was meaningful for Augustine because one of his biggest obstacles to faith was sexual immorality. In fact, Augustine introduced the entire Ponticianus encounter

---

64. For a helpful discussion on parallels between the conversion experiences of Victorinus and Augustine, especially regarding the relationship between humility and baptism in both men's spiritual journeys, see Alexander, *Augustine's Early Theology of the Church*, 67–79.

65. Augustine *Confessions* 8.4.9.

66. Ibid., 8.7.17.

67. Ibid., 8.6.14.

with this prayerful commentary: "Now I will relate how you set me free from a craving for sexual gratification."[68] Third, Augustine, who had been quite infatuated with career ambitions, identified with the two officials who set aside their careers for the sake of the gospel. At the conclusion of his conversion account, Augustine testified that he was "no longer . . . entertaining any worldly hope."[69] As a result, he also resigned from his imperial post before moving back to Africa to pursue a monastic lifestyle.[70]

While his account of Simplicianus' story of Marius Victorinus impacted some readers, Augustine's narrative of Ponticianus telling the story of Antony and the two officials probably reached others with the gospel. Surely, there were those whose career ambitions were poisoning their spiritual lives, while others struggled like Augustine with sexual immorality. Perhaps Augustine's African readers were especially attracted to the African angle of Ponticianus' story. Hence, the example of Antony, the two officials, and now Augustine provided models for imitation.

Augustine's testimony in *Confessions* is one of the most celebrated conversion accounts from the early church. Moreover, by narrating faith stories within his own faith story, Augustine does seem to have an evangelistic purpose for his contemporary readers, who could probably identify with at least one of the characters mentioned in Augustine's narrative.

Discipleship Forms and Values

In the early church, there seemed to be an organic relationship between evangelism and discipleship. In fact, within the gospel accounts, it is difficult to show the precise point when the Twelve were converted and when they began discipleship. In the fourth and fifth centuries, one key evangelistic strategy of the church was inviting non-believers to put their name in for baptism, which set in motion a period of catechesis (instruction) leading up to the actual day of baptism.[71] With this in mind, let us

---

68. Ibid., 8.6.13.
69. Ibid., 8.12.30.
70. Ibid., 9.2.2.
71. See Ferguson, "Baptism," 160–63; and also Ferguson's recently released expansive work, *Baptism in the Early Church*.

briefly survey two forms of patristic discipleship. The first, catechesis, will be explored as a means of lay discipleship; while the second, monasticism, will be considered as a means of forming spiritual leaders.

Catechesis

The early church did not espouse an "easy believism." After submitting their name for baptism, petitioners were scrutinized by the church leadership and, if accepted, were admitted as catechumens—those preparing for baptism.[72] From the early second century, there is evidence that instruction was given prior to baptism.[73] In the early third century, Hippolytus (c. 170–236), in his *Apostolic Tradition*, referred to a fairly developed system of catechesis in Rome that included three years of pre-baptismal teaching.[74] In the fourth century, the catechumenate was largely confined to the forty-day Lenten period leading up to Easter, when new believers were baptized.

What was the content of a catechumen's instruction?[75] New believers, many of whom came from pagan backgrounds, were provided with moral instruction from the Scriptures.[76] At the same time, they were exorcized and invited to renounce their former life. At various stages in the patristic period, exorcism took place at the outset of the catechumenate, during Lent, and just prior to baptism.[77] Irenaeus and Augustine both included a survey of biblical and salvation history in their catechesis.[78] Eventually, the focal point of pre-baptismal catechetical instruction became the so-called Nicene Creed. During the Lenten period, catechu-

---

72. This term developed in the third century and was used in *Passion of Perpetua and Felicitas* 2; and Tertullian *Prescription against Heretics* 41; see also Yarnold, *Awe-Inspiring Rites of Initiation*, 2–6.

73. *Didache* 7.1; Justin *First Apology* 61; also Ferguson, "Catechesis, Catechumenate," 223.

74. Hyppolytus *Apostolic Tradition* 17.1.

75. For a thorough discussion of each stage of the catechumenate, including baptism, see Yarnold, *Awe-Inspiring Rites of Initiation*, 2–40.

76. See *Didache* 1–6; Justin *First Apology* 61.

77. Yarnold, *Awe-Inspiring Rites of Initiation*, 5, 9, 18–20.

78. See Irenaeus *Proof of the Apostolic Preaching*; and Augustine *Instructing Beginners in Faith*.

mens received lectures in which each line of the Creed was expounded and then, just prior to baptism, they "handed it back" *(traditio)* in a public declaration of faith.[79] In some churches, the Lord's Prayer was also recited in a similar manner.[80] In the week following baptism, further instruction was given on the meaning of baptism, chrism (anointing with oil), and the Eucharist.[81]

Discipleship Values in Catechesis

Given the significant number of treatises and sermons devoted to catechesis in the patristic period, including manuals written to train and equip catechists, it is quite evident that teaching new believers both before and after baptism was a priority for the early church.[82] What were the prevailing discipleship values for catechumens?

First, the church recognized that many came from pagan backgrounds and had much to learn about the gospel and much to change in their lives. The emphasis on exorcism also reveals a worldview that acknowledged the presence and work of the Evil One. Hence, with conversion, the new believer also had a great deal to renounce from the former life.[83]

Second, and related, there was significant emphasis on moral and character change. Perhaps the *Didache*'s emphasis on choosing the "way of life" over the "way of death" best communicates this value.[84] Though he spoke of a three-year catechumenate in his *Apostolic Tradition*,

---

79. Yarnold, *Awe-Inspiring Rites of Initiation*, 12–13.

80. Ibid., 14.

81. Ferguson, "Catechesis, Catechumenate," 224.

82. Though my discussion has primarily dealt with catechesis in the Western church, the following sermons and treatises on catechesis show a rich catechetical tradition in the Western and Eastern church: Irenaeus *Proof of the Apostolic Preaching*; Hippolytus *Apostolic Tradition* 16–20; Cyril of Jerusalem,*Catechetical Lectures*; author unknown, *Mystagogical Catecheses*; Theodore of Mopsuestia *Catechetical Homilies*; John Chrysostom *Baptismal Catecheses*; Ambrose *On the Mysteries, On the Sacraments*, and *Explanation of the Symbol*; and Augustine *Sermons* 56–59, 212–18, 363. Training guides and manuals for catechists included: Gregory of Nyssa *Catechetical Orations*; Augustine *Instructing Beginners in Faith* and *On Faith and the Creed*.

83. See Justin *First Apology* 14; Augustine *Sermon* 215.1; also Merdinger, "Do You Renounce Satan?"; and Kreider, "'They Alone Know,'" 177.

84. *Didache* 1–6; also Ferguson, "Catechesis, Catechumenate," 223.

Hippolytus indicated that the most important consideration was whether the catechumen had experienced life change: "Have they honored the widows? Have they visited the sick? Have they done every kind of good work?" In this case, "the time shall not be judged, but only [the candidate's] conduct."[85]

Third, there was an emphasis on sound doctrine. As noted, every believer needed to be able to hand over the Creed prior to being baptized. Thus, Gregory of Nyssa's fourth-century observation that common people were debating the Trinity in Constantinople should not be a surprise, because even the simplest layman was required to be doctrinally literate before being baptized.[86]

Fourth, catechesis required new believers to be conversant with the content of Scripture. This was best modeled by Irenaeus and Augustine, who included a survey of biblical and salvation history as part of their teaching. Scripture's importance did not diminish at the end of the catechumenate as the reading and preaching of Scripture occupied a central place in communal worship in the patristic period. In *Letter* 71 to Jerome in c. 403, Augustine raised the issue of how Jerome rendered "gourd" in Jonah 4:6 in the Vulgate translation.[87] Augustine's concern was prompted by news that when the new translation was read in a church assembly in Libya, the people rioted when they heard that "gourd" *(cucurbita)* had been changed to "ivy" *(hedera)*. Though Augustine and Jerome's correspondence gives us an appreciation for the challenges of Bible translation in this period, it more significantly shows how well the faithful knew the Scriptures: they could recognize a single word change in the book of Jonah!

Finally, the process of the catechumenate also pointed to the sanctity of worship. Catechumens as well as non-believers were dismissed from the worship assembly before the Eucharist was celebrated. This opportunity for worship was reserved for those who had shown themselves faithful to learn the Scriptures and the Creed, to declare their faith

---

85. Hippolytus *Apostolic Tradition* 19; 17 (Kreider, "'They Alone Know,'" 176).
86. See Gregory of Nyssa *Oration on the Deity of the Son and the Holy Spirit*.
87. Augustine *Letter* 71.3.5.

publicly in baptism, and thus to appreciate the importance of corporate worship in the community of believers.

Monastic Community

In recent years, an increasing amount of scholarship has been devoted to the fourth-century phenomenon of the monk-bishop. That is, monks were being ordained as bishops (i.e., Basil of Caesarea, Augustine) or some bishops were embracing at least some aspects of monastic living (i.e., Athanasius, Ambrose).[88] As a result, the bishops' monastic programs directly influenced how they discipled other spiritual leaders. Let us briefly survey the spiritual formation strategy of two monk-bishops, Basil of Caesarea (c. 329–79) and Augustine (354–430).

Raised in an ascetic family, Basil was a protégé of the ascetic Bishop Eustathius of Sebaste, and then later founded his own monastic retreat on his family's estate in Pontus.[89] Compelled to defend the church against the Arian threat that was raging in Asia Minor, Basil accepted ordination and eventually became the bishop of Caesarea in 370. Though occasionally taking retreats back to the family estate, Basil established a monastery in Caesarea that included both ordained clergy and laymen. His daily monastic program included singing Psalms, Scripture reading and memorization, doctrinal training against heresy, and ascetic discipline. His monastic *Rules (Long Rules* and *Short Rules)* provided direction for communal living, and his *Morals* gave instruction on how spiritual leaders should conduct themselves. While his monastic labor was pastoring the church at Caesarea, Basil also established a hospice for the poor on the outskirts of the city. Though the monastery and hospice were not deliberate training centers for church leaders, clergy were nevertheless being discipled in this context and, at times, Basil ordained some qualified monks to church leadership.[90]

---

88. See Rousseau, "Spiritual Authority of the 'Monk-Bishop,'" 380–419; Sterk, *Renouncing the World*; Demacopoulos, *Five Models of Spiritual Direction*; and Smither, *Augustine as Mentor*.

89. Basil *Letters* 207.2; 223.5; Gregory of Nazianzus *Letter* 6.37; also Rousseau, *Basil*, 68–69, 84–85; and Sterk, *Renouncing the World*, 35–40.

90. See Sterk, *Renouncing the* World, 27, 136, 147–50; and Rousseau, *Basil*, 142.

Learning from Patristic Evangelism and Discipleship

Augustine's ascetic "itinerary" began at Cassiciacum soon after his conversion and continued in an increasingly monastic trajectory at Tagaste prior to his ordination as a priest at Hippo in 391.[91] Despite Demacopoulos' assertion that Augustine "rarely utilized his ascetic training with respect to the priesthood," Augustine effectively combined the contemplative life and active life and mentored the Hippo clergy in monastic community.[92] Augustine reports that upon his consecration as priest, Bishop Valerius, approving of Augustine's continuation of a monastic lifestyle, gave him land next to the Hippo basilica on which to build a monastery.[93] The garden monastery attracted monks from all walks of life, including ordained ministers.[94] The daily routine included personal and corporate prayer, Scripture reading, other spiritually nourishing reading, common meals, mealtime theological discussion, and work. For the ordained clergy, their work was, of course, service in the Hippo church.[95]

When Augustine succeeded Valerius as bishop of Hippo in 396–97, he established the *monasterium clericorum*, a monastery comprised solely of the ordained clergy at Hippo.[96] While the daily schedule and disciplines resembled those in the garden monastery, the clergy house was distinct in that it was open to visitors. Though Augustine's duties as a bishop pulled him more from a life of contemplation, it would be an overstatement to conclude that he abandoned his monastic convictions altogether.[97]

---

91. For a further discussion on Augustine's journey in monasticism, see Smither, *Augustine as Mentor*, 135–58; Ladner, *Idea of Reform*, 353; and Lawless, "Augustine's First Monastery," 65–78.

92. Demacopoulos, *Five Models of Spiritual Direction*, 85; see my discussion on Augustine using the monastery as a means of mentoring clergy in Smither, *Augustine as Mentor*, 146–48.

93. Augustine *Sermon* 355.2.

94. Augustine *Letters* 64.3; 209.3; also Zumkeller, *Augustine's Ideal*, 37.

95. Smither, *Augustine as Mentor*, 146–47.

96. The two had served as co-bishops since 395.

97. Mandouze, *Saint Augustine*, 219.

Monastic Discipleship Values

Despite significant linguistic, cultural, and theological differences in their contexts, there are at least two common themes in the monastic discipleship strategies of Basil and Augustine. First, they were both convinced that community itself was an essential means of spiritual growth. As noted, Basil's *Long* and *Short Rules* provided direction, even down to the smallest detail, for how a monastic community should function. In *Morals,* he encouraged spiritual leaders to benefit from the godly influence of a spiritual community, to give priority to the community's needs, and to confront the sins of one another in the community.[98] Brian McGuire correctly concludes that in Basil's writings "community is exalted as desirable in itself," and that "Basil is the first monastic writer in the East to be totally convinced that a common life provided the best way of bringing individual men to God."[99]

As Augustine's pre-conversion life was characterized by friendship and friends were present even when he made his commitment to Christ, it is hardly surprising that Augustine would also view the group as vital to spiritual growth. In fact, the only formal vow that Augustine's monks made upon entering the monastery was the commitment to communal living.[100] In his commentary on Psalm 132,[101] Augustine defined unity in the monastic context as brothers having "one heart and soul toward God."[102] As Augustine believed that the ascetic disciplines of prayer, fasting, study, and work were key to making spiritual progress, he was also convinced that the monk or spiritual leader needed the accountability and support of a community in order to succeed in the monastic venture. Thus he exhorted the more mature to stand with the weaker ones in their common goal: "Will he who makes good progress retreat so that he permits no human company at all? What if before he made progress no

---

98. Smither, *Augustine as Mentor,* 66; also Basil *Morals* 16.1; 27; 30–31; 33–34; 37–38; 42–46; 48.5; 52.1; 60; 70; and Ladner, *Idea of Reform,* 341–42.

99. McGuire, *Friendship and Community,* 25, 31.

100. Augustine *Rule* 1.2–4; *On the Work of Monks* 17.20, 25, 32, 38; *Sermon* 356.1; and Possidius *Life of Augustine* 5; also Zumkeller, *Augustine's Ideal,* 131.

101. Psalm 132 in the Vulgate is Psalm 133 in English translations.

102. Augustine *Exposition of the Psalms* 132.2 (Zumkeller, *Augustine's Ideal,* 398).

one wished to suffer him at all? ... Let your love then pay attention. The apostle says 'bearing with each other in love, eager to preserve the unity of the Spirit in the bond of peace.'"[103]

A second key discipleship value for Basil and Augustine was a commitment to sound doctrine. Both men's ministries were marked by prolonged battles with heretical and schismatic movements that threatened the health of the church. Both believed that the canonical Scriptures were the basis for sound doctrine. In *Morals*, Basil insisted that the Scriptures were vital to spiritual growth and ministry, and they were to be believed, followed, obeyed, and taught faithfully.[104] In the *Long Rules*, Basil taught that the Scriptures should be the basis of monastic education and that a key role of the monastic overseer was teaching Scripture.[105] In *Letter* 101, Augustine described the training of Possidius, a member of the Hippo monastery who later became bishop of Calama: "For he was nourished through our ministry, not in that literature that those enslaved to various desires call liberal, but with the bread of the Lord."[106] Writing Augustine's biography years later, Possidius added that a major outcome of Augustine's training program was that ten ordained clergy emerged from the Hippo monastery to serve the church in North Africa. Possidius described them as "venerable men of continence and learning" whose "zeal for the spread of God's word increased."[107]

Conclusion: Points of Recovery?

Since a great historical and cultural distance separates the early church from the modern evangelical church, one wonders what can be reasonably recovered from the fathers in evangelism and discipleship. I would like to conclude with some ancient-modern "talking points" as well as some questions for reflection.

First, the socially integrated evangelistic witness of the early Christians offers a model for modern Christians wanting to be *in* but not

103. Ibid., 99.9 (Zumkeller, *Augustine's Ideal*, 388).
104. Basil *Morals* 8; 12.2; 17.1; 18; 26.12; 28; 41; 44; 70.12.
105. Basil *Long Rules* 15, 41, 47; also Sterk, *Renouncing the World*, 51.
106. Augustine *Letter* 101.1 (Teske, *Letters 100–155*, 17).
107. Possidius *Life of Augustine* 11.3–4 (Fellowes, *Life of Saint Augustine*).

of the world. On the whole, North American and European evangelicals in the last century have tended to be marginalized from the greater society largely by our own doing. While living in a secular culture requires much wisdom, the early church seemed to continue the integrated model of Jesus, who proclaimed an uncompromising message of repentance, yet had table fellowship with the likes of Zacchaeus.

A second value is the emphasis on lay witness. The eighteenth-century Moravian conviction that "every Christian is a missionary" could have also applied to second- and third-century Carthage. While more recent groups like the Moravians, Methodists, and even twentieth-century parachurch groups like Campus Crusade for Christ and ministries such as Evangelism Explosion have emphasized training lay people in evangelism, too many evangelicals continue to be persuaded that such spiritual work is the work of a paid, spiritual professional. If our neighbors are interested in the gospel, are we capable of witnessing to them or must we make an appointment with the pastor?

On a positive note, globalization is actually fostering anonymous missionary movements in many parts of the world today. For instance, Filipino, Indian, and Pakistani guest workers have been instrumental in bringing the gospel to the Gulf region and North Africa. Peruvian missiologist Samuel Escobar estimates that for every official missionary sent from Latin America, another ten Christians have gone abroad for work, and some of those have had remarkable success in evangelism and church planting.[108]

Regarding discipleship, the modern church has much to glean from the early church in its commitment to learning Scripture and doctrine—resounding themes observed both in catechetical and monastic contexts. What is a modern new believer receiving in the way of teaching before being baptized?[109] For that matter, what is the average church member learning in modern churches that have succumbed to pragmatism, that overemphasize technology, and that expect Attention Deficit Disorder? I submit that a revival of biblically focused and doctrinally rich disciple-

---

108. Escobar, *Changing Tides*, 160–63.

109. Clinton Arnold has offered a very helpful reflection on new members' classes in light of the early church model in "Early Church Catechesis," 39–54.

ship would be very useful and strategic for the church as she presses on to be salt and light in an increasingly secular culture.

Finally, the evangelical church in the West today has much to glean from the conviction of Basil and Augustine that spiritual growth happens best in community. Unfortunately, it seems that the church has overly catered to an individualistic culture and attempted to disciple isolated believers. How would Augustine feel about the multi-site church revolution? Would he forsake rich spiritual and theological mealtime discussions for a chance to blog instead?

Indeed, there is significant cultural and historical distance between the early church and the modern evangelical church, and our issues today were not necessarily theirs then. However, this study has shown that there are a number of principles for evangelism and discipleship that should encourage, inspire, and even instruct.[110]

---

110. I wish to thank Emily Heady, Bryan Liftin, Brian Shelton, Rex Butler, Frank Gumerlock, Glen Thompson, and David Alexander, who read initial drafts of this paper and provided helpful feedback.

3

Learning from Patristic Community Formation

REX D. BUTLER

❧ THE NEW trend among evangelicals is something old—the early church. As promoted by the late Robert Webber in his Ancient-Future Faith Series[1] and reported by Chris Armstrong in a recent issue of *Christianity Today*,[2] many evangelical congregations are looking back to the patristic church for patterns of corporate Christian life and worship. These young Christians (and some older ones) have become dissatisfied with church buildings that resemble malls, worship services that sound like rock concerts, and programs that are patterned after consumer-oriented businesses.[3] As a result, they are now engaging in such ancient practices as observation of the liturgical calendar, weekly celebration of the Eucharist, recitation of creeds, and public confession.[4]

My responsibility in this paper is to discuss what the contemporary church might learn from the early church in the areas of community formation and maintenance, including baptismal practices, the Eucharist, and other acts of worship, and church discipline. First, I present selected

---

1. See especially Webber's *Ancient-Future Faith* and *Ancient-Future Worship*.
2. Armstrong, "Future Lies in the Past," 23–29. This topic has also been reported by the secular press; for example, Salmon, "Feeling Renewed by Ancient Traditions;" and Tolson, "Return to Tradition," 42–48.
3. Armstrong, "Future Lies in the Past," 26.
4. Tolson, "Return to Tradition," 44.

descriptions of these rituals as practiced in the patristic period, focusing on the second- and third-century church in the West[5] and glancing backward, forward, and toward the East. Then I show how some contemporary congregations are appropriating these ancient practices today. Finally, I briefly offer my own recommendations concerning ancient-future lessons, emphasizing a circumspect *ressourcement*.

Baptism in the Early Church

During the early centuries of the church, baptism and the Eucharist became more elaborate as symbolic actions were added to the simple rites described in the New Testament. The rich imagery attempted to communicate through symbolism the work of Christ in believers both in their initiation and in their continued communion in the church. The symbolic actions served an educational function in congregations where the members were largely illiterate. Some of the most detailed descriptions of early baptismal rites conducted in the ante-Nicene church are found in Justin Martyr's apologetic writings;[6] the *Apostolic Tradition*, attributed to Hippolytus of Rome;[7] and several of Tertullian's treatises, especially *On Baptism*.[8]

---

5. Webber, *Common Roots*, 8, expressed a partiality toward the second-century church. The reason that I concentrate on the ante-Nicene church is that the period reflects earlier Christianity and influenced the post-Nicene church. I focus on the Western church simply because I must narrow the parameters further. Certainly the Eastern church is significant in a study of patristic formation and maintenance, and is referenced occasionally.

6. Justin Martyr was executed in Rome about 165. His major extant writings are the *First Apology*, the *Second Apology*, and *Dialogue with Trypho*. All quotations are from ANF. Everett Ferguson's recently published tome, *Baptism in the Early Church*, was received after the completion of this essay.

7. The *Apostolic Tradition* reflected the order of the Roman church in the second and third centuries. Its enduring influence, however, was strongest in the East, especially Egypt and Syria. For this reason, a study of the baptismal practices reflected in this treatise provides a broad understanding of the ritual throughout the early church. See Easton, introduction to *Apostolic Tradition of Hippolytus*, 27–78. All quotations from the *Apostolic Tradition* are from Bradshaw et al., *Apostolic Tradition*. The citations are numbered according to the system devised by Bernard Botte.

8. Written around the turn of the third century, Tertullian's treatise *On Baptism* is the earliest surviving monograph on Christian baptism. All translations of Tertullian's writings are mine.

Early in church history, candidates for baptism underwent a period of catechesis before their initiation into the church.[9] Around the middle of the second century, Justin wrote, "As many as are persuaded and believe that what we teach and say is true, and undertake to live accordingly" are brought to the water of baptism (*1 Apol.* 61). Tertullian reported that, about fifty years later, candidates in Carthage received pre-baptismal instruction (*Bapt.* 18.4) but gave no clue to its duration. According to Hippolytus, one of Tertullian's contemporaries, catechesis in the Roman church usually lasted for three years.[10] Zealous individuals, however, were permitted to be baptized earlier if their character permitted (*Trad.* 17.1–2). By the time of Augustine, about two centuries later, catechumens who were deemed worthy of baptism were encouraged to enroll before Lent.[11] During that forty-day period, they entered into a rigorous regimen of preparation, which included daily instructions on the baptismal creed and the Lord's Prayer, fasting, prayer, almsgiving, frequent exorcisms, and abstention from sexual activities and bathing.[12]

As the time for baptism approached, the examination of the catechumens intensified to determine "if they lived virtuously while they were catechumens, and if they honored the widows, and if they visited those who are sick, and if they fulfilled every good work" (*Trad.* 20.1). During the final week, they were exorcised daily. On Thursday, they bathed, and, after fasting on Friday, they assembled on Saturday to kneel in prayer before the bishop, who laid his hands upon them to exorcise all evil spirits so that they would flee and never return.[13] Afterward, the bishop is instructed: "Let him blow into them. And when he has sealed their foreheads, and their ears and nostrils, let him raise them up" (*Trad.* 20.8).[14] This ritual has been interpreted in opposite ways: as a rite of

---

9. The earliest non-canonical example of pre-baptismal instruction is found in the *Didache*. The teaching about the way of death and the way of life, found in chapters 1–6, was intended to be reviewed with those about to be baptized. *Did.* 7.1.

10. See Folkemer, "Study of the Catechumenate," 244–65.

11. Harmless, "Catechumens, Catechumenate," 147–48.

12. Harmless, "Baptism," 85.

13. Augustine explained that the bath was necessary because the candidates had abstained from ablutions during Lent. Augustine *Ep.* 54.10.

14. Touching the nose was substituted for touching the mouth out of concern for propriety in the baptism of women. Cabié, "Christian Initiation," 35.

Learning from Patristic Community Formation

opening, or "Ephphetha," which recalled the deaf mute of Mark 7:32-35 and indicated that the initiates' ears were opened to the mysteries of the liturgy;[15] and as a rite of closing the senses to evil.[16]

Tertullian acknowledged that any Lord's Day was acceptable for baptism but suggested that Easter and Pentecost added solemnity to the occasion (*Bapt.* 19). On whatever day was chosen for baptism, the preparations were very elaborate. At dawn, prayers were made to implore God to consecrate the baptismal water through the descent of the Spirit. In this way, the water was imbued with sacramental power to sanctify the one who was immersed therein (*Bapt.* 4). According to Tertullian, there was no difference between water that was running or still, outside or indoors (*Bapt.* 4.3).[17]

The candidates were baptized in a certain order: children, men, then women.[18] All catechumens removed their clothing;[19] the women loosened their hair and put aside all jewelry. The bishop prepared two kinds of oil, one of thanksgiving, and the other of exorcism. Two deacons, each bearing the oil, attended the presbyter, who commanded the catechumen to renounce Satan, his demons, and his works (*Trad.* 21.3-9; *Cor.* 3.2).[20]

15. Yarnold, *Awe-Inspiring Rites*, 17-18.

16. Bradshaw et al., *Apostolic Tradition*, 111.

17. In the *Didache* 7.1-3, there is a preference for "living" or running water, perhaps derived from Jesus's baptism in the Jordan River, but it offered alternatives in descending order: cold water, collected fresh at its natural temperature; warm water that had stood in a cistern; or affusion, if sufficient water for immersion was lacking.

18. The practice of infant baptism had already begun: "And first baptize the small children. And each one who is able to speak for themselves, let them speak. But those not able to speak for themselves, let their parents or another one belonging to their family speak for them." *Trad.* 21.4. This practice, however, was not universal yet, for Tertullian, writing just prior to Hippolytus, discouraged it as an innovation. *Bapt.* 18.5.

19. Guy suggested that, in most cases, the baptismal candidates set aside only the outer garments due to the impropriety of the baptism of naked women by male clergy. Guy, "'Naked' Baptism in the Early Church," 133-42. Van der Meer argued for naked baptism with the contention that public baths had minimized modesty between men and women. Van der Meer, *Augustine the Bishop*, 367.

20. In Augustine's church, the candidates faced west to renounce Satan and then east to proclaim their allegiance to Christ: "'As far as the east is from the west has he distanced our sins from us'.... When sin is pardoned your sins set and your grace rises: it is sunset for your sins and sunrise for the grace that liberates you." Augustine *Expsitions of the Psalms* 102.19 (Boulding, *Expositions of the Psalms*, vol. 5).

After the renunciation, the presbyter anointed the candidate with the oil of exorcism immediately before the baptismal rite (*Trad.* 21.10).

Baptism was conducted by triple immersion in the name of the Father, the Son, and the Holy Spirit while those being baptized responded with what Tertullian described as "a slightly broader answer than the Lord has commanded in the Gospel" (*Cor.* 3.3; see also *Bapt.* 6.2). This "broader answer" was presented fully in the *Apostolic Tradition* in the form of a baptismal creed, which includes all the elements of the *regula fidei*.[21] In baptism, it was presented in interrogatory form to the candidates to give them an opportunity to express their solidarity with the Rule of Faith:

> Do you believe in God the Father Almighty? . . . Do you believe in Christ Jesus, the Son of God, who was born by the Holy Spirit from the Virgin Mary and crucified under Pontius Pilate, and died and was buried and rose on the third day alive from the dead, and ascended into heaven and sits on the right hand of the Father, and will come to judge the living and the dead? . . . Do you believe in the Holy Spirit and the holy church and the resurrection of the flesh? (*Trad.* 21.12–17)[22]

Following each question, the candidate responded, "I believe," and was immersed.

In the *Apostolic Tradition*, various duties were ascribed to bishops, presbyters, and deacons. According to Tertullian, the primary authority for baptism belonged to the bishop, but that authority could be delegated to priests and deacons or even laymen—but not laywomen (*Bapt.* 17.1–2, 4–5). After emerging from the baptismal water, the one newly baptized was anointed with the oil of thanksgiving (*Trad.* 21.19, 22; *Bapt.* 7), signed with the cross (*Trad.* 21.23; *Res.* 8.3), given the kiss of peace (*Trad.* 21.23), and had the administrator's hands imposed in welcome of the Holy Spirit (*Bapt.* 8.1). After the descent of the Spirit and the ascent

---

21. See Litfin's entry in this present work.

22. The first question is omitted from the Sahidic version, although it is implied by the inclusion of the second and third questions. Likewise, the Latin fragment is missing the first question but includes the other two. Therefore, this quotation begins with the question as presented in the *Canons of Hippolytus*, a derivative of *Apostolic Tradition* composed in Egypt in the mid-fourth century. Bradshaw et al., *Apostolic Tradition*, 10–11.

of the neophyte from the font, the time had come to ask for spiritual gifts (*Bapt.* 20.5)[23] and to dress again (*Trad.* 21.20).[24]

At the conclusion of the baptismal service, the entire community prayed together and closed the prayer service with the kiss of peace (*Trad.* 21.25-26; *Bapt.* 20.5), which was a sign of filial love and of welcome into God's family. Until the completion of the initiation, catechumens were not allowed to pray with or give the kiss of peace to the faithful. The culmination of the initiation was another first: the baptismal Eucharist, which included bread and three cups—one of wine; another that was a mixture of milk and honey, symbolizing entrance into the Promised Land (*Trad.* 21.27-28; *Cor.* 3.3); and, finally, a cup of water, which provided the inner person with the baptism just received by the body (*Trad.* 21.29).

These descriptions of the baptismal ceremonies of the early church reveal both a departure from the simplicity of New Testament baptism and also the development of rich imagery of the conversion experience: the candidates renounce Satan and pledge allegiance to Christ; they strip off the old selves and clothe themselves with the new; the water cleanses from sin; the triple immersion emphasizes the operation of the Trinity; the imposition of hands summons the ministry of the Holy Spirit and the endowment of spiritual gifts; the oil seals the believers; the new members of the body of Christ partake of the bread and wine of the Eucharist; and the new citizens of the Promised Land drink of milk and honey.

The Eucharist in the Early Church

The baptismal ceremony described in the *Apostolic Tradition* closed with a Eucharist that involved three cups. This expanded ritual, however,

23. In *Passio de Perpetuae et Felicitatis*, Perpetua reported her experience with the Spirit following baptism: "The Spirit directed me to request nothing else after the water except endurance of the flesh." *Pass. Pert.* 3.5. Her experience reflected Tertullian's exhortation to catechumens in his treatise *De Baptismo*: "Therefore, blessed ones, ... when you ascend from that most holy bath of new birth and spread out your hands for the first time, ... ask from the Father, ask from the Lord, to receive personal resources of grace and distributions of gifts." *Bapt.* 20.5. Translations are mine.

24. By the time of Augustine, the neophytes, as they were called, received a white linen robe that symbolized the spotless purity of the newly baptized, who wore these robes for the following eight days. Van der Meer, *Augustine the Bishop*, 369-70.

was reserved for the conclusion of baptism, and a simpler rite was the more regular pattern in the early church. Justin Martyr, Hippolytus, and Tertullian provided early descriptions of the Eucharist in the Western church.

As a second-century apologist, Justin Martyr attempted to communicate to his Roman community the truth about Christian life and worship, including the Eucharist,[25] which he outlined in his *First Apology*. After the reading of Scripture, a sermon, and congregational prayers, then bread and a cup of wine mixed with water[26] were brought by the deacons to the president (the bishop, *Trad.* 4.1), who lifted up the prayer of thanksgiving to God the Father through the name of the Son and of the Holy Spirit.[27] At the conclusion of this eucharistic prayer, all the people said "Amen," which Justin explained to his readers is Hebrew for "so be it." Afterward, in order to maintain the unity of the church, deacons carried a portion of the Eucharist to those absent from the congregation (*1 Apol.* 67). Thus, the eucharistic service consisted of two acts: consecration and communion.[28]

---

25. Historians such as González reported that the Christians' pagan neighbors circulated rumors about ritual cannibalism during the Eucharist. See González, *Story of Christianity*, 50. McGowan argued instead that the charges of cannibalism originated not in the "body and blood" of the Eucharist but in the pagans' perception of Christians as threats to society and, as such, as aliens and practitioners of evil taboos. McGowan, "Eating People," 413–42. Justin referred to accusations of "eating human flesh" (*1 Apol.* 26) and drinking blood (*2 Apol.* 12) but did not tie them to the Eucharist. Minucius Felix (*Oct.* 9) and Tertullian (*Ad. Nat.* 1), Latin writers of the second to third centuries, did connect charges of cannibalism to initiatory rituals. Therefore, it seems possible in my opinion (*contra* McGowan's) that, at some point, the pagans found, in addition to their general suspicions, a basis for their accusations of Christian cannibalism in stories about the "body and blood" of the Eucharist.

26. Ferguson explained, "The common table beverage of the ancient world was wine diluted with water. Justin thus counters wild pagan stories about the Christian meal by saying that Christians ate ordinary bread and drank the common table beverage (not something more intoxicating)." Ferguson, "How We Christians Worship," 13.

27. According to Justin, this prayer was offered at "considerable length." *1 Apol.* 65. In the *Apostolic Tradition*, the bishop could pray a grand and elevated prayer, if he were able, or he could pray a brief and fixed prayer. *Trad.* 10.4–5. For an example of a Eucharistic prayer, see *Trad.* 4.4–13.

28. Ferguson, "How We Christians Worship," 13.

In his *Dialogue with Trypho*, Justin described the Eucharist not only as a thanksgiving but also as a memorial. The Lord Jesus Christ prescribed the celebration

> in remembrance (ἀνάμνησις) of the suffering which He endured on behalf of those who are purified in soul from all iniquity, in order that we may at the same time thank God for having created the world, with all things therein, for the sake of man, and for delivering us from the evil in which we were, and for utterly overthrowing principalities and powers by Him who suffered according to His will. (*Dial.* 41)

Justin restricted the Eucharist to baptized converts:

> For not as common bread and common drink do we receive these; but in like manner as Jesus Christ our Saviour, having been made flesh by the Word of God, had both flesh and blood for our salvation, so likewise have we been taught that the food which is blessed by the prayer of His word, and from which our blood and flesh by transmutation are nourished, is the flesh and blood of that Jesus who was made flesh. (*1 Apol.* 66)

Furthermore, Justin saw the celebration of the Eucharist predicted in Malachi 1:10–12:

> I have no pleasure in you, saith the Lord; and I will not accept your sacrifices at your hands: for, from the rising of the sun unto the going down of the same, My name has been glorified among the Gentiles, and in every place incense is offered to My name, and a pure offering: for My name is great among the Gentiles, saith the Lord: but ye profane it. (*Dial.* 41)

Expanding on this text, Justin interpreted the prophecy as a rejection of the Jewish sacrifices in favor of the Gentiles' pure offering, which was the bread and cup by which the Lord's name was glorified (*Dial.* 41).

Hippolytus, in his instructions about the Eucharist, warned bishops to keep the liturgy a secret from the uninitiated: "This is the white stone of which John said, 'There is a new name written on it, which no one knows except the one who will receive the stone'" (*Trad.* 21.40). With this warning, Hippolytus expressed the concept of the Eucharist as a mystery, revealed only to believers after baptism. Therefore, the unbaptized seekers and catechumens were dismissed before the Eucharist, and the worship service was divided into two parts: the *synaxis*, the open gathering for all worshippers; and the Eucharist proper.²⁹

Paul used the Greek word μυστήριον in such passages as Ephesians 1:9–10, 3:8–9, and 5:32 to speak of the "mystery of His will," "the administration of the mystery which for ages has been hidden in God," and the fact that the "mystery is great; but I am speaking with reference to Christ and the church" (NASB). For Paul, this "mystery" referred to God's hidden plan of salvation through Christ for the church. For Hippolytus and Tertullian, however, the saving work of Christ was revealed to the church through rites such as the Eucharist and baptism. Tertullian translated the Greek word μυστήριον into the Latin term *sacramentum*,³⁰ which meant, in one sense, "something set apart as sacred," and thereby introduced early sacramental language into the Western church.³¹ The Eastern Orthodox Church still refers to sacraments as mysteries.

In a liturgy separate from the eucharistic service, Hippolytus described the *agape*, or love feast (*Trad.* 23.3–4; 26–29). This meal was distinct in several ways: the bread was described as "blessed" (εὐλογητός) as opposed to the Eucharist; the feasts were held in private homes; the guests broke their own bread and gave thanks for their own cups; and, in return for their invitations, they were expected to pray for their hosts. Hippolytus issued warnings that alluded to the abuses reported by Paul in 1 Corinthians 11:20–22 and condemned by other church fathers, such as Tertullian (*De ieiun.* 17). Due to such controversies, the *agape* was separated from the Eucharist in the mid-second century; however, the meal was not discontinued altogether until the end of the patristic period.³²

---

29. Guy, *Introducing Early Christianity*, 196.

30. Tertullian *Adv. Marc.* 5.17.1; 5.18.2; 5.18.9; *De an.* 21.2; *De ieiun.* 3.2. For a recent study of how the use of the word *sacramentum* changed over time, see Van Slyke, "Changing Meanings of *sacramentum*," 245–79.

31. Crehan, *Early Christian Baptism*, 103.

32. Davies, *Early Christian Church*, 153.

Learning from Patristic Community Formation

Worship in the Early Church

Justin Martyr and other church fathers indicate that, from at least the second century, the Eucharist was administered as a part of every worship service. In his *First Apology*, Justin explained that Christians met on Sunday because it commemorated both the day that God began to make the world and the day that Jesus Christ rose from the dead (*1 Apol.* 67). As Everett Ferguson points out, "Thus, the Christian day of assembly was connected by Justin with the beginning of the physical creation and with the beginning of the new creation at the Resurrection."[33] Tertullian mentioned that Christians met also on other days, such as anniversaries of martyrs' deaths, and did so before dawn (*Cor.* 3).[34]

The church calendar of the ante-Nicene church was very simple. Outside of the weekly celebration every Sunday, there were two annual celebrations: the Pascha and Pentecost. The Pascha, which was the Christian Passover, commemorated the cross and resurrection of Christ. In the days of preparation, Christians engaged in fasting and vigils, which consisted of prayer and the reading of Scriptures. Pentecost was the period of fifty days following the Pascha, and Tertullian said of that season that "we celebrate that occasion with excessive rejoicing" (*De ieiun.* 14). For the early Christians, these few weekly and annual observations sufficed and served to express their eschatological joy.[35]

This simple calendar contented the early church until the Constantinian era, when the union of church and state allowed a more elaborate system of festivals and holy days. The liturgical celebration of Christmas Day on December 25 was instituted at least by 336.[36] Even ear-

---

33. Ferguson, "How We Christians Worship," 12.

34. For a non-Christian reference to early worship, see the letter of Pliny the Younger to Trajan, in which he reported that Christians were accustomed to go to a "meeting on a given day before dawn, and singing responsively a hymn to Christ as to God, swearing with a holy oath not to commit any crime ... When all this was finished, it was their custom to go their separate ways, and later re-assemble to take food of an ordinary and simple kind." Pliny *Ep.* 10.96–97 (Harris, "Pliny, *Epistulae*").

35. Davies, *Early Christian Church*, 154.

36. Davies repeated an often-stated belief that December 25 was chosen specifically to coincide with the pagan celebration of the nativity of the *Sol Invictus*. Ibid., 210. According to William J. Tighe, however, the influence was reversed: Aurelian, Roman emperor from 270–75, instituted the pagan festival on December 25 in order to establish

lier, Lent had been developed as a six-week preparation of catechumens for baptism on Easter but later was asserted upon the entire church as a period of self-renunciation. The forty days of fasting corresponded with Christ's forty days in the wilderness.[37] Cyril of Jerusalem (d. 386) shaped the Holy Week, which included Palm Sunday; Maundy Thursday; Good Friday; Holy Saturday, which featured a night-long vigil in preparation for baptism; and, of course, Easter Sunday, with the Eucharist at dawn. Forty days after Easter Sunday came the Feast of the Ascension. Pentecost came ten days later and recalled the descent of the Spirit. Ultimately, the entire year was organized into a liturgical cycle designed "to set the facts of the gospel before the many nominal Christians who flocked into the Church."[38]

Justin, Tertullian, and other Christians met in house churches as had their forebears in the New Testament.[39] In about 165, at the trial that led to his martyrdom, Justin was asked by the prefect, "Where do you meet?" and he answered, "Wherever it is each one's preference or opportunity . . . In any case, do you suppose we all meet in the same place? Not so . . . I have been living above the baths . . . and for the entire period of my sojourn at Rome . . . I have known no other meeting-place but there. Anyone who wished could come to my abode and I would impart to him the words of truth" (*Acts of Justin* 3).[40] Justin's testimony indicated that, "although the Christians in Rome were becoming fairly numerous, they did not abandon meeting in homes, even if that meant the Christian com-

---

a pagan alternative because this date was already significant to Roman Christians. See Tighe, "Calculating Christmas." This "Calculation hypothesis" proposes that Christ's conception occurred on the same date as his death, which was supposed to occur on March 25, and that his birth followed exactly nine months later, on December 25. For a thorough discussion of this theory along with the one put forth by Davies, known as the "History of religions hypothesis," see Roll, *Toward the Origins of Christmas*.

37. Davies, *Early Christian Church*, 210. See also Dix, *Shape of the Liturgy*, 353–57.

38. Davies, *Early Christian Church*, 210–11.

39. Christians met privately in other meeting places, such as Tyrannus' school (Acts 19:9) and a warehouse on the edge of Rome mentioned in the apocryphal Acts of Paul (*Passio Pauli* 1). See White, *Social Origins of Christian Architecture*, 105.

40. In *1 Apol.* 61.3, Justin informed his readers that candidates for baptism were "brought by us where there is water." White suggested, "If these two texts of Justin can be tied together, then baptism might well have been performed downstairs at the baths." White, *Social Origins of Christian Architecture*, 110.

munity could no longer assemble in one place."[41] In Tertullian's Carthage as well, it has been estimated that there were five or six house churches, comprising three to four hundred members total.[42]

The use of homes for worship provided important advantages for evangelism during the early centuries of Christianity. The small gatherings in the intimate setting of a home church enjoyed interaction between the preacher and the hearers, free discussion among the participants, a relaxed, informal atmosphere, and Christian hospitality.[43]

A shift in the house church pattern developed before the mid-third century, as houses were converted to accommodate Christian congregations. One such building has been discovered in Dura-Europos, a town located on the banks of the Euphrates River near the eastern frontier of the Roman Empire.[44] Christopher Haas described the church at Dura-Europos:

> The private residence was modified by removing one interior wall in the dining area, creating a larger room for Christian services. A small dais at the eastern end of the hall probably served as the worship center. Benches were installed around the walls of an interior courtyard, perhaps to mark off a place of instruction. In yet another room, a canopied baptismal font was erected, flanked by frescoes of Adam and Eve, and the Good Shepherd—perhaps signifying the Fall and Redemption.[45]

Throughout the Roman world, in regions that included Croatia, Britain, Tunisia, Numidia, and Egypt, house churches were remodeled similarly.[46] This new kind of church building, known as *domus ecclesiae*,

---

41. Haas, "Where Did Christians Worship?" 32.

42. Tabbernee, "To Pardon or not to Pardon?" 381.

43. Green, *Evangelism in the Early Church*, 207–8.

44. The building at Dura-Europos, which was renovated about 240, provides the "earliest and clearest archaeological evidence" of a private house that converted to a Christian building, but, considering its geographical isolation, it probably was not the first. White, *Social Origins of Christian Architecture*, 110. Some archeologists have recently claimed that they have found earlier church buildings in Jordan and Megiddo.

45. Haas, "Where Did Christians Worship?" 34.

46. In Oxyrhynchus, Egypt, "a municipal survey of street wardens for around 295 listed two streets known as North-Church and South-Church," indicating that two church buildings were prominent landmarks. White, *Social Origins of Christian Architecture*, 123.

became necessary because many congregations outgrew private dining rooms; Christians of higher social standing were able to finance buildings devoted to Christian worship; and changes in the liturgy, especially the separation of the agape meal from the Eucharist, demanded larger rooms for assembly.[47] As the assemblies grew, so did the expansiveness of the renovations, and the *aula ecclesiae*, or "hall of the church," marked the next stage of development.[48]

Toward the end of the third century, church buildings of the next phase were designed and built specifically for Christian gatherings. Many new buildings were located adjacent to the renovated house churches and/or in the vicinity of cemeteries hallowed by martyrs' graves, where congregations had been accustomed to gather. The extent of the expansive building program during the second half of the third century was remembered by Eusebius: "[M]ass meetings gathered in every city, and congregations worshiped in new, spacious churches that replaced the old" (*Hist. eccl.* 8.1.5).[49] Most of these prayer halls were destroyed during the Great Persecution (303–11), but after Constantine's conversion, his subsequent patronage of the church led to the even larger and more splendid basilicas of the post-Nicene era.[50]

During Justin's era, when congregations met in simple house churches, the worship services were simple as well. In his *First Apology*, Justin provided an outline of a typical Sunday morning: reading of Scriptures, sermon, congregational prayer, the Eucharist, the offering. The Scriptures to which Justin referred included specifically "the memoirs of the apostles or the writings of the prophets," and the lector read "as long as time permits" (*1 Apol.* 67). In Tertullian's description of the Scriptures, he listed "the law and the prophets . . . with the writings of evangelists and apostles" (*de Praes.* 36) as well as the psalms, which were chanted (*de An.* 9).

The sermon was delivered by the president (literally "the one presiding over the brethren"), whom Everett Ferguson describes as "a congre-

---

47. Haas, "Where Did Christians Worship?" 34–35.
48. White, *Social Origins of Christian Architecture*, 128–29.
49. From Maier, *Eusebius*, 289.
50. Haas, "Where Did Christians Worship?" 35.

Learning from Patristic Community Formation

gational overseer or pastor, not a diocesan bishop."[51] Justin emphasized the expository nature and moral content of the sermon, which was typical of preaching in the early church: "the president verbally instructs, and exhorts to the imitation of these good things" (*1 Apol.* 67).[52]

At the conclusion of the sermon, all the congregants "rise together and pray" (*1 Apol.* 67). The standing posture of this corporate prayer indicated generally "joy and boldness, showing the freedom of God's children to come boldly into his presence," and specifically a celebration of the resurrection on the Lord's Day. Ancient depictions of worship show Christians standing and praying with outstretched arms in honor of Christ on the cross. Some congregations faced east, toward the Holy Land, in expectation of Christ's return.[53]

This congregational prayer evidently was extemporaneous. Elsewhere in the *First Apology*, Justin provided an example of its content:

> ... worshipping as we do the Maker of this universe, ... whom we praise to the utmost of our power by the exercise of prayer and thanksgiving for all things wherewith we are supplied, ... and with gratitude to Him to offer thanks by invocations and hymns for our creation, and for all the means of health, and for the various qualities of the different kinds of things, and for the changes of the seasons; and to present before Him petitions for our existing again in incorruption through faith in Him. (*1 Apol.* 13)[54]

This model prayer contained the pattern of other ancient prayers: "it begins with an address to God as Father and Creator, praises him for his mighty acts, moves from thanksgiving to petition, and closes with a doxology—all being done with reference to Christ."[55] Tertullian, in his own *Apology*, mentioned also these petitions in the public prayers: the

---

51. Ferguson, "How We Christians Worship," 12. The ecclesiastical hierarchy of bishop, presbyter, and deacon is evident elsewhere: in Ignatius' letters (for example, *Smyrn.* 8), which were written half a century earlier, and in the *Apostolic Tradition*, which was written about half a century later.

52. See Ferguson, "How We Christians Worship," 12.

53. Ibid., 13.

54. In *ANF* 1:166.

55. See Ferguson, "How We Christians Worship," 13.

welfare of the emperors, of all those in authority, and of the world; peace; and the delay of judgment (*Apol.* 39).

Justin said nothing specifically about hymn singing in his congregation, although Everett Ferguson, in translating the conclusion of the Eucharistic prayer (*1 Apol.* 67), indicated that "the people sing out their assent, saying the 'Amen.'"[56] Elsewhere, Justin wrote that "we have been taught that the only honour that is worthy of Him is not to consume by fire what He has brought into being for our sustenance, but to use it for ourselves and those who need, and with gratitude to Him to offer thanks by invocations and hymns" (*1 Apol.* 13). Other sources from this era provided evidence that chanting psalms and singing hymns were part of early Christian worship.[57] For example, Pliny the Younger described one Christian activity as "singing responsively a hymn to Christ as to God" (*Ep.* 10.96). Tertullian reported that his congregation participated in "singing of psalms" (*De an.* 9) and that "each individual was encouraged to sing to God, in the midst of the assembly, either from the holy Scriptures or according to his or her own ingenuity" (*Apol.* 39). Tertullian's eastern contemporary, Clement of Alexandria, recorded the earliest extant Christian hymn composed in Greek meter at the conclusion of the *Paedagogus*.[58] By the fourth century, as church buildings became larger and worship became more sophisticated, large choirs developed for processionals and antiphonal hymn singing.[59]

In Justin's congregation, the corporate prayer was followed by the Eucharist, which was conducted every Sunday (*1 Apol.* 67; *Dial.* 41). Although Paul, in his instructions about the Lord's Supper, said only, "as often as you eat this bread and drink the cup" (1 Cor 11:26, NASB), Christians soon began to celebrate the Eucharist on each Lord's Day (Acts 20.7; *Did.* 14.1).[60] Robert Cabié explained this development by pointing

---

56. Ibid., 14. McKinnon, however, failed to see any example of psalmody in Justin's description of worship in this text. McKinnon, *Music in Early Christian Literature*, 20.

57. For a sourcebook on early Christian texts about music in worship from the New Testament to the fifth century, see McKinnon, *Music in Early Christian Literature*.

58. Guy, *Introducing Early Christianity*, 206; and Ferguson, "Hymns," 550.

59. White, *Social Origins of Christian Architecture*, 138; and Guy, *Introducing Early Christianity*, 206.

60. At the turn of the fifth century, Augustine wrote that "some partake daily of the

out that Christians lived in a pagan world and that they retained their identity "due largely to their assembly on Sundays. The Church to which they belonged became a visible reality for them there, and they renewed their strength by sharing the Word and the Bread."[61]

The sense of Christian identity and communion inherent in the Eucharist was so vital to Justin's community of believers that, at the conclusion of the Eucharist, the deacons of that congregation carried the elements to members who were unable to attend (*1 Apol.* 67). According to Gregory Dix, in order to maintain the corporate fellowship in some cities where there were multiple congregations, "deacons . . . carried portions of the Bread to all who could not be at the Sunday *ecclesia*."[62]

The final act of the worship service outlined by Justin Martyr was the offering, by which the congregation further maintained its connection with the broader community. The freewill gifts were deposited with the president, who then distributed them among orphans and widows; the sick and aged; "those who are in bonds," perhaps for their Christian faith;[63] strangers who were passing through; and, "in a word . . . all who are in need" (*1 Apol.* 67).

In summary, the elements of worship listed by Justin Martyr are the Word of God, corporate prayer, the Eucharist, and the offering. Ferguson, in his study of early Christian worship, discovered

> two balanced pairs of activity. In the service of the Word, God speaks to human beings. In prayer, human beings speak to God. The Word of God to us calls forth the response of our words to him. In the second pair, the Eucharist represents God's gift to us—spiritual life through Christ. The offering or contribution represents the gifts of his people to God. God gives, and we give in return.[64]

---

body and blood of Christ, others receive it on stated days: in some places no day passes without the sacrifice being offered; in others it is only on Saturday and the Lord's day, or it may be only on the Lord's day." Augustine *Ep.* 54.2 (*NPNF1* 1:300).

61. Cabié, *Eucharist*, 19.

62. Dix, *Shape of the Liturgy*, 105. Elsewhere, Dix referred to this portion of the bread as the *fermentum*. Ibid., 21, 285.

63. See also Tertullian *Apol.* 39.

64. Ferguson, "How We Christians Worship," 15.

Early Christian worship, therefore, like true worship in every era, was communion with God and with others.

Church Discipline in the Early Church

Maintenance of that communion depended upon church discipline, which focused on two goals: the purity of the church and forgiving restoration. Public confession in the church was practiced as early as the turn of the first century, but it began developing into the penitential system during the next century.[65]

The question of penance began with the problem of post-baptismal sin. In the *Shepherd of Hermas*, which originated in the Roman community during the second century, two principles were presented. First, it was understood that "there is no other repentance beyond that which occurred when we descended into the water and received forgiveness of our previous sins." Stated another way, the *Shepherd* affirmed that "the one who has received forgiveness of sins ought never to sin again, but to live in purity" (*Herm. Mand.* 4.3.1–2). Second, the Shepherd warned that "if, after this great and holy call, anyone is tempted by the devil and sins, he has one opportunity for repentance. But if he sins repeatedly and repents, it is of no use for such a person, for he will scarcely live" (*Herm. Mand.* 4.3.6).[66] The process for this one opportunity for post-baptismal repentance became known as *exomologesis*, a severe confession, which included "a period of penance and exclusion from communion, and formal absolution and restoration" granted by a bishop or, in his absence, a priest.[67]

Tertullian's change of position on the issue of post-baptismal sin is well-known. In his treatise *On Repentance*, written around the turn of the third century, Tertullian allowed a second but final opportunity for repentance and forgiveness of sin committed after baptism. The penitent must undergo *exomologesis*, which included prostration before the elders of the church in sackcloth and ashes, fasting, praying, and confessing be-

---

65. *Didache* 4.14.
66. Davies, *Early Christian Church*, 107.
67. Kelly, *Early Christian Doctrines*, 216.

fore the congregation. Though strict, this penitence afforded absolution for both spiritual and carnal sins (*De paen.* 7.10; 9.1–6; 3.8).

About a decade later, after his adherence to the rigorous sect known as Montanism, Tertullian wrote a treatise *On Modesty*, which expounded a decidedly more severe restriction on post-baptismal forgiveness. In its introduction, he repudiated his earlier views and insisted instead that indulgence must not be granted to believers who commit the most extreme sins, such as adultery and fornication (*De pud.* 1.6). In his offensive against such practices, he condemned the *Shepherd of Hermas*, which he named "Shepherd of adulterers" (*De pud.* 20.2) because it permitted one opportunity for repentance after baptism. Later, Tertullian included apostasy, murder, and idolatry in the list of sins that were unpardonable by the church (*De pud.* 22.11). Among his concluding arguments is this citation: "I have the Paraclete himself speaking in the new prophets: 'The church has the power to forgive sin, but I will not do it, lest others also sin'" (*De pud.* 21.7).[68] Tertullian's stricter views, inspired as they were by a sect that was ultimately rejected by ecclesiastical hierarchy, did not prevail.

Tertullian's views, however, were echoed by Hippolytus, who also found himself in opposition to leadership in the Western church. In his *Refutation of All Heresies*, Hippolytus wrote a scathing report on Callistus, bishop of Rome (217–22), who evidently adopted a policy of leniency toward post-baptismal sin. Based upon such biblical texts as Romans 14:4, the parable of the wheat and tares (Matt 13:24–30), and the story of Noah's ark, where clean and unclean animals were mixed, Callistus asserted that the church should include sinners. Furthermore, according to Hippolytus, Callistus abrogated to himself the authority to forgive even adultery and murder and instituted the practice of second baptism presumably to pardon post-baptismal sins (*Ref.* 9.7). Although Hippolytus' report was highly prejudiced, Tertullian issued his own condemnation of a Roman bishop (*De pud.* 1.6), who probably can be identified as Callistus. Evidently, however, a more lenient approach to post-baptismal sin eventually developed in the church. For example, Cyprian, bishop of

---

68. Daly, *Tertullian the Puritan and His Influence*, 128–29.

Carthage in the mid-third century, admitted that "to adulterers even a time of repentance is granted by us, and peace is given" (*Ep.* 51.20).[69]

Perhaps the most significant development of the penitential system in the ante-Nicene Western church came during Cyprian's episcopacy. In the aftermath of the Decian persecution, controversy arose over the reinstatement of the lapsed into the church. This issue was made even more complex by the varied responses to persecution: some had apostatized by sacrificing to pagan gods; some had satisfied the imperial requirements by producing certificates of compliance, either purchased or forged; and others, who became known as confessors, had remained steadfast and had suffered for their Christian faith.

When the persecution ended and the lapsed began to return to the church, there were three distinct responses. The confessors, who believed that they had the authority and the merit to pardon, wanted to reinstate the lapsed freely. Novatian, a Roman presbyter who led a party of rigorists, insisted that idolatry was unpardonable, refused to restore the lapsed, and sentenced the repentant to lifelong penance. Cyprian, with the support of Bishop Cornelius of Rome and a synod of North African bishops, instituted a moderating position whereby the lapsed, through a protracted period of repentance, could seek pardon and reinstatement (*Ep.* 51.6).[70] The key components of the penitential system that developed from this critical decision were the balance between the purity of the church and forgiving love, and the authority of the bishops to assign the acts of penitence and to pardon sins.

In his discussion of the penitential discipline of the ante-Nicene church, J. N. D. Kelly pointed out that the system was public and that there was no evidence of penance as a sacrament that involved private confession to a priest and absolution.[71] Allowances were made, however,

---

69. Kelly, *Early Christian Doctrines*, 218.

70. Those who had obtained certificates fraudulently, the *libellatici*, were subject to varying terms of penance, depending upon the amount of pressure applied to them. Those who actually had sacrificed, the *sacrificati*, could not be admitted until they were on their deathbeds. See Frend, *Rise of Christianity*, 323.

71. According to Kelly, the first reliable reference to private penance as a sacrament came in 589 at the third council of Toledo, which condemned the practice as an execrable presumption. Kelly, *Early Christian Doctrines*, 439. Watkins contended that John Chrysostom, at least, proved to be an exception in the East since he allowed private confession

for a Christian to seek private counsel from a sympathetic and compassionate priest, who then could recommend a course of action that might be private or public.[72] For lesser sins, those which scarcely can be avoided by even good Christians, individuals could find forgiveness through prayer, almsgiving, and mutual forgiveness. Public penance was reserved for the graver sins, which included apostasy, adultery, and murder. The church continued to allow post-baptismal forgiveness for such sins only once and to claim for ordained clergy alone the exclusive authority to reconcile such sinners to the church.[73]

Summary of Formation and Maintenance in the Early Church

This brief sketch of community formation and maintenance in the ante-Nicene church has alluded to two subtexts. First, at this point in Christian history, the catholic, or universal, church was unified in a way that has not been seen since. At no other time could it be said more truly of the visible church: "There is one body and one Spirit, just as also you were called in one hope of your calling; one Lord, one faith, one baptism, one God and Father of all who is over all and through all and in all" (Eph 4:4–6, NASB). This unity was seen most clearly in the practice of sharing the Eucharist among the missing members of a congregation and the sister congregations of a city. Unity in early church life was further expressed through such actions as the kiss of peace following baptism; collecting and distributing offerings brought at the conclusion of a worship service; and the balance of purity and love sought through church discipline.

The second subtext of ante-Nicene Christianity was the hostility of the society in which this unified church existed. Two of the writers highlighted in this sketch were the apologists Justin Martyr, whose very nickname testifies to the animosity of his culture, and Tertullian. Their motivation to write their apologies was to communicate to their antagonists the truth about Christian beliefs and practices. In doing so, they

---

to a priest, who assigned private penance and granted absolution. Watkins, *History of Penance*, 475–77. See Chrysostom *De. Sacerd.* 3.5.

72. Origen *In Ps.* 37; *Hom.* 2.6 (cited in Davies, *Early Christian Church*, 154).

73. Kelly, *Early Christian Doctrines*, 216–17.

provided glimpses into the early church not only for their contemporaries but for us in the twenty-first century as well.

Appropriation of the Early Church by the Contemporary Church

Robert Webber, who is considered the father of ancient-future worship, advocated a return to classical worship, or "worship renewal," in order to communicate to a postmodern generation that is audiovisual and, therefore, responsive to symbolism.[74] One of his goals, however, was not merely to recreate ancient rituals in modern churches but "to recover . . . the symbolic actions of worship" in several ways: "space, the order of worship, music, baptism, the Eucharist, the Christian year, and the arts."[75]

One practice that mirrors the early church, perhaps unintentionally, is the use of cell groups meeting in private homes. The ancient and modern home groups are not completely analogous because, in current usage, many of these gatherings function as ministries of megachurches.[76] More closely aligned to the patristic practice are those "new, largely self-organizing groups of young Christian adults who meet in private homes, church basements, or coffee-houses."[77] Members of cell groups and churches meeting in homes and other private settings have reported benefits in their evangelistic outreach, as did their patristic forebears, and many have selected such venues in order to achieve an ambience similar to that of ancient worship.

Webber, in his description of an ideal space for worship, called for a people-centered design that facilitates participation by the congregants. In this format, the seating is arranged in a semicircle around a more centralized space where the table of the Eucharist is the focal point. The pulpit is set to one side, and the baptismal pool or font is placed at the entry to the sanctuary, symbolizing baptism as the entrance into the

---

74. Webber, *Ancient-Future Faith*, 15, 94.

75. Ibid., 107.

76. Even within this paradigm, however, I know of one church in Atlanta whose cell groups adopted the practice of sharing the *fermentum* among themselves in conscious imitation of the patristic pattern.

77. Tolson, "Return to Tradition," 44.

church. An open, spacious design, as opposed to one that is longitudinal, is effective for the music and arts that Webber envisioned for worship renewal.[78]

Webber's order of worship was heavily influenced by the liturgies preserved by Justin Martyr and Hippolytus, both of whom he frequently cited. From these and other early church fathers, he developed a basic structure for a worship service built around Word and Sacrament and outlined in four acts: "assembling, hearing God's Word, responding at Eucharist, and being sent forth into the world."[79] His suggested service of the Word can include confession of sin; readings from the Scripture, including the Old Testament, the Epistles, and the Gospels; recitation of creeds; a sermon that declares God's word and calls hearers to imitate Christ; and congregational prayers. The service of the Sacrament begins with the sharing of the kiss of peace, which signifies reconciliation among the participants; continues with the partaking of the bread and wine; and concludes with a dismissal formula that sends the congregants out into the world to serve the Lord, whose death and resurrection they had just celebrated.[80] Webber's order of service clearly reflects influence from Justin's *First Apology* and the *Apostolic Tradition* and, in turn, is reflected in the worship practices of some contemporary, evangelical congregations, which have been reported to "engage in ... ancient liturgical practices, including creedal declarations, public confession," and "weekly Eucharist."[81]

Indeed, a hallmark of ancient-future worship is the weekly celebration of the Eucharist, a pattern that surprises many traditional evangelicals. However, Thomas Howard, who signed the 1997 "Chicago Call" for a return of modern evangelicalism to historic Christianity, insisted that "[t]he notion that this is somehow 'too frequent' is a very late one, wholly

---

78. Webber, *Worship Old & New*, 144–46; and *Ancient-Future Faith*, 108.

79. Webber, *Common Roots*, 101; and *Worship Old & New*, 151.

80. Webber, *Common Roots*, 101–2; *Worship Old & New*, 165–66, 248–49; and *Ancient-Future Faith*, 108–9.

81. These young Christians "may use a piece of bagel as the body of Christ" (Tolson, "Return to Tradition," 44, 47) or "take communion from bread purchased at a nearby grocery store and sip wine out of a pottery chalice or grape juice from plastic cups" (Salmon, "Feeling Renewed by Ancient Traditions").

at odds with the testimony of the faithful who return to this table week by week, and even day by day."[82]

Webber referred to the Eucharist as well as baptism as "symbols" and "sign-acts," but he did not hesitate to describe them also as "sacraments." His understanding of the Latin *sacramentum*, however, is to "make holy," and, "[i]n this sense there is only one sacrament, Jesus Christ," who "is *the* sacrament of the church because only Jesus Christ can make one holy." This power is communicated through baptism and the Eucharist, "[b]ut water, bread, and wine do not save us; they are the signs of the salvation that comes from Jesus Christ."[83] Howard, who expanded on "A Call to Sacramental Integrity," one aspect of the Chicago Call, charged the church to "return to an authentically *gospel* sacramentalism that embraces, proclaims, and enacts as it should its part in the great mysteries of redemption.[84]

In discussions of ancient-future worship, less is said about baptism than the Eucharist, probably because the latter is more prominent in weekly worship. Nonetheless, the rite of initiation is important to evangelical communities that are using worship renewal to reach out to a postmodern generation. Webber encouraged the return to such patristic practices as the renunciation of evil and the threefold affirmation of the Father, Son, and Holy Spirit, expressed in the interrogatory baptismal creed.[85] At the Church of the Apostles, an "emerging" congregation in Seattle, candidates for baptism engage in a "rite of enrollment" during which they sign a book to indicate their commitment to God. As in Augustine's church, these catechumens often enroll on the first Sunday of Lent, and those who do are baptized after an Easter vigil. Other feast

---

82. Howard, *Evangelical Is Not Enough*, 153. See also Webber and Bloesch, *Orthodox Evangelicals*, for a full discussion of the Chicago Call. Howard, although he signed the Chicago Call as an evangelical, eventually converted to Roman Catholicism. In *Evangelical Is Not Enough* he also advocated "a return to the episcopate" (152) Similarly, his co-signer, Peter Gillquist (author of *Becoming Orthodox*), joined the Antiochian Orthodox Church and was ordained an archpriest.

83. Webber, *Worship Old & New*, 229–30.

84. Howard, "Call to Sacramental Integrity."

85. Webber, *Worship Old & New*, 235.

days on which baptism is celebrated are "the Baptism of Jesus, the day of Pentecost, Holy Trinity, and Christ the King."[86]

A feature of worship renewal is the liturgical calendar, which was developed by the church fathers and is common among Catholics, Orthodox Christians, and mainline Protestants, but is "new again" among evangelicals.[87] Webber promoted the liturgical calendar in several books,[88] and Howard called for evangelicals to "return to the Christian year":

> To move, with all the faithful everywhere, through Advent to the Nativity and thence to the Epiphany and the Presentation in the Temple and from there to Lent, Holy Week, the great Pasch, the Ascension, and the season of Pentecost is to have the Scriptures kept marvelously alive. To remember Paul and Peter, Timothy and Titus, Polycarp and Ignatius, and a host of others is to have one's imagination filled with gratitude for these forerunners in the Faith and to be *helped*.[89]

As Webber pointed out—with justification—evangelicals observe a secular calendar highlighted by New Year's Day, Memorial Day, Mother's Day, Father's Day, the Fourth of July, and Labor Day.[90] Even Thanksgiving, although more religious in tone, had its origin as a patriotic celebration. The liturgical calendar focuses the Christian's attention on Christ and his church.

This discussion of patristic community maintenance appropriated by contemporary evangelical churches concludes with a look at the practice of church discipline. One section of the Chicago Call, "A Call to Church Authority," includes a charge to church leaders to discipline members of their flocks in the areas of morality, stewardship of money and time, and relationships with God and others.[91] In the early church, the disciplinary process involved public confession, penance, and priestly absolution,

---

86. Ward, "Emerging Church and Communal Theology," 174.

87. Armstrong reported that even Liberty University celebrated Lenten season. Armstrong, "Future Lies in the Past," 23. See also Salmon, "Feeling Renewed by Ancient Traditions."

88. See especially Webber, *Ancient-Future Time*.

89. Howard, *Evangelical Is Not Enough*, 153.

90. Webber, *Common Roots*, 108–9; and *Ancient-Future Faith*, 111.

91. Braun, "Call to Church Authority."

but contemporary methods can look very different. At Seacoast Church in Charleston, South Carolina, "worshipers write their sins on pieces of paper and pin them to a cross." Later, volunteers pray over these confessions. According to the pastor, Greg Surratt, this practice "has ramped up the sense of God's presence and power in incredible ways."[92] Technology has made it possible for thousands of people to post anonymous confessions on Web sites such as mysecret.tv, which is operated by Lifechurch.tv, an Internet-based megachurch. Pastor Bobby Gruenwald affirmed, "We do believe there is value in confessing our sins to each other. . . . This process may be a more modern way of people discovering the value of that tradition."[93] One wonders, however, if this electronic method of accountability actually undermines traditional community formation.

Assessment of Ancient-Future Formation and Maintenance

Each new generation of Christians seeks to reach their world with the message of the gospel. Interestingly, fathers of the early church are inspiring evangelicals in the twenty-first century, as they seek to appropriate ancient practices in modern ways. These evangelicals in a postmodern era recognize a similar goal and challenge faced by their patristic counterparts: the desire for unity in the church in the face of a hostile culture. Because many postmoderns respond to audio-visual, symbolic communication, the rich symbolism inherent in the ancient practices of baptism, the Eucharist, and worship and in the personal discipline of confession could be effective in contemporary churches if implemented circumspectly.

As a Baptist, I do not subscribe to the sacramental theology prevalent throughout much patristic literature, and I oppose the development of penitential theology.[94] Therefore, I would not support a facile adoption of certain practices found in patristic communities.[95] Nevertheless, I believe there are various lessons one can glean from the early church

---

92. Salmon, "Feeling Renewed by Ancient Traditions."
93. Ibid.
94. See the "2000 Baptist Faith and Message," article 7, for a characteristically Baptist perspective on baptism and the Lord's Supper.
95. And I would differ in my approach from Webber.

in matters of community formation and maintenance. While many postmodern individuals want the comfort of community, they must also understand the necessity of communal boundaries and of covenanted responsibility.[96] The very nature of community implies that some are "in" and some are "out," as evidenced by the initiatory role of baptism and the excommunicatory role of church discipline.[97] Early Christians understood that sin affects communities and not only individuals, and thus implemented church discipline in cases of moral and doctrinal failure. One can appreciate the early Christian recognition of the "sinfulness of sin" without adopting the excesses of *exomologesis* (which may mitigate the "graciousness of grace").

One may also learn from the patristic emphasis upon instruction for new community members, even if one demurs from a three-year wait for baptism.[98] Perhaps evangelicals could rediscover a more regular celebration of the Lord's Supper and a re-emphasis upon the public reading of Scripture (especially in view of the increasing biblical illiteracy of our culture).[99] "Non-liturgical" assemblies might consider the commemoration of Pentecost, which has a far more central role in biblical theology than such holidays as Mother's Day or Memorial Day—even though the latter often receive more attention in our church services.[100] Moreover, we can learn from the formation of contemporary communities of faith, which seek to be closely united fellowships that serve as havens from a sometimes hostile society.

---

96. See Hellerman, "Ancient-Future Community."

97. As mentioned above, churches vividly symbolized the initiatory role of baptism through the placement of the font near the sanctuary entrance.

98. See Arnold, "Early Church Catechesis," 39–54. Historic Baptist catechisms include Keach's Catechism of 1677, the Charleston Catechism of 1813, and Spurgeon's Catechism of 1855. Cf. Nettles, "Encouragement to Use Catechisms."

99. 1 Tim 4:1–3. Cf. Robinson, "Whitney: Worship Should Be God-Centered and Biblical."

100. See Adams, "Significance of Pentecost."

4

Learning from Patristic Use of the Rule of Faith

Bryan M. Litfin

❈ *Introduction*

In the preface to his magisterial work *Medieval Exegesis: The Four Senses of Scripture*, the great French Jesuit scholar Henri de Lubac issued a call that rings true in our generation as well. "We must," he writes,

> abandon a certain tone, all too frequent yet, of smirking condescension . . . there ought to be a refusal to see even the greatest of these men as nothing more than "overgrown children." . . . [There is no longer] any excuse for anyone who thinks that he is under an obligation never to admire any one of their works, except when he honors it by judging it worthy to stand alongside our modern works. Let us allow ourselves to be persuaded that their writings, even though they are quite different from ours, can furnish us with more than just childish babblings. It is well worth the effort to endeavor to understand the serious lines of their thought, even if we are under no obligation to adopt and follow them.[1]

De Lubac's words with respect to the medieval exegetes apply no less to the early church fathers. All too often, we subject the ancients to the criteria of our own age as a means to evaluate their merits. When we find a patristic writer doing exegesis in ways congruent with how we have been trained—for example, when Theodore of Mopsuestia articulates an

---

1. De Lubac, *Medieval Exegesis*, xvii.

interpretive vision grounded in literalism and sober restraint—we celebrate his prescience in adopting methodologies that will reign supreme in the twenty-first century. However, when we find Origen discovering mystical significance in the garments of the high priest, or the trappings of the tabernacle, we look down our noses at his primitive approach.

But what if the critical spirit were allowed to move in the opposite direction? What if a patristic writer were genuinely allowed to teach *us* something about biblical interpretation? In other words, what if we "retrieved the tradition," as Dan Williams has urged us to do, not as archaeologists picking out treasures from the debris of the ages, but as students at the feet of brilliant masters?[2] This is not to say we should be naïve, that we should uncritically endorse the patristic sources and subject ourselves to them as inerrant. For evangelicals, only Scripture can demand this kind of unquestioned loyalty. Nevertheless, perhaps the time has come for a new perspective on the writings of the early Christians—one in which they are allowed to function as authorities, though not the final authority.

The issue I am raising, more broadly put, is the question of "Scripture and tradition." It is something I have been thinking about for the past fifteen years. In fact, it was this very issue that first awakened my professional interest in patristics. I can well remember my frustration as I began to write exegetical papers in seminary, only to discover that various well-trained commentators were all reading the same biblical texts, yet reaching different conclusions about their meaning. One scholar was convinced the Greek genitive was objective, another insisted it was subjective, or appositional, or partitive, and so on. The experts were studying the same words, but coming to different interpretations. Somewhere in the midst of all those commentaries spread out on my desk, I lost the confidence that a rigorous exegetical method, dutifully applied, would always yield certain and consistent results in all the details. What I did not lose, however, was the confidence that Holy Scripture is God's authoritative Word. Could there be, I wondered, a better way forward?

In the crisis precipitated by my realization that learning Greek and Hebrew would not unlock a secret garden of indubitable interpre-

---

2. Williams, *Retrieving the Tradition*.

tive conclusions, I began to long for a friend to assist me—some wise counselor who could point me in the right direction as I considered the meaning of the biblical text. I wanted a helpful voice to inject wisdom and discernment into the cacophony of arguing commentators, and my own perspectival opinions. I was not looking for an authoritative magisterium to give me the dogmatic answers; I was merely looking for insight. It was at this critical juncture that I was introduced, for the first time in my life, to the "church fathers."

They were entirely unknown to me. I had never met the body of Christian writers from the second through fifth centuries. I recall one of my high school teachers attempting to teach me about some guy named Augustine, but I did not have "ears to hear" at that point in my life. However, a few years later as a young graduate student at Dallas Seminary, I was ready. As I got to know the church fathers over the years, I began to appreciate the subtle nuances of their Scripture study. At last I had found a helpful voice to come alongside my biblical interpretation.

My interest in the interplay between Scripture and tradition led me to a decade of research and publication on the role of the *regula fidei,* or Rule of Faith, in patristic hermeneutics. Although much scholarly ink has been spilt on this subject, it is not my intent to speak only to professional academics. I harbor a profound interest in the task of *ressourcement* as it is being attempted in the pews and pulpits (or couches and barstools!) of today's churches. If the ancient-future discourse is carried out only in the halls of academe, or in certain elite conferences, we will have missed the opportunity to let the church fathers speak anew to the people of God. Therefore, it is to the pastor preparing a sermon in his study, no less than to professional academics in their offices, that I address this essay.

There is a lot of talk about the Rule of Faith in early Christian studies; yet the Rule is often discussed in abstraction, or selectively quoted, without actually putting the relevant texts before the reader. The goal of this chapter is to lay out, in one convenient place, all the instances of the Rule of Faith in patristic writings through the ante-Nicene era. Only after we have a clear sense of exactly what the Rule of Faith is will we be in a position to draw some conclusions about its relevance today.

My central thesis on these matters is simple. The interpretive value of *tradition* has for too long been associated only with Roman Catholicism.

It is time for Protestant evangelicals to reclaim their own proper understanding of tradition. Our study of God's Word—alone inspired and inerrant—will be the stronger for it.

What Is the Rule of Faith?

The term "Rule of Faith" has become conventional in the scholarly literature on the subject of patristic tradition; and indeed, the Latin writers often did use the term *regula fidei*. Yet the fathers could just as easily call it the "rule of truth," "ecclesiastical rule," or "catholic rule" (using *regula* or κανών with the appropriate modifier). What did the ancient Christians mean by this term?

According to my research, the Rule of Faith was this: *a confessional formula (fixed neither in wording nor in content, yet following the same general pattern) that summarized orthodox beliefs about the actions of God and Christ in the world.* Though it was originally used as a catechetical summary for baptismal candidates, or as a set of inquiries for the font itself, the Rule came to be seen more broadly as a convenient summary of catholic orthodoxy. Its theological flow moves from the one Creator God to his Son Jesus Christ, who was prefigured in the Old Testament and openly revealed in the New. He was born of a virgin, ministered, suffered, died, rose again, and ascended to heaven. The apostolic, Spirit-led church awaits his return to resurrect the dead and dispense eternal punishment or rewards. There is hardly any soteriology or bibliology in the Rule, its eschatology is very basic, and its ecclesiology is meager (though we should note the Rule's very existence presupposes a robust view of the church).

By no means do all instances of the Rule of Faith in the church fathers contain the full set of concepts I have just enumerated. In fact, only a few times does the Rule appear with all the details as described above. Nevertheless, whenever the partial confessions were mentioned, they were understood to be attached to a broader nexus of ideas that the apostolic church had embraced. In other words, the Rule of Faith was essentially "presumed" by the ancient Christians—perceived intuitively rather than mandated for everyone with fixed, inflexible wording. Once that crystallization process began to occur in the fourth century, we pass from the great age of the Rule of Faith to the age of solidified creeds.

Instances of the Rule of Faith in the Ante-Nicene Church

There is no single place where all *regulae fidei* are collected in one handy tome. August Hahn's 1897 work purports to do so, and it does a marvelous job of collating many relevant texts in the original languages.[3] The book is a starting point for anyone doing creedal studies. A more recent and equally masterful work is that of Jaroslav Pelikan and Valerie Hotchkiss.[4] The authors list fourteen distinct sources for the *regula fidei*, although on closer inspection, some of them fall short of a true Rule.[5] Furthermore, in my studies of the secondary literature on patristic tradition, I discovered other instances of the Rule of Faith.[6] In order to survey the church fathers' use of the Rule, I will now provide a complete list of all relevant sources. This is something I have never seen accomplished in one place.

An immediate problem one faces in attempting such a task is deciding what counts as an instance of the *regula fidei*, and what is simply bare-bones confessional material. I think I can safely say that a complete Rule of Faith is not to be found prior to Irenaeus. The great bishop of Lyons, writing circa 180, was the first to articulate it in detail and to make programmatic use of it theologically. Earlier writers, even up to Justin Martyr (who died around 165), do not provide a full Rule, nor do they

---

3. Hahn, *Bibliothek der Symbole*.

4. Pelikan and Hotchkiss, *Creeds & Confessions*.

5. The sources given by Pelikan and Hotchkiss that I omit from my compilation are: *Didache* 7, because it deals more with the method of baptism than actual confessional content; Polycarp, *Philippians* 2, because its collection of sayings is too scattered to be considered a Rule; and Gregory Thaumaturgus' *Declaration of Faith*, which Gregory of Nyssa considers to be the baptismal creed taught to Macrina the Elder in the late third century, but which possesses Trinitarian language that would more properly situate it in the fourth-century age of synodal creeds. In my present list, I also omit the snippets of confessional formulae found in the New Testament. Though obviously creedal in nature, they represent primitive kerygma rather than a true Rule of Faith.

6. The most useful overviews of the subject of creeds and the *regula fidei* are: van den Eynde, *Normes de l'Enseignement Chrétien*; Kelly, *Early Christian Creeds*; Flesseman-Van Leer, *Tradition and Scripture*; and Hanson, *Tradition in the Early Church*.

Learning from Patristic Use of the Rule of Faith

use it extensively in their argumentation. It seems Irenaeus was the first to recognize that the church's baptismal symbol could carry theological and exegetical firepower if it were borrowed from the catechetical/liturgical setting, to be marshaled in an apologetic/polemical context.

There are thirteen distinct sources from the second and third centuries that deserve to be called instances of the *regula fidei*. As I have said, many of these can hardly be considered a true Rule of Faith, if we take Irenaeus' or Tertullian's full-fledged statements as the standard. Nevertheless, I would argue that the thirteen sources provided here have enough theological content and confessional structure to be cited as examples of the patristic Rule.

1. Ignatius of Antioch primarily provides us with Christ-kerygma. Ignatius' docetic opponents were always in his sights, so he insisted on the true birth, life, death, and resurrection of the Lord. Christ has a twofold aspect: "both from Mary and from God"; "both from the seed of David and of the Holy Spirit"; "Son of Man and Son of God."[7]

In two places, Ignatius provides a more substantial confession that can be considered a nascent Rule of Faith. His letter *To the Trallians*, chapter 9, outlines the following: the Davidic lineage, birth from Mary, true eating and drinking, crucifixion under Pilate, the resurrection of Christ by the Father, and the resurrection of the saints. In *To the Smyrnaeans* 1, Ignatius emphasizes the same elements: Son of David and Son of God, born of a virgin, baptized, truly crucified under Pilate, resurrected from the dead, and providing resurrection to the saints, that is, to all "faithful people, whether among Jews or among Gentiles, in the one body of his church." While we do see a little ecclesiology included in the formula, in which Jew and Gentile are united by God into one body, nevertheless, Ignatius' primary emphasis is on Christ himself. Jesus is linked to the history of the Jews through his lineage as the son of David through Mary; yet he is God's own Son as well. Ignatius' Rule of Faith is essentially christological, emphasizing the Savior's earthly and heavenly origins.

---

7. Ignatius *Ephesians* 7.2; 18.2; 20.2. Quotations from the letters of Ignatius are taken from Holmes, *Apostolic Fathers*.

2. Aristides of Athens was a second-century apologist about whom we know very little. His *Apology* represents the earliest extant example of that genre. Eusebius states that the *Apology* was addressed to Emperor Hadrian, which would date it to the first quarter of the second century.[8] Today it survives only in a partial Syriac translation, along with some late Armenian and Greek fragments.

The *regula fidei* of Aristides is presented in a way that normally characterized its earliest versions, namely, it was not expressed as a single cohesive unit, but as a series of doctrinal assertions inserted among running commentary or polemic. When we tease out the constituent elements of the Rule from Aristides' own comments, we find, first of all, God as Creator, and some theology proper.[9] Next comes Christology: Jesus was born of a virgin and was incarnate in flesh, called twelve disciples, died, was buried, and rose again after three days. Aristides also mentions the evangelistic work of the apostles as the source of Christian belief. Of course, this is not really ecclesiology; nor is there any pneumatology or eschatology. Perhaps the most significant element here is the Jewish context: Jesus is born of a "Hebrew virgin" and from "the tribe of the Hebrews," and he was "pierced by the Jews." Like Ignatius, Aristides locates the origins of Christianity within Jewish history by connecting Jesus to the Creator God of Israel.

3. Justin Martyr offers quite a bit of confessional material in his writings, especially Christ-kerygma (birth, death, resurrection, ascension, return), but also some early Trinitarian formulae.[10] The closest thing to a Rule of Faith in Justin is found in his *First Apology* 13, where he describes God, the Maker of the Universe, and offers some comments on appropriate worship.[11] He then describes Jesus's birth, ministry as a teacher, and crucifixion under Pontius Pilate. Jesus is the Son of God and is second in rank, with the prophetic Spirit in third place. When Justin refers to "the prophetic Spirit," we can cross-reference *First Apology* 61, where he men-

---

8. Eusebius *Hist. eccl.* 4.3.3.

9. Aristides *Apology* 1–2 (ANF 9:263–65; or Pelikan and Hotchkiss, 52).

10. Kelly, *Early Christian Creeds*, 71–75.

11. Barnard, *St. Justin Martyr*, 30–31. Justin's use of the phrase "we have been taught" indicates he is citing standard Christian material as found in the Rule of Faith.

tions "the Holy Spirit, who through the prophets foretold all the things about Jesus." Likewise, in *First Apology* 31, the "prophetic Spirit" is said to have inspired the Jewish prophets. The Old Testament predicted that Christ would be born of a virgin, do miracles, be crucified, die, and rise again to ascend to heaven. The apostles were sent to preach these things to the Gentiles. In Justin's confessions of faith, the two Testaments are related to each other as christological prophecy and fulfillment.[12]

4. *The Epistle of the Apostles* is an apocryphal letter supposedly written by the disciples of the Lord after his ascension, though it is actually an anonymous work dating to the mid second century. At the outset, Jesus is connected with the work of the Creator God, whose creative activity is described in vivid detail. God is said to have spoken "in parables through the patriarchs and prophets, and in truth through him whom the apostles declared and the disciples touched."[13] Once again, we discover a feature that is becoming a common refrain in the Rule of Faith: the Old Testament is a prophetic prediction of the fuller revelation that Jesus Christ brings. According to the *Epistle*, he became flesh in Mary's womb through the Holy Spirit, was born from her at Bethlehem, and went forth doing miracles. Christians are said to believe in "the Father, the Ruler of the entire world, and in Jesus Christ our Savior, and in the Holy Spirit, the Paraclete, and in the holy church and in the forgiveness of sins."[14] Although this apocryphal document does not represent a mainstream Rule of Faith, its christological focus and prophecy-fulfillment motif is consistent with other ancient *regulae*.

With 5. *Irenaeus of Lyons*, we cross a boundary of sorts. For the first time, the scattered creedal comments found in earlier writers become an organized Rule of Faith that can be deployed for theological and polemical purposes. The Rule also loses, on three occasions, its random, off-the-cuff character, becoming a distinct entity that Irenaeus quotes in a formulaic

---

12. Ignatius would have agreed with that idea, though he did not include it as part of the Rule of Faith. For example, he writes of "Jesus Christ, our only teacher ... whom even the prophets, who were his disciples in the Spirit, were expecting as their teacher." *Magnesians* 9 (Holmes, *Apostolic Fathers*, 209).

13. *Epistle of the Apostles* 3 (Pelikan and Hotchkiss, 54).

14. *Epistle of the Apostles* 5.

way.[15] What has caused such remarkable advancement here? Perhaps the easiest explanation is the brilliant theological creativity of the bishop of Lyons (although anti-Marcionite apologetics probably played a role as well). In any case, it is now possible to speak of the church's official Rule. Irenaeus' Latin translator typically calls it the *regula veritatis*, and the original Greek may have been either ὑπόθεσις or κανών τῆς ἀληθείας.[16]

Irenaeus' use of the Rule of Faith has been intensively studied.[17] Among the many investigations, Philip Hefner has offered an important perspective on the narrative function of the Rule.[18] Likewise, Richard Norris argues that the Rule, or ὑπόθεσις, refers to "what we would call a 'plot,' a coherent story-structure of some sort that involves and identifies a particular set of characters."[19] The insights of Hefner and Norris give us every reason to believe that the Rule of Faith articulated for Irenaeus a world-encompassing metanarrative. An essential element of this narrative was its unified nature. Or put another way, the events of the old dispensation are intimately related to those of the new, comprising a harmonious whole.[20] The narrative is continuous, yet consists of two main chapters: before and after Christ. There is much more that could be said about Irenaeus and the Rule, but for now I highlight his *unifying* use of it, by which the dispensations are joined into a single narrative of salvation history, centered on Jesus Christ. This is consistent with what we have seen in earlier writers, though Irenaeus has now developed the point much more thoroughly.

---

15. Irenaeus *Proof of the Apostolic Teaching* 6 (Smith, 51); and *Adversus Haereses* 1.10.1 and 3.4.2 (Grant, *Irenaeus of Lyons*, 70–71, 127).

16. Flesseman-Van Leer, *Tradition and Scripture*, 125–28. With respect to the terminology used by Irenaeus, there may have been antecedents in Philo of Alexandria. See Lanne, "Règle de la Vérité," 70.

17. Ammundsen, "Rule of Truth in Irenaeus," 574–80; Ochagavía, *Visible Patris Filius*; and Donovan, *One Right Reading?*

18. Hefner, "Saint Irenaeus and the Hypothesis of Faith," 300–306; and "Theological Methodology and St. Irenaeus," 294–309.

19. Norris, "Theology and Language in Irenaeus of Lyon," 289.

20. See *Proof* 6; *Adv. Haer.* 1.10.1; 3.11.7; 3.16.6; 4.9.3; 4.33.7; and 4.35.4.

6. *Tertullian of Carthage* does much the same thing as Irenaeus in his approach to the Rule of Faith, but goes even further. He makes the Rule the lynchpin of his apologetic defense against the heretics—and in fact, of his theological system as a whole. Three main instances of the *regula fidei* appear in Tertullian's writings.[21] Perhaps the archetypical Rule of Faith in all patristic literature is given in *Prescription against Heretics* 13, where we find every classic element included: God the Creator; the Word who was born of Mary, lived, died, rose again, and ascended to heaven; the Holy Spirit who guides the church; and the promise of Christ's return for resurrection, judgment, and rewards. For Tertullian, as for Irenaeus, these basic elements come together to form a cosmic Christian metanarrative.[22]

One of the most valuable features of the Rule's narrative was its usefulness in refuting heresy. Though the narrative was subject to variety in how it was expressed, nevertheless it retained a definite plotline that would exclude radically different recitations. Tertullian echoed his predecessor Irenaeus when he claimed the gnostics constructed a brand new myth from the biblical corpus, just as the ancient poets would audaciously "update" their received literary classics.[23] The heretics wrongly appropriated biblical language and refashioned it into a story of their own devising. In so doing, they produced an entirely different narrative. Their words may have been borrowed from the Bible, but when they were compared to the handy summary provided by the Rule, it became obvious that the heretics' story was *not* the biblical one.

---

21. *Prescription against Heretics* 13; *Veiling of Virgins* 1; and *Against Praxeas* 2. The texts can be found in various editions and translations, but are most easily accessed in Pelikan and Hotchkiss, 56–57.

22. The skeptic may wonder if we are justified in speaking of such an ancient "narrative" theology, yet contemporary scholars believe this was in fact a common understanding of the Rule of Faith. Paul Blowers contends that "in the crucial 'proto-canonical' era in the history of Christianity, the Rule, being a narrative construction, set forth the basic 'dramatic' structure of a Christian vision of the world, posing as an hermeneutical frame of reference for the interpretation of Christian Scripture and Christian experience, and educing the first principles of Christian theological discourse and of a doctrinal substantiation of Christian faith." Blowers, "*Regula fidei*," 202. See also Di Berardino and Studer, *History of Theology*, 34–39; and Countryman, "Tertullian and the *regula fidei*," 208–27.

23. Irenaeus *Prescription against Heretics* 39 (Greenslade, *Early Latin Theology*, 59–60). Cf. Irenaeus *Against Heresies* 1.9.4 (Grant, *Irenaeus of Lyons*, 69–70).

For Tertullian, the metanarrative encapsulated in the Rule did not only serve as a polemical tool for fighting heretics; it also had positive value for doing systematic theology. The cosmic Christian story functioned as an interpretive key for Scripture by emphasizing the christological harmony between the Old and New Testaments. Christ was "seen in diverse ways by the patriarchs, was ever heard in the prophets."[24] In fact, the church "unites the Law and the Prophets with the writings of the evangelists and apostles."[25] As we have already seen in earlier figures, so we find in Tertullian, that the Rule of Faith joined Jesus Christ to the Creator God of Israel and the Jewish prophets. The notion that the Rule unites the two dispensations—thereby serving as an interpretive guide for all of Scripture—is central to Tertullian's theology.

Taken together, Irenaeus and Tertullian do two things with the Rule of Faith. First, they understand it to summarize a cosmic Christian narrative of salvation history. Specifically, they join the Creator God of the Old Testament and his work among the Jews to the Christian economy and the revelation of Jesus Christ. Both eras, both covenants, both Testaments, reveal the one God and his Christ. Though this is not an altogether new idea, it is now much more developed theologically.

Second, and based on this first principle, Irenaeus and Tertullian used the Rule as an interpretive guide to elucidate Scripture's meaning. Since the Rule summarized the whole revelation of God, it could be used as a synopsis of what the Bible is about. In this way, heretical falsehood could be excluded, for no interpretation can violate the Rule's basic contours. As Tertullian said, "To know nothing against the Rule is to know everything."[26]

7. Clement of Alexandria, our next patristic figure, understood the Rule in a unique way: it provided secret tradition or special knowledge passed down from Christ and the apostles to the intellectual Christian, or what Clement called the "true gnostic."[27] While Clement may have known the contents of a baptismal symbol, that was not what he had in mind when

---

24. Irenaeus *Prescription against Heretics* 13 (Greenslade, *Early Latin Theology*, 40).
25. Ibid., 36 (Greenslade, *Early Latin Theology*, 57).
26. Ibid., 14 (Greenslade, *Early Latin Theology*, 40).
27. Hanson, *Origen's Doctrine of Tradition*, 53–72.

he talked about the Rule. Rather, he referred to an esoteric reading of Scripture and Christian theology that allowed the "true gnostic" to delve into mysteries not ordinarily accessible to everyday believers. This Rule was unwritten and was ἀπόρρητος ("not to be spoken")—at least not in broader circles.

For Clement, the Rule was certainly hermeneutical in character. R. P. C. Hanson writes, "In most of his references to this tradition, Clement seems to have conceived of it as nothing else than an interpretation of the Scripture."[28] Of course, the interpretation was spiritual. Allegorization is an inherent part of the Rule of Faith.[29] Clement says he will deliver the truth "sublimely," and "in a lofty strain," by interpreting the Scriptures "according to the canon of truth."[30] What will this look like? Clement goes on to explain that "the ecclesiastical rule is the concord and harmony of the law and the prophets with the covenant delivered at the coming of the Lord."[31]

In a lengthy discussion in *Stromateis* 7.16–17, Clement says only those who have received the church's Rule can properly understand the Scriptures.[32] In contrast, those who have spurned the ecclesiastical tradition have fallen away into heresy. By their own intellectual laziness, they have dismissed the Bible as superficial, not taking a comprehensive view of salvation history from creation to the prophets to the gospel. It is the church's tradition alone that can reveal the inner meaning of Scripture. In particular, the ecclesiastical tradition reveals that the two Testaments are united. The church has the true entrance key, "the tradition of the Lord," as opposed to the heretics' counterfeit key. Only "the ancient and catholic church" can create a unity of faith built on the two Testaments—or rather, "the one Testament [revealed] in different times by the will of the one God, through one Lord."[33] For Clement, the church's tradition, as encapsulated in the Rule of Faith, provides the interpretive key for

---

28. Ibid., 58.
29. Ibid., 59.
30. *Stromata* 6.15 (*ANF* 2:509).
31. Ibid. (*ANF* 2:509).
32. Ibid., 7.16–17 (*ANF* 2:550–55).
33. Ibid., 7.17 (*ANF* 2:555).

unlocking Scripture's hidden meaning. And this hidden meaning, which must be accessed through allegorical exegesis, displays the unity of the Old and New covenants under the one God.

What can we say by way of assessing Clement? He clearly departs from the other church fathers when he makes the *regula fidei* a source of secret wisdom for intellectual Christians. The public and open nature of the Rule of Faith upon which anti-gnostic apologists such as Irenaeus and Tertullian had insisted is turned on its head. Clement's understanding of the Rule as recondite oral tradition sets him apart in the ancient church. On the other hand, when he uses the Rule as a hermeneutical device to elucidate Scripture's holistic metanarrative against the heretics, he is not far from what earlier writers had done. Even so, Clement's insistence that allegorical exegesis is a component of the Rule goes beyond anything that had yet been said, setting the stage for Origen's approach to the *regula fidei*.

8. *Hippolytus* was a presbyter and later a schismatic bishop in early third-century Rome. At two points he provides us with a Rule of Faith: *Against Noetus* 17–18 and *Apostolic Tradition* 21.[34] In the first example, Hippolytus gives the Rule in the way we have already noticed in Aristides of Athens: as a series of assertions accompanied by running commentary. It is necessary to tease out the actual elements of his Rule, or what he calls, the "tradition of the apostles" (παράδοσις των ἀποστόλων).[35] He speaks of God the Word becoming incarnate of Mary for the salvation of all who believe, then backtracks to mention the one Father who created all things with the Word at his side. "This was he who was proclaimed through the Law and the Prophets," Hippolytus says, expressing a sentiment that has apparently become a requisite aspect of the Rule of Faith. The two natures of Christ are then described, with emphasis on his true divinity and humanity. The trial under Pilate and the crucifixion next appear, then the resurrection on the third day. Backtracking again,

---

34 There are scholarly debates about the origins of these works, but it is best not to become embroiled in the question of authorship so that we may consider the sources themselves. For a discussion of the authorship issues, see Shelton, *Martyrdom and Exegesis in Hippolytus*, ch. 1.

35. Hippolytus *Contra Noetum* 17.2 (Butterworth, 84).

Hippolytus describes Jesus's birth and miracles, then closes with the bestowal of the Spirit upon the apostles, the ascension to the Father's right hand, and his role as judge of the living and the dead. There is also a mention of the "holy Church." Here we certainly have an ample *regula fidei*.

The Rule of Faith is presented in *Apostolic Tradition* 21 in a more stylized, less discursive way because Hippolytus is supplying the actual baptismal creed.[36] The three articles are as follows: first, God the Father; second, Jesus Christ the Son of God, born of the Spirit and of Mary, crucified under Pilate, died, risen again, ascended to heaven, and returning as judge of the living and the dead; and third, the Holy Spirit, the holy church, and the resurrection of the dead. All the major elements of the Rule of Faith appear here, including the proclamation of Christ in the "Law and the Prophets." Hippolytus provides a helpful witness to the content of the church's Rule, though he does not employ it theologically to the degree that Irenaeus and Tertullian do.

9. The *Didascalia Apostolorum* is a Greek work from northern Syria dating to around AD 230.[37] It survives in Syriac in its entirety, in a partial Latin translation, and in the fourth-century *Apostolic Constitutions* in Greek. The *Didascalia*'s final chapter contains a summary of the apostles' teachings, forming a brief Rule of Faith.[38] It is primarily christological. No mention is made of the Father's creative work or the Spirit-filled church. Yet several other traditional elements are there: the crucifixion under Pilate, resurrection from the dead, ascension to the Father's right hand, and a promised return to judge the living and the dead. Interestingly, there is also a statement about Christ's proclamation of victory to the Old Testament saints during his three days in the grave; but the origin of the "descent into hell" theme is beyond the scope of this paper.[39] For our purposes, let us note that the *Didascalia*'s Rule is centered on the actions of Christ. However, there is no mention of finding Christ proclaimed in the Old Testament.

---

36. Dix and Chadwick, *Treatise on the Apostolic Tradition*, 35–37.
37. Bradshaw, *Search for the Origins of Christian Worship*, 88.
38. Connolly, *Didascalia Apostolorum*, 258.
39. See Kelly, *Early Christian Creeds*, 378–83.

10. Novatian, a mid third-century Roman presbyter and schismatic, is next on our list. His *De Trinitate* is actually an extended commentary on the Rule.[40] Novatian opens the treatise by saying, "The Rule of Truth requires that we believe, first in God the Father and almighty Lord." Later, in chapter 9, he says, "The same Rule of Truth teaches us, after we believe in the Father, to believe also in the Son of God." And in chapter 29, Novatian says that the "authority of faith" as found in the "digest of the words and writings of the Lord" likewise commands belief in the Holy Spirit promised to the church. Thus, the *De Trinitate* is structured around the frequent threefold pattern of the Rule: Creator God, actions of Christ, and Spirit in the church.

Novatian makes a noteworthy statement when he quotes the christological portion of the Rule. He says Jesus Christ "was not only promised in the Old Testament, but also has been manifested in the New Testament."[41] The dynamic of prophecy and fulfillment is not new, of course, but Novatian goes on to assert that Christ "fulfills the shadows and types of all the prophecies concerning the presence of His Incarnate Truth."[42] The phrase "shadows and types" hints at the language of allegorical exegesis, which we have so far seen only in Clement of Alexandria. Other than the addition of this subtle expression, Novatian's Rule follows the generally established pattern.

11. Origen brings us to one of the most significant theologians of the ancient church. We should not be surprised, then, to find that his understanding of the church's Rule has been well examined.[43] Origen clearly

---

40. The original title of the work appears to have been *De Regula Veritatis* or *De Regula Fidei*. It received its current title in the manuscript tradition only after the fourth-century Trinitarian controversies emerged. For an English translation of the text, see DeSimone, *Novatian*.

41. Novatian *De Trinitate* 9 (DeSimone, *Novatian* 42).

42. Ibid. (DeSimone, *Novatian* 42).

43. Key studies on the Rule of Faith in Origen include: Bardy, "Règle de Foi d'Origène," 162–96; Hanson, *Origen's Doctrine of Tradition*; Trevijano Etcheverría, "Orígenes y la 'regula fidei,'" 327–38; Outler, "Origen and the *Regulae Fidei*," 133–41; and Cocchini, "Dalla regula fidei riflessioni origeniane sullo Spirito Santo," 593–603. My thanks go to Amanda Lehman and Nathan Erickson for translating Trevijano Etcheverría for me, and to Mark Brucato for his translation of Cocchini.

had a catechetical précis available to him.[44] Yet for Origen, the Rule was broader than the baptismal symbol he would have known in Egypt.[45] His central discussion of the Rule, found in the preface to *Peri Archon*, immediately reveals he was not reproducing a fixed creed drawn from the baptismal font, but was using the church's historic summary of faith in a more fluid way: as the building blocks of theological argumentation. We do not discover in Origen the stereotyped language of a creed. The Rule of Faith instead provides the fundamental data from which to do constructive theology. In this regard, Origen is squarely in line with writers such as Irenaeus and Tertullian.

What about the *content* of the Rule for Origen? We should note that Origen offers two types of material in *Peri Archon*.[46] He distinguishes between material that is part of the church's official teaching, and material about which Christians (or those claiming to be Christians) still debate. The fixed material includes God the Creator, who was at work in the Old and New Testaments; Jesus Christ, incarnate in flesh, born of a virgin and the Holy Spirit, who suffered, died, rose again, and ascended to heaven; the Holy Spirit who is united with the Father and Son, and who inspired the prophets of the Old Covenant and the apostles of the church; and an eschatological article which promises the final resurrection of the soul with judgment and rewards. This is the clear teaching of the church's *regula fidei*. In addition, those matters about which there is still debate (being matters only for the intellectual Christian to explore) include certain arcane points of pneumatology, psychology, angelology, demonology, cosmology, and theology proper. These points are *not* part of the Rule.

Interestingly, there are also some unique elements that Origen says are part of the church's established teaching, but which have not appeared in any earlier Rule of Faith (except perhaps in Clement). These doctrines include the free will of the soul; the existence of Satan and the demons; a non-eternal universe and its current state of dissolution; the hidden meaning of Scripture, to be accessed through spiritual exegesis;

44 Bardy, "Règle de Foi d'Origène," 196.

45 Trevijano Etcheverría, "Orígenes y la 'regula fidei,'" 338; and Outler, "Origen and the *Regulae Fidei*," 134.

46. Origen *Peri Archon* 1.pref.4–10 (Butterworth, *On First Principles*, 2–6).

and the existence of good angels. For Origen, these are not part of the *debated* doctrinal points, but the *certain* doctrines. Thus we encounter the curious development that Origen's Rule of Faith included, in addition to the standard catechetical summary, some extra truths that he takes to be essential Christian principles. Why does Origen have this unique Rule of Faith? As a catechist, he was well acquainted with the content of the church's basic instruction. Yet for him, the Rule of Faith included more. Apparently he viewed these extra doctrines as a given in the church at Alexandria. He could conceive of no other Christianity than one in which these doctrines inherently belonged, so he included them in his description of the *regula fidei*.

Despite this difference in the Rule's actual content, we find that Origen used the Rule of Faith theologically very much like his patristic predecessors. We have seen how the church fathers joined the two Testaments by means of the Rule's overarching narrative. Irenaeus and Tertullian clearly did so; but even the less theological writers taught the unity of salvation history by emphasizing prediction and fulfillment. When Origen advocated allegorical exegesis as part of the Rule, he was making the same point. He wanted to join the two covenants by accessing the spiritual meaning that would place Christ everywhere in the Bible. Thus, Origen was not out of step with the rest of the fathers in his use of the Rule. Admittedly, he added other doctrines to the traditional baptismal confession. Yet these doctrines were quite orthodox, and he knew the difference between them and the matters still under debate. Though Origen had a fuller Rule of Faith, it was not a heretical one; and in terms of how he *employed* it, he was very much in keeping with earlier attempts to unify the law and the gospel.

12. Cyprian, bishop of Carthage until his death in 258, mentions the Rule of Faith often but quotes it infrequently.[47] In his *Epistle 73, To Jubaianus*, Cyprian lists the beliefs the orthodox accept, but the heretic Marcion does not: God, the Father and Creator; and the Son of God, born of the Virgin Mary, the Word made flesh, who died for sins and conquered

---

47. For some of the places where Cyprian mentions the Rule and/or the baptismal symbol, see van den Eynde, *Normes de l'Enseignement Chrétien*, 244–45, 298.

death and was raised in the flesh.[48] Elsewhere, Cyprian quotes part of the baptismal interrogation: "Do you believe in remission of sins and eternal life through the holy Church?"[49] Most of the traditional elements of the church's Rule—the Creator God, the life and work of Christ, the Holy Spirit, and the Church—are present in Cyprian, with nothing out of the ordinary. Nevertheless, we do not get much indication from Cyprian's creedal material of a twofold salvation history, or of the prediction of Christ in the Old Testament. Cyprian was more concerned with church unity in his own day than solidarity with the Old Covenant.

13. *The Baptismal Creed of Alexandria* is our final example to be mentioned. Though the extant sources are from a slightly later period, they represent the creed as Origen would have known it in the mid third century. Our earliest source is Dionysius of Alexandria, who was the head of the catechetical school in Alexandria, and later a bishop there until he died in 265. Unfortunately, not much of his literary corpus has survived. However, in his *Letter to Pope Stephen*, some creedal material is preserved in a Syriac translation. Though it is not a full-fledged Rule of Faith, Dionysius does call it the "sound words of faith."[50] We find once again the traditional Christ-kerygma affirming that Christ is God, became a man, died, rose, and will come again to judge the living and the dead.

Another source of the Alexandrian baptismal creed is the *Dêr Balyzeh Papyrus*, which apparently derives from the late third or early fourth century. It runs: "I believe in God the Father almighty, and in His only-begotten Son our Lord Jesus Christ, and in the Holy Spirit, and in the resurrection of the flesh in the holy Catholic Church."[51] A letter from Bishop Alexander, dated to around 318, likewise confesses the Egyptian church's faith in the unbegotten Father, the only begotten Son, and the Holy Spirit who "made new both the saints of the old covenant and the

---

48. Greenslade, *Early Latin Theology*, 160.

49. Cyprian *Epistle* 69.7 (Greenslade, *Early Latin Theology*, 155).

50. Feltoe, *Saint Dionysius of Alexandria*, 53. See also Hanson, *Tradition in the Early Church*, 91.

51. Kelly, *Early Christian Creeds*, 89.

inspired teachers of the so-called new covenant."⁵² Then a christological section appears, delineating the Virgin Birth, the crucifixion, the resurrection, and the ascension to the Father's right hand. The contemporaneous creed of Arius, which he submitted to the bishop of Constantinople in 327, covers the same ground: God the Father; Jesus Christ, who was born, suffered, rose again, and will return in judgment; the Holy Spirit; and the church which awaits the resurrection of the flesh and eternal life.⁵³ Another creed in the fourth century, attributed to the Egyptian monk Macarius the Great, affirms these same points as well.⁵⁴ As we consider the Alexandrian symbol, we see all the traditional elements found in other *regulae*.

The thirteen sources surveyed above represent a comprehensive look at the Rule of Faith in its heyday during the second and third centuries. Of course, references to the Rule did not disappear overnight. J. N. D. Kelly speaks of a "movement toward fixity," culminating in the establishment of the authoritative Old Roman Creed and its daughter creeds in the fourth and fifth centuries.⁵⁵ Nevertheless, the earlier, more fluid concept of the *regula fidei* continued to be found among the patristic writers. For example, Augustine mentioned the Rule approximately fifty times in his writings, and he used it theologically much like his forerunners. It was by no means limited to baptismal catechesis or liturgical recitation, but was employed as a hermeneutical device.⁵⁶ The church fathers of the second and third centuries set a precedent for later generations, not only in the structure and content of the Rule, but in its theological, polemical, and exegetical usage.

Summary and Conclusions

From the earliest figures like Ignatius or Justin Martyr, to the more comprehensive theologians like Irenaeus, Tertullian, Clement, or Origen, the

---

52. Ibid., 188–89.
53. Socrates Scholasticus *Ecclesiastical History* 1.26 (*NPNF2* 2:28).
54. Kelly, *Early Christian Creeds*, 190–91.
55. See in particular ibid., chs. 3–6.
56. Grech, "Regula Fidei as a Hermeneutical Principle." See also Litfin, "Rule of Faith in Augustine."

Rule of Faith functioned in distinct and consistent ways. From the beginning, confessions about Jesus (among the proto-orthodox, at least) located him in the context of Jewish life and Israel's God. The one Creator God was active among the patriarchs and prophets through the Spirit, until the fullness of the incarnation finally came. At first, the church fathers understood this point only in a basic way. But when we get to Irenaeus and Tertullian, we find salvation history being united into a cosmic narrative, in which the writings of the Old Testament must be theologically joined with the New. When figures such as Clement or Origen spoke of "allegorical exegesis," they were referring to a christological reading of the Old Testament as a book replete with veiled references to Christ in an effort to find New Testament truth in the prophetic Scriptures.

The fathers were nearly unanimous that the Bible must be read as a canonical whole, as a single story with one great plotline. The narrative is encapsulated in the Rule of Faith, making it an accurate summary of the Bible. Practically speaking, that meant intentional agreement with the Rule of Faith must be the goal of any interpretive move. Far from being in competition with Scripture, the church's received tradition was seen by the fathers as an accurate guide to the more comprehensive revelation found in God's Word. Therefore, each and every biblical verse must be interpreted in light of the totality of Christian truth.

What, then, can we learn from the church fathers' use of the Rule of Faith? We must understand that for them it was a summary of catholic orthodoxy. The Rule of Faith was a synopsis of what the Christian faith was all about. Today we might call it "mere Christianity." I wish to draw three specific conclusions from the patristic understanding of the *regula fidei*.

The Rule of Faith Emphasized Unchanging, Absolute Truths

Immediately, in using the word "truths," we run the risk of supposing the fathers were concerned only with doctrinal propositions. While doctrine was an important part of the life of the ancient church, let us note that the "truths" found in the Rule of Faith were *actions in the world*. This is precisely why the Rule can be construed as a narrative: it celebrated the mighty deeds accomplished by God on the world's stage. Specifically, these deeds are:

1. The act of Creation by the Father God
2. The act of Prediction through the Spirit in the Old Testament
3. The act of Incarnation by the Holy Spirit through the Virgin Mary
4. The act of Ministration in which Christ serves the world, preaches, and works miracles
5. The act of Crucifixion for the purpose of salvation
6. The act of Resurrection in triumph
7. The act of Ascension to the Father's right hand
8. The act of Proclamation by the Spirit's power in the apostolic church
9. The act of Consummation in which the dead will be raised by Christ for final judgment

At its heart, Christianity is about these nine things. It is a message of divine action, not a collection of theoretical axioms. Notice also that the divine actions center on Jesus Christ. The one who is both God and man accomplished the will of the Father in the power of the Spirit. The gospel, as summarized in the Rule of Faith, is a proclamation of what Christ has done. These facts are unchanging and absolute. To relinquish any of them is to abandon Christianity for something else.

Though the Rule of Faith Summarized Core Truths, It Omitted Many Other Points

One of the most surprising aspects of the *regula fidei* is not what it contains, but what it leaves out. We might wish to find within its contours a comprehensive survey of all Christian doctrine, but it simply is not there. For example, the formal language of Trinitarianism is absent, for obvious reasons of historical development. Nor is bibliology included, again for historical reasons (i.e., Trinitarianism and the official recognition of a closed canon both belong to the fourth century). Ecclesiology and eschatology are limited to only the most basic points: the existence of the Spirit-filled church, and the promise of Christ's return to resurrect, punish, and reward. What is perhaps even more perplexing from an evangelical point of view is that formal soteriology is entirely missing. The church fathers apparently did not think it necessary to include the "plan of salvation" in their summary of the Christian faith. Of course, concepts such as faith, grace, righteousness, sin, baptism, and atonement are to be found in the patristic writings. Yet the Rule of Faith was content to omit any discussion of the human side of salvation, focusing solely on the actions of God in Christ. It recorded only the essential Christian truths about God's saving work. Thus, it created a springboard for further theological investigation, allowing "room to roam," while still providing fixed boundaries that limited speculation.[57]

The Rule of Faith, as a Summary of Mere Christianity, Was a Useful Exegetical Authority

The church fathers frequently employed what I call "regular exegesis." That is to say, they refused to read Scripture from a neutral stance, with their minds a *tabula rasa* awaiting the input of information. Rather, they read Scripture with the intent to arrive at an orthodox conclusion—and the Rule of Faith handily summarized what the intended goal should be. The ancient Christians did not seek to be objective; their approach was not scientific in the traditional sense of aloof detachment. How could believers in the risen Christ ever be neutral toward the writings that testified about their Lord? No, the church fathers were not modernists. They

---

57. Tertullian expressed the Christian's exegetical freedom this way: "Let us seek only what can come into question without disloyalty to the Rule of Faith ... Provided the essence of the Rule is not disturbed, you may seek and discuss as much as you like. You may give full rein to your itching curiosity where any point seems unsettled and ambiguous or dark and obscure." *Prescription against Heretics* 12, 14 (Greenslade, *Early Latin Theology*, 39–40). Augustine said something similar when he offered his own interpretation of a psalm, then wrote, "Some other person may produce a better interpretation, for the obscurity of the scriptures is such that a passage scarcely ever yields a single meaning only. But whatever interpretation emerges, it must conform to the rule of faith." *Expositions of the Psalms* 74.12 (Boulding, 4:50). For more on this subject, see Litfin, "Rule of Faith in Augustine," 97–100.

read every verse of Scripture with a specific outcome in mind: orthodoxy, or "right belief" about the things of God.

In the Rule of Faith, the fathers possessed a useful tool that always kept before their eyes the essentials of Christianity, the metanarrative of God's great plan. Though the Rule could not solve every exegetical conundrum, it certainly could guide the interpreter toward the bigger picture. As was noted above, one of the key elements of that picture was the unity of the two Testaments. Therefore, any contemporary interpreter who wishes to be illumined by the patristic witness will inevitably seek to discover Christ in the Old Testament. Early church tradition, as found in sources like the *regula fidei*, gives us an authoritative guide to the christological heartbeat of Holy Scripture. The Lord Jesus must be the center of all exegesis, the goal of every interpretation, the hermeneutical key to the entire Bible. The exegete who takes his cues from the ancients will never be aloof or objective, but will unapologetically drive his interpretations back to Jesus Christ.

Are the interlocutors in the ancient-future conversation willing to hear the church fathers? If so, then hear these final remarks. The early Christians definitely believed in absolute truths. In a 2004 article in *Christianity Today*, one Emergent leader was quoted as saying, "I grew up thinking we had figured out the Bible, that we knew what it means. Now I have no idea what most of it means."[58] To the extent that such skepticism reflects a general distaste within Emergent circles at making unequivocal truth claims, it ceases to be truly ancient. The church fathers made very clear and very bold affirmations of what the Bible had to say about the great christological purposes of God. So too, the contemporary church must not fail to preach the truths of Christian theology. There is much we know for certain about God, because he has given us his Word.

At the same time, the postmodern reluctance to make overly detailed or sweeping truth claims authentically retrieves the patristic preference for emphasizing core truths, while leaving others open to debate. The fathers certainly engaged in vigorous theological exchange. Yet when it came time to be baptized, it was the core confession of God's actions in Christ that really mattered. In the early church, truth was not grounded

---

58. Crouch, "Emergent Mystique," 38.

Learning from Patristic Use of the Rule of Faith

in philosophical premises, but in God himself, who acts in our world in dramatic fashion, most vividly in Jesus Christ. To be ancient-future is to be centered on Christ as the protagonist in a great drama, one in which we ourselves are co-actors. Therefore, what is often called a "narrative" approach to theology is an entirely patristic instinct.

Finally, an ancient-future Christianity must include a new respect for tradition as an interpretive authority. We must begin to employ a "regular exegesis" that is intentional about making our interpretive conclusions square with the Rule of Faith. We must not shrink back in fear at the word "eisegesis," as if bringing our presuppositions to the text—and indeed, even knowing the outcome ahead of time—somehow taints the interpretive task. As long as our conclusions are orthodox, we will not have "led in" a foreign meaning. Where the tradition is unclear, we will not force the issue. But where historic orthodoxy has clearly spoken, our handling of the text must be *inclined* in that direction. To take one prominent example, the virgin birth is not up for debate; it is part of the received deposit of the faith.

The church fathers are good friends to evangelicals. Let us recognize and celebrate that fact. A truly ancient-future exegesis will not only make room at the table for the received wisdom of the ancients, it will humbly seat them at the table's head, so that together we may feast on the Bread of Life.

5

Learning from Patristic Responses to Cultural Opposition

W. BRIAN SHELTON

❖ IN THE early second century AD, the Roman historian Tacitus wrote the *Annals of Imperial Rome* with a critical eye on the Roman emperor. The work was a strategic response to what Tacitus believed was an office that had dulled the moral conscience of Roman leaders. His history provides a rare Roman reference to the early church that describes the cultural opposition facing it. Notice the pejorative representation of early believers: "Nero fabricated scapegoats—and punished with every refinement the notoriously depraved Christians (as they were properly called). Their originator, Christ, had been executed . . . but in spite of this temporary setback the deadly superstition had broken out afresh, not only in Judea (where the mischief had started) but even in Rome. All degraded and shameful practices collect and flourish in the capital."[1]

Soon after, Justin wrote his *First Apology*, also with a critical eye on the emperor. The work showed a strategic response to what Justin believed was a philosophical double standard. His history provides a rare second-century insight into how the early church handled persecution. He hoped to persuade the emperor himself that Roman persecution, and not Christian citizenship, was fraudulent and immoral.

---

1. Tacitus *Annals of Imperial Rome* 15:44 (Grant, *Tacitus*, 365).

Justin argued that Christians are "unjustly hated and wantonly abused."[2] Christians were in fact excellent Roman citizens, as they paid their taxes, avoided fornication, refused to commit perjury, encouraged rational thinking, and protected unwanted children exposed to weather.[3] In fact, Justin argues, Christians are ideal Roman citizens and other Roman citizens are the recipients of their civil benevolence. In the face of cultural opposition, one Christian in ancient Rome responded journalistically and intellectually.

What various types of responses to opposition did ancient Christians make from which we, the contemporary church, can profit? The early church encountered opposition and persecution on several levels, and their types of responses ranged from integrative and accepting to dissociative and rejecting. This essay considers the ways that particular patristic writers responded to the pressures of Roman culture that threatened their faith. Foundational to their response was their identity in Christ and their relationship to the world in which they lived. I hope this explanation will reveal why spiritual preparation, perseverance, thoughtful and biblical reflection, strategic response, and cultural apologetics matter for the contemporary church. Our study begins with some groundwork concerning Christianity's relationship to culture that the early church first determined for itself.

Theory of Christ and Culture

Jesus was not without culture in mind when he warned his disciples about the opposition that comes with following him: "If the world hates you, you know that it has hated Me before *it hated* you. If you were of the world, the world would love its own; but because you are not of the world, but I chose you out of the world, because of this the world hates you" (John 15:18, NASB).

Our study of the "cultural opposition" that the early church encountered begins with a definition of culture. In his classic work *Christ and Culture*, H. Richard Niebuhr remarks that "culture is the 'artificial,

---

2. Justin *First Apology* 1 (*ANF* 1:163).

3. Justin *First Apology* 10 (rational thinking), 17 (taxes), 27 (infanticide), and 29 (fornication); and *Second Apology* 2 (perjury).

secondary environment' which man superimposes on the natural. It comprises language, habits, ideas, beliefs, customs, social organization, inherited artifacts, technical processes, and values."[4] Although culture's essence cannot be defined, some characteristics can be laid out. It is always social, it is a human achievement associated with human values, it must be realized in temporal and material forms, and it has numerous and disparate values to develop and adopt.[5] Yet, the nature of culture is not as important as the church's relationship to it, which finds precedent in God's relationship to the world.

The chart below provides Niebuhr's five categories of Christ's relationship to culture. Craig Carter provides a similar illustration and thorough summary of the categories, and this table is adapted from it:[6]

	Christ _____ culture				
relationship	*against*	*of*	*above*	*paradoxes*	*transforms*
Niebuhr's label	radicals	liberals	synthesists	dualists	conversionists
biblical examples	1 John, Revelation	apocryphal Gospels	sayings about God's transcendence	Paul's letters	John's Gospel
historical examples	Tertullian, monasticism, Mennonites, Tolstoy	gnosticism, Abelard, Kant, Schleiermacher, Ritschl	Justin, Clement of Alexandria, Aquinas, Butler	Marcion, Luther, Kierkegaard, Roger Williams	Augustine, Calvin, F. D. Maurice

Notice the ways that Christ relates to culture: *against* it, *of* it, *above* it, *paradoxical to* it, and *transformative of* it. We will not elucidate each here,

4. Niebuhr, *Christ and Culture*, 32.
5. Ibid., 32–39.
6. Carter, *Rethinking Christ and Culture*, 36.

allowing the examples from the patristic era to illustrate the various ways that Christ might relate to culture.[7]

Finally, some conceptualization about the otherworldly nature of Christianity is in order. Given the character of the Judeo-Christian religious tradition, conflict between the early church and the Roman Empire was inevitable. The patristic differences with pagan culture were similar to the experiences of the Israelites going into the land of Canaan, when God designated his people to be holy, separated from the neighboring cultures with practices foreign to the character of God. The patristic era's experiences were not different than the apostles' conflict recorded in Acts, when Jews accused them of blasphemy, and then resorted to conspiracy, mobs, persecution, and even murder to prevent the spreading of the gospel. Despite the success of Christianity, the persecutions of entire religious communities yet today remind us of the never-ending opposition to Christianity in the world. The stark opposition is what the New Testament writers had in mind when they spoke of "the world" as alien to the faith.[8]

This brings us to how the contemporary church can profit from the early church. Accounts of patristic experiences of persecution and cultural opposition provide several different responses that can be neatly collected into the two categories of *integrative* and *dissociative*. Integrative responses were ways of accepting or partially accepting tenets of culture. Such responses interactively engaged and related to culture, and in a sense cooperated with it. The effect was to assimilate and to convince. Meanwhile, dissociative responses opposed cultural features and were more antagonistic, often appearing defiant but rarely hostile to culture. When Christians disagreed with cultural values, they responded by contesting them and standing against them.

This essay will consider the perspectives of early Christians who employed culture through integrative responses or resisted culture

---

7. Both Craig Carter and D. A. Carson offer excellent treatments of Niebuhr's work, and also present a vision for the contemporary church in its relationship to culture. See Carson, *Christ & Culture Revisited*.

8. In John's Gospel one finds the strongest depiction of the "world" as alien to God: "The world, then [in John's cosmology], is not a neutral place.... the *world* is thus a *theological* term for humanity set against God." Burge, *John*, 63.

through dissociative responses. Using an account from Justin's life as an introductory sketch to each category, the essay provides applications in different scenarios encountered by many different early Christian writers. It does not critically examine their uses, but for this essay recognizes with Paul McKechnie that "people's allegiance to Christ was expressed in a variety of theoretical frameworks."[9] The variety of responses mirrors Niebuhr's range of Christian understanding of culture in relationship to the faith. The end effect is one of strategic intentionality, even as a thoughtful and biblical understanding of culture is required by the contemporary church today.

Integrative Responses

As Justin wrote his *First Apology* to the emperor, his appeal was particularly noteworthy because it sought to defend a religion alien to the recipient by using the values of that same recipient. Trained in the philosophies of Stoicism, Aristotelianism, Pythagoreanism, and Platonism, Justin built his case for Christianity by using these systems, employing their principles in methodology or in direct citation. For example, Justin argued that Plato spoke rightly on matters of truth because he in fact borrowed from the writings of Moses in the Hebrew Scriptures.[10] With impressive theological breadth and imagination, Justin linked John's depiction of Christ as *Logos* with the *logos* notion popular in the Middle Platonist tradition.[11] G. L. Carey declares that Justin "sums up in one bold stroke the whole history of mankind as finding its consummation in Christ."[12] He integrated the values seen in Greek philosophy and popular culture into a Christian worldview, "the first Christian thinker after Paul to grasp the universalistic implications of Christianity."[13] Justin's efforts are the most recognized integrative measure taken against cultural opposition to Christianity, and his efforts more specifically illustrate the category of "legal responses."

9. McKechnie, *First Christian Centuries*, 19.
10. Justin *First Apology* 59 (*ANF* 1:182).
11. Kretschmar, "Early Church," 40.
12. Carey, "Justin Martyr," 558.
13. Ibid.

Legal Responses

Some patristic writers systematically sought to justify Christianity by synthesizing the new faith with contemporary culture through legal compatibility arguments. The implication was that the new faith was related to other dimensions of culture. As an intellectual appeal, it sought to assimilate cultural values with Christian values. The inculturation process was crucial to the church's self-identity as it confronted the culture, trying to appeal to Christianity's legitimacy by recognizing its similarities with what was already valued and affirmed. With the posture of a legal defendant, Justin accused the pagan critic Crescens of slander, because the critic in ignorance claimed that "Christians were atheists and impious" yet was unable to answer the most fundamental questions about Christianity. This argument was more than just an exposé of an opponent's inconsistencies; it was an affirmation of certain true and consistent principles found in pagan philosophy. Justin said that Crescens denied both Socratic and Cynic principles of fairness when he falsely and ignorantly accused Christians.[14]

John Renard calls this method of Justin the "inculturation and conflict" model. Renard argues that in such cases a theological adaptation takes place, as the apologist assimilated the Christian faith into culture and vice versa.[15] Georg Kretschmar argues that the success of the later theological and christological controversies greatly rested on such inculturation, which he reduces to a Christian integrative response to Greek metaphysics.[16]

Athenagoras exhibited apologetic methodologies that sought to elevate Christ *above* culture by showing the weak arguments used by critics to judge Christian thought. He argued that the gods were historically recent inventions, that the Greek poets insisted the gods were created, and that the philosophers acknowledged a one, true, uncreated God. He argued that Plato would never be considered a Roman criminal, so why should Christians be treated so?[17] Such approaches were called

---

14. Justin *Second Apology* 3 (*ANF* 1:189).
15. Renard, "Comparative Theology," 8–9.
16. Kretschmar, "Early Church," 43.
17. Athenagoras *Plea for the Christians* 5–7 (*ANF* 2:131–32).

"apologetic" because they offered a defense of the faith. Early Christian legal-looking works can be seen in the list of *contra* titles below, but more directly in works like Tertullian's *Apology*, Justin's *First* and *Second Apologies*, Aristides' *Apology*, and Commodian's *Song of Apology*.

Trained in law, Tertullian of Carthage defended the faith through legal argumentation to become a premier apologist. Some readers may be surprised to find him listed here under "integrative responses," but Tertullian has often been misrepresented as a separatist who rejected culture. This bias centers on a misunderstanding of his famous quote: "What has Athens to do with Jerusalem? What concord is there between the Academy and the Church? What between heretics and Christians? . . . Away with all attempts to produce a mottled Christianity of Stoic, Platonic, and dialectic composition! We want no curious disputation after possessing Jesus Christ . . . With our faith we desire no further belief."[18] Reconciled with the rest of Tertullian, this is not a rejection of the same Greek philosophy and rhetoric whose methods he appreciates and employs.[19] Rather, this is a dramatic moment of poetic exaggeration in which he does indeed caution against overvaluing culture. In this rhetorical flourish he condemns pagan philosophies, but he does not practice this negative critique comprehensively. Elsewhere, he remarks about the continuity of culture and faith. For example, "What poet or sophist has not drunk at the fountain of the prophets? Thence, accordingly, the philosophers watered their arid minds, so that it is the things they have from us which bring us into comparison with them. . . . Finding a simple revelation of God, they proceeded to dispute about Him."[20]

One cannot overemphasize the importance of articulating true ideas within the boundaries of creation and culture for contemporary evangelicalism. The survival of the church requires effectively introducing the gospel to a world in its own context, one that is cultural and in a fallen state. Augustine's experience with intellectual uncertainty during his time pursuing Manichaeism illustrates this. As he searched for an-

---

18. Tertullian *Prescription against Heresies* 7 (ANF 3:246); *Apology* 46 (Niebuhr, *Christ and Culture*, 54).

19. Osborn, "Was Tertullian a Philosopher?" 322–34; and Litfin, *Getting to Know the Church Fathers*, 277.

20. Tertullian *Apology* 47 (ANF 3:51–52).

swers, his colleagues could not provide them but referred him to a leading Manichaean teacher, Faustus, who would be arriving soon. Augustine's expectations grew, but when the legendary teacher arrived, Augustine "was bitterly disappointed to find out that [Faustus] relied on rhetorical skills and eloquence to persuade. . . . yet his answers were shallow and poorly reasoned."[21] On the other hand, Augustine's later encounters with Ambrose and Pontitianus proved to be intellectually illuminating, leading to the conversion of one of the most significant figures in Christian history.

These examples demonstrate how Christ is *above* culture. Niebuhr appropriately uses the term "synthesists" to describe these legal and philosophical arbitrators. However, to a lesser degree, they viewed Christ as being *of* culture.[22] It is still a Christian effort; after all, they employed the methods of contemporary culture against itself in order to further the cause of the gospel. They acknowledged the truth contained in literature and historical writings, works still appreciated by modern-day culture. Much of evangelicalism lacks an appreciation of such breadth and can be very skeptical of general revelation, of any product of a non-Christian culture, and anything associated with practices outside of one's own faith community. Even John Calvin, with a strong view of depravity, admitted that humankind's natural abilities are not wholly extinguished, but common grace allows humanity to make cultural advances that are inherently good. He explains: "Still, we see in this diversity some remaining traces of the image of God, which distinguish the entire human race from the other creatures."[23]

For these legal and philosophical *synthesists*, any indication of cultural goodness ultimately finds its source in the divine. In this sense the apologists find their best classification in Christ *over* culture. This tendency is apparent in Clement of Alexandria and Irenaeus, who were philosophical synthesists.

---

21. Moreland, *Love Your God*, 42.

22. Although the label is now pejorative, Niebuhr's term "liberal" describes the freedom these writers employed and the breadth of epistemology from which they comfortably drew.

23. Calvin, *Institutes of the Christian Religion*, 2.2.17.

Philosophical Synthesis Responses

Much overlap exists between the categories of legal response and philosophical synthesis, and Justin could easily be placed in this latter category as a premier philosopher. However, Justin primarily intended to represent the faith legally in ways that other philosophical synthesists did not. These writers acknowledged the value of some components of a system, but they did not necessarily affirm them all. These other apologists of the second century subtly assessed subjects like Greek philosophy as not fully adequate, and they carefully depicted a similar, Christian form to be superior. This is an important tenet to preserve when Christianity confronts culture.

Clement of Alexandria viewed philosophy as a divine creation, the gift of the Logos.[24] For him, much of what seemed to be cultural opposition was not necessarily threatening but could be easily incorporated to serve Christianity. Culture "at least prepares the way for the teaching that is royal in the highest sense of the word, by making men self-controlled, by molding character and making them ready to receive the truth."[25] For Clement, those who absolutely reject culture as pagan are foolish. He wrote of how "the multitude are frightened at the Hellenic philosophy, as children are at masks," declaring that the knowing Christian "will not then be deficient in what contributes to proficiency in the curriculum of studies and the Hellenic philosophy."[26]

However, the Greek perspective does not fully comprehend the whole truth of creation like the Christian Scriptures and so has its limitations. Clement's ultimate allegiance to Christ alone is seen at the close of *Stromateis* 6, when he declares that if a ruler ever prohibited Greek philosophy, then it would vanish. The word of Christ, however, cannot die.[27] Thus, Clement does not see culture and corresponding learning as the end goal, but his Christ-*of*-culture model is ultimately balanced by one of Christ *above* culture, although the balancing moments are few. God "ad-

---

24. Clement *Stromata* 7.6 (*ANF* 2:531–37).
25. Clement, cited in Frend, *Martyrdom and Persecution*, 259.
26. Clement *Stromata* 6.10 (*ANF* 2:498).
27. Ibid., 6.18 (*ANF* 2:520). This inferiority of even a good culture is also illustrated in *Stromata* 1.5, when he labels philosophy as the handmaiden of theology.

monishes us to use indeed, but not to linger and spend time with, secular culture. For what was bestowed on each generation advantageously, and at seasonable times, is a preliminary training for the word of the Lord."[28] Niebuhr believes that for Clement, "His Christ is not against culture, but he uses culture's best products as instruments in his work of bestowing on men what they cannot achieve by their own efforts."[29] For Clement, Christians ought to prepare "for a life in which they no longer care for themselves, their culture, or their wisdom. Clement's Christ is both the Christ of culture and the Christ above the culture."[30]

In his case against gnosticism, Irenaeus reveals a familiarity with contemporary Roman rhetorical styles that illustrates an appreciation and integration of culture. Gerard Vallée shows how Irenaeus' methods of argumentation belong to popular philosophy, employing polemics found in Greek philosophical debate.[31] Irenaeus claims that gnostic pastors and writers employ "gnosis falsely so-called," contradict right reason, teach novelty and not classical thought, are subtle and not clear, disagree within their own community, and lack practical knowledge and virtue.[32] These are all violations of traditional standards for maintaining a valid position. Although Irenaeus integrates cultural elements in his encounter with cultural opposition, he also clearly argued for Christ *against* one cultural trend: gnosticism.[33]

The examples of intellectual integration are numerous. Two more will suffice to demonstrate how the fathers viewed Christ as being *of* but still *above* culture. Like Paul in Romans 13, *1 Clement* sees obedi-

28. Ibid., 1.5 (*ANF* 2:306).
29. Niebuhr, *Christ and Culture*, 127.
30. Ibid., 127–28.
31. Vallée, *Anti-Gnostic Polemics*, 7.
32. Ibid., 14–15. His summary provides a sample from Irenaeus' *Against Heresies*.
33. In a similar vein, the contemporary phenomenon of "comparative theology" often neglects this latter safeguard of Christian integration. Represented by authors like Francis X. Clooney and David Tracy, this is "the study of inter-religious relations, and of the implications of serious interchange between and among religious traditions for the future of Christian theology." Renard, "Comparative Theology," 6. Depending on the comparative theologian, the methodology may neglect the important principles of "truth" and "error" that patristic writers like Irenaeus insisted upon as they confronted a diverse religious culture.

ence to governmental rulers as obedience offered to God. His prayer for Christians in Corinth is that "we render obedience to your almighty and most excellent name, and to our rulers and governors on earth." He says they were placed by God's sovereignty, and the practice of being subject to them accepts God's appointment of them.[34] This exhortation probably came under the reign of Emperor Domitian, notorious for severe persecution of the church.

Macrina was a woman prized by her brother Gregory of Nyssa as the epitome of both Christian values and Greek ideals. In the biographical *Life of Saint Macrina*, she is presented as a Christian who is honorable, knowledgeable, teachable, philosophical, and virtuous—superlative Greek values cherished in a woman who is presented to be like Christ. Kenneth Steinhauser writes, "Macrina is the perfect embodiment of the philosophical life, or Christian *paideia*. In the literary composition of her story, Gregory has merged a Christian message with a classical Greek genre because in her person she represents the amalgamation of biblical Christianity with classical Greek thought."[35]

Augustine serves as our sole example of the Christ-*transforms*-culture model. In contrast to the pessimistic view among "radicals" of Christ *against* culture, for Augustine the great story of creation, the fall, and salvation can be viewed optimistically because of the victorious Christ who cannot help but affect Christian efforts on earth. His own *Confessions* parallel this dramatic shift from alienation from God toward transformation in God. The optimistic shift is most clearly seen in his *City of God*, whose thesis is that the kingdom of the world (Roman Empire) is passing away as the kingdom of God (Christ's body the church) is becoming established. Niebuhr remarks of him: "Christ is the transformer of culture for Augustine in the sense that he redirects, reinvigorates, and regenerates that life of man, expressed in all human works, which in present actuality is the perverted and corrupted exercise of a fundamentally good nature."[36]

---

34. *1 Clement* 60.4—61.1 (Holmes, *Apostolic Fathers*, 127); and Niebuhr, *Christ and Culture*, 51.

35. Steinhauser, "Aesthetics of Paradise," 59.

36. Niebuhr, *Christ and Culture*, 209.

As Augustine looked back only four hundred years to the reign of Tiberius Caesar and the initially little-known death of Christ, he could not help but appreciate the powerful progress that Christianity had made. He rightly serves as a capstone to our survey of intellectual and philosophical integration responses to cultural opposition. In the triumphal language of Philip Schaff, "Christianity was called to pass through an equally important intellectual and literary struggle with the ancient world; and from this also it came forth victorious, and conscious of being the perfect religion for man."[37]

Integrative Lessons for the Contemporary Church

Bruce Nicholls remarks, "Within a pluralistic culture it is hard to produce a lifestyle that cuts clean against the general way of life of the culture. . . . [Culture] is constantly changing, and therefore the task of contextualization, however understood, is always a continuing one."[38] He offers a caution to a conservative evangelical church that seems overly skeptical of culture. In particular, we unknowingly tend to reject the intellectual dimension for the heartfelt dimension. J. P. Moreland remarks about these early centuries of the church: "Faith and a disciplined mind were not natural enemies then. A well-formed mind held a place of honor. And it was believed that the Christian mind could be the best mind."[39]

Unfortunately, the evangelical culture values faith and heartfelt religion but does not characteristically prize knowledge and intellectual activities. Moreland points out: "Step one generation away from the New Testament writers to meet the men who were discipled by the apostles and you find treatises, apologies, and circular letters of stunning intelligence from those intensely devoted Church fathers."[40] We ought to be more like them, not less like them. Moreland further exhorts: "We need the mind disciplined in Christ, enlightened by faith, passionate for God and his creation, to be let loose in the world."[41] Meanwhile, the great evangelical

---

37. Schaff, *History of the Christian Church*, 86.
38. Nicholls, "Towards a Theology of Gospel and Culture," 35, 70.
39. Moreland, *Love Your God*, 15.
40. Ibid.
41. Ibid., 16.

Carl Henry wrote: "Training the mind is an essential responsibility of the home, the church, and the school. Unless evangelicals prod young people to disciplined thinking, they waste—even undermine—one of Christianity's most precious resources."[42]

In a culture of relativism and religious pluralism, the church must find new ways to integratively connect without compromising its core identity and values. Like Justin, contemporary Christianity needs to strategically confront culture, as Hauerwas and Willimon call for in works such as *Resident Aliens*.[43] They describe how the church took for granted its foothold in Western culture from 313 to 1961, from the Edict of Milan granting Christianity freedom to the watershed opening of a South Carolina Fox Theater that avalanched in the abolishment of blue laws and heralded the end of Christian dominance in American culture. Hauerwas and Willimon insist that Christians can no longer presume the upper hand in culture. Such attitudes have led to a failed presumption among evangelicals who have believed "we could fit American values into a loosely Christian framework, and we could thereby be culturally significant."[44]

Concerning legal responses, the contemporary church could take a lesson in consistent, logical argumentation. At the very least, dialogical approaches to training are still effective in our still somewhat oral culture. Perhaps the church can adapt rational gospel presentation to an increasingly visual, postmodern culture rather than catching up in the next generation. Gene Veith remarks, "Postmodern ideas are revitalizing the arts, opening them up to the past and to ordinary human life . . . Relating art to the rest of reality is promising, opening up possibilities for art that fully engages moral and spiritual values."[45]

Concerning philosophical synthesis, evangelicals could employ culture's positive components for understanding the kingdom of God. In a

---

42. Henry, *Christian Mindset*, 145–46. Some classic books written to challenge evangelicalism intellectually include: Noll, *Scandal of the Evangelical Mind*; Moreland, *Love Your God with All Your Mind*; and Sire, *Habits of the Mind*.

43. Hauerwas and Willimon, *Resident Aliens*.

44. Ibid., 17.

45. Veith, *Postmodern Times*, 93–96. See especially Veith's treatment of postmodern art and its use by the church (93–109).

postmodern age in which rational cases for truth become less convincing, we must adjust without forsaking truth arguments that still convince. Abraham Kuyper sums up the goodness of these things in his famous declaration: "There is not a square inch on the whole plain of human existence over which Christ, who is Lord over all, does not proclaim, 'This is mine!'"[46] We should recognize culture as a gift of God, a product of his common grace. To weigh culture, however, is a different process, and the "emerging" church should beware of so accommodating postmodernism that significant theological meaning becomes negotiable or harmfully deconstructed. D. A. Carson remarks how "emerging" church theology is often theologically shallow "because it overlooks the basic fact that no worldview, no epistemological system developed by us in this fallen world, is entirely good or entirely bad."[47]

Evangelicals associated with "emerging" movements are characterized by a dissatisfaction with the contemporary model of devotions, worship, and church activities, and this has led some to "go ancient." Books such as Tony Jones's *The Sacred Way: Spiritual Practices for Everyday Life* are a typical alternative, laying out a plan to engage in ancient practices centering on the *Via Contemplativa* (quiet) and *Via Activa* (active).[48] This interesting trend appears like a Christ-*transforms*-culture model in which ancient practices reemerge to find validity in contemporary circles. Still, best viewed as a Christ-*above*-culture model, these Christians embrace liturgical practices because they are ancient, perhaps showing the variety of potential devotional and worship styles, perhaps revealing greater continuity with the past. Such seemingly bizarre amalgams remind us that often there is no single Christian answer on secondary things. Niebuhr, sounding like "emerging" author Brian McLaren, insisted in 1951 that "there are possibilities at many points among the many various positions."[49]

---

46. Benne, *Quality with Soul*.

47. Carson, *Becoming Conversant*, 68.

48. Jones, *Sacred Way*, esp. 15–21. This works is also a good example of uncritical acceptance of historical practices, even encouraging combinations of practices as if they are void of any context beyond personal significance.

49. Niebuhr, *Christ and Culture*, 231; and McLaren, *New Kind of Christian*, 54. McLaren describes faith to be like a spider web with many anchor points, not just Scripture

Niebuhr maintained that the synthesists teach us about "concern for wise Christian participation in the common life."[50] Strategic integrative responses must be applied repeatedly to the Christian confrontation with culture still today. Kretschmar claims: "Faith needs to take shape in every culture," and the process is "the gift and work of the Holy Spirit."[51]

Dissociative Responses

Rusticus the prefect had ordered the recently arrested Justin to offer libations to the gods: "Obey the gods at once, and submit to the emperors." Justin responded that he obeyed Christ, an act unworthy of blame or condemnation: "We worship the God of Christians, whom we reckon to be one from the beginning, the maker and fashioner of the whole creation." Justin defended Christ as Son of God and subject of the prophets. The final line of Justin's defense is recorded as, "Yes, I am a Christian." Rusticus the prefect asked Chariton for a defense, and he similarly responded, "I am a Christian." The prefect then asked Charito, and she responded, "I am a Christian." Euelpistus also remarked, "I am a Christian," as did Hierax and Paeon. The ancient account records their deaths: "The holy martyrs having glorified God . . . were beheaded, and perfected their testimony in the confession of the Saviour."[52] This same response is echoed in the *Passion of the Scillitan Martyrs*, where each Carthaginian Christian on trial declared, "I am a Christian." All these believers responded to cultural opposition in simple, humble sacrifice for the Lord who had died for them. Martyrdom is one example of a dissociative response that early Christians made against a culture that acted and believed contrary to the faith.

---

alone. Speaking through one of the book's fictional characters, he says, "Those points might be spiritual experiences, exemplary people and institutions whom one has come to trust, that sort of thing." Although in different contexts, these two authors comment similarly on the Christian use of the temporal in understanding and articulating the eternal.

50. Niebuhr, *Christ and Culture*, 138.
51. Kretschmar, "Early Church," 44.
52. *Martyrdom of Justin Martyr* 1–5 (ANF 1:305–6).

Martyrdom Responses

The most radical form of resistance occurred when Christians were persecuted under the threat of physical harm. The Greek word μάρτυς indicates a "witness" who testifies about a given fact. Even by the time of the writing of Revelation, the term already indicated those who died for the faith.[53] Christ calls one Antipas "My witness, My faithful one, who was killed among you [in Pergamum], where Satan dwells" (Rev 2:13, NASB). The fifth seal reveals souls under the altar in heaven "who had been slain because of the word of God, and because of the testimony [μαρτυρίαν] they had maintained" (Rev 6:9). This becomes the most popular usage in the early church: the powerful witness that came through surrendering one's life for the faith. Faithful Christian witness under increasing persecution became a powerful response to culture, and acts of martyrdom had a particularly noteworthy effect on the Roman Empire that inflicted it.[54]

Persecution came in various forms, but none were ultimately effective in snuffing out Christianity. The book of Acts captures the initial persecutions by the Jews, as early as the prohibition from the Sanhedrin not to preach (4:18) and the stoning of Stephen (7:58). During this time, the church enjoyed some freedom from Roman legal action, as the Empire viewed Christianity as a Jewish sect and not a violation of the *religio illicita* policy that forbade new religions.[55] The Roman emperor Nero blamed Christians for causing the fire at Rome in AD 64. Imprisonment and execution by the government became more common during his reign as Christianity also became more common. Tacitus records the events, and so preserves one sample of suffering for the contemporary church: "Their deaths were made farcical. Dressed in wild animals' skins, they were torn to pieces by dogs, or crucified, or made into torches to be ignited after dark as substitutes for daylight. Nero provided his gardens for the spectacle, and exhibited displays in the Circus, at which he mingled with the

---

53. For a nuanced presentation, see Dehandschutter, "Meaning of Witness in the Apocalypse."

54. One of the best overviews of persecution can be found in Lesbaupin, *Blessed Are the Persecuted*. The most comprehensive, detailed analysis remains in Frend, *Martyrdom and Persecution*.

55. See Winter, "Gallio's Ruling on the Legal Status of Early Christianity."

crowd—or stood in a chariot, dressed as a charioteer. Despite their guilt as Christians, and the ruthless punishment it deserved, the victims were pitied. For it was felt that they were being sacrificed to one man's brutality rather than the national interest."[56]

This becomes the story line of the early martyrs: although the Roman Empire found its own due cause for execution, the gratuitous suffering and the sacrificial willingness of the Christians won the day. The effect of the Christian response is unparalleled in history. Among the most quoted patristic sayings, Tertullian's great expression captures the effect: *semen est sanguis Christianorum* "the blood of Christians is seed," depicting how the faith spread by the witness of the martyrs.

In the late first century, Emperor Domitian's fear of Christian influence led him to act adversely against the church. Mob violence occurred under the reigns of Trajan, Hadrian, Antoninus Pius, and Marcus Aurelius, although the acts of violence were local and sporadic. The emperors Septimus Severus, Decius, and Diocletian were among the worst persecutors, the latter of whom issued an edict to demolish churches, confiscate scriptures, torture clerics, deprive civil servants of citizenship, and even execute the unrepentant. Meanwhile, there were times of peace, and there were local churches that probably never faced persecution. However, Christians united to refuse public acknowledgment of Caesar's divine honor. People castigated Christians as "irreverent to the Caesars, enemies of the Caesars, of the Roman people."[57] Believers refused to participate in public festival ceremonies with idols, to enlist in imperial military service, to attend theatrical performances that practiced immorality on stage, and to join in political and civil service opportunities.

Exhortations for the contemporary church can be drawn from the actual reflections of Christian writers during this time. Concerning the reality of harmful cultural opposition, Cyprian of Carthage remarked: "The day of persecution has begun to be over our heads. . . . A severer and fiercer combat is now threatening for which, with an incorrupt faith and robust courage, the soldiers of Christ ought to prepare themselves, considering, therefore, that they daily drink the Chalice of the Blood of

---

56. Tacitus *Annals* 15.44 (Grant, *Tacitus*, 366).

57. *Irreligioses in Caesares, hostes Caesarum, hostes populi Romani.* See Neander and Schneider, *General History*, 91.

Christ so that they themselves may also be able to shed their blood for Christ."[58] This struggle defines the nature of the Christian life, living in a world that is alien to the things of God (1 Cor 1:18). Wayne Grudem remarks: "We should see all the hardship and suffering that comes to us in life as something that God brings to us *to do us good*, strengthening our trust in him and our obedience, and ultimately increasing our ability to glorify him."[59]

The story of imperial persecution comes to an end in 311 as Galerius issued an edict to tolerate a peaceful Christianity. Licinius and Constantine issued the Edict of Milan in 313, bringing formal freedom to Christianity. Constantine's official declaration of his own Christian faith ended centuries of uncertainty and obstacles facing early believers. Through a faithful, sacrificial response, they overcame opposition ranging from disparity with Greek religious and philosophical culture to official rejection and numerous martyrs by the Roman state, Jewish zealots, and local mobs. Yet the need for Christian cultural critique did not wane, even though the nature of critique was transformed as a predominantly Christian society now sought to express itself culturally.

Contra Responses

The Christian apologist Tatian was declared heretical in the early fifth century, but his position illustrates a denunciation of Greek philosophy. A former student of Justin, he also engaged in a defense of the faith against contemporary representation, but through ridicule and disdain for pagan philosophy in his *Address to the Greeks*. Aggravated at the unwarranted mistreatment of Christians, he wrote an apology that did not synthesize cultural tenets with the Christian faith like his master, but rejected them in a passionate Christ-*against*-culture fashion. Such writings I call *contra* responses, named after numerous dissociative book titles rejecting individuals, their theological positions, and the cultural tenets they espoused.

Another explicit rejection of a religious cultural trend was the denial of gnostic theology in the life of the early church. Gnosticism was

---

58. Cyprian *Letter* 58.1 (Donna, *Letters*, 163).
59. Grudem, *Systematic Theology*, 812.

a cultural phenomenon, attractive for its mysterious and intellectual elements. Birger Pearson has shown how gnostic communities adopted rabbinical traditions, biblical characters, and basic theological precepts from Judaism and Christianity.[60] The result for the fathers was not a pagan source adjusted by Christian truth, but an absolute perversion of the Judeo-Christian revelation. In the process of theological synthesis, gnostics transformed these well-defined features into something mythical and modified to fit their theories of a creator demiurge, a theory of Seth as progenitor of a gnostic race, and a cosmic redemption. The church responded, not in friendly integration, but in absolute rejection of gnostic methodology, claims to authority, scriptures, and theology.

Unlike the model of integrating philosophy and rhetorical argumentation found in their Western counterparts Justin and Tertullian, Irenaeus and Hippolytus sought no common ground in their response to cultural opposition when countering the gnostics. The common ground between these anti-heretical writers and their opponents could only be the Christianity that those antagonists sought to exploit. The apologists of the era had to ascertain how to engage the gnostics in an effective way, and their success can be measured by the waning of gnostic theology. Irenaeus described how gnostic authors "promulgate such a kind of religion, and who so frigidly and perversely pull to pieces the greatness of the truly unspeakable power." He polemically responded to how they impiously misrepresent God: "Such an opinion we should detest and execrate, while we ought everywhere to flee far apart from those that hold it."[61]

Instead, for Irenaeus the revelation of God is found in Scripture, corresponding to God's economies of work in creation, delivered by the apostles, and residing in the community of faith. Irenaeus develops a summary of theological truth termed the "rule of faith," with the technical name *regula fidei*. This standard is the tradition of the apostles, evidenced in the church and recorded in an early notion of Scripture that was, for Irenaeus and others, handed down to the true church and its

---

60. Pearson, *Gnosticism*.
61. Irenaeus *Against Heresies* 1.16.3 (*ANF* 1:341–42).

Learning from Patristic Responses to Cultural Opposition

leaders everywhere.[62] For our purposes, we ought to affirm John O'Keefe and R. R. Reno who caution against any assumption that this second-century use of Scripture "was nothing more than an exhaustive exercise in proof-texting animated by an anti-intellectual submission to doctrinal authority."[63] Instead, it was an intentional, thoughtful, and faithful effort by church leaders to employ Scripture and the apostolic tradition against what they viewed as inferior and dangerous false doctrine.

One direct lesson from the patristic rejection of gnosticism finds application today, as critical historical scholarship seeks to legitimize gnostic theology as an alternative Christianity that was marginalized by early catholic churches through political and ecclesiastical means. Walter Bauer contended that during the first few centuries of Christianity, Rome in particular used persuasive and polemical tactics to further the orthodox agenda. What has come to be termed the "Bauer thesis" insists on the dictum, *audiatur et altera pars*, "Let the other side also be heard."[64] The 1990s saw the gathering of the Jesus Seminar, a collection of scholars who produced *The Five Gospels: The Search for the Authentic Words of Jesus*, their pronouncement of the "authentic" sayings of Jesus.[65] The presence of the *Gospel of Thomas* in the volume illustrates contemporary efforts to validate gnostic gospels and similar materials.[66] Elaine Pagels's more recent *Beyond Belief: The Secret Gospel of Thomas* reports her own spiritual journey to recognize the "breadth of God," including a diversity of gospel texts and interpretations of Christ.[67]

The accusation of patristic exploitation is not without some merit, as writers like Irenaeus, Hippolytus, Tertullian, and Epiphanius sought every means to eliminate the gnostic threat to the church. However, their rationale was not merely manipulative and political, but a philosophical concern for Christian revelation and a pastoral concern for congregations of Christians throughout the empire. These writers rejected gnosticism

62. Note the essay in this book by Litfin, "Learning from Patristic Use of the Rule of Faith."

63. O'Keefe and Reno, *Sanctified Vision*, 126.

64. Bauer, *Orthodoxy and Heresy*, xxi.

65. Funk et al., *Five Gospels*.

66. The gnostic (or non-gnostic) nature of the Gospel of Thomas is debated. For one important evaluation, see Perrin, *Thomas*.

67. Pagels, *Beyond Belief*.

because it was inferior and false, not merely because it was a competing Christianity. These authors wrote large, comprehensive assessments of such heresies with clear *contra* intent. Their titles alone betray their positions, such as Irenaeus' *Against Heresies*, Athanasius' *Orations against the Arians*, and Augustine's *Contra Faustus the Manichean*.[68]

Having presented Tertullian's Christ-*over*-culture penchant, it is important to balance it with his dissociation with cultural practices. He denounced participation in political life, military service, and even trade and business. For Tertullian, corrupt tendencies in philosophy and the arts lead to idolatry, and the theater's tragedy, music, and graphic practices are equally corrupt. Yet Niebuhr points out that Tertullian's Christ-*against*-culture paragon "sounds both more radical and consistent than he really was."[69] Still, Niebuhr insists that for Tertullian "it is in culture that sin chiefly resides. Tertullian comes very close to the thought that original sin is transmitted through society."[70]

Monastic and Apocalyptic Responses

Two somewhat radical responses to cultural opposition are grouped together here because of their shared value of retreat—separation from culture for the sake of faith. These should not be viewed as cowardice, for in fact their painful and sacrificial components demonstrate that the opposite is true.

The first radical response to cultural opposition was the practice of withdrawing into the desert for great spiritual devotion. Anchorites were individuals who intentionally became hermits in order to prioritize spiritual growth. Society distracts from spirituality, so many left society to seek solitude and an environment for spiritual growth that comes with desert life. Solitary living and self-denial allow for greater spiritual prog-

---

68. Additional examples include Basil's *Contra Euplomius*; Cyril's *Contra Julian*; Epiphanius' *Refutation of All Heresies*; Hegesippus' *Memoirs against the Gnostics*; Jerome's *Contra Jovinian* and *Contra Rufinus*; Leontius' *Contra Nestorians and Eutychians*; Origen's *Contra Celsus*; and Tertullian's *Contra Marcion, Contra Praxeus*, and *Prescription against Heretics*.

69. Niebuhr, *Christ and Culture*, 55. References to Tertullian's censures can be found here, taken from his works *On Idolatry, Prescription sgainst Heresies*, and *Apology*.

70. Niebuhr, *Christ and Culture*, 52.

ress and even perfection. The surrendering of goods, food, and clothes permits greater opportunity for prayer, focus on the Word, and spiritual warfare. The desert experience becomes a kind of iconic suffering and transformative event. Belden Lane captures the spirit of sacrificial desert affliction: "In wild places, terror and growth-toward-wholeness walk hand in hand ... the liminality of desert and mountain terrain redefines every boundary giving shape to one's life."[71]

In these lives of the desert fathers, asceticism was highly valued, over against a society characterized by personal indulgence. Devotion to spiritual practices such as fasting, praying, and meditating were frequent. Sacraments, discipleship, and mentoring seem to have been common. Mortification of the flesh was not uncommon. For example, one anchorite named Theodora warned a fellow monk: "You should realize ... [evil] attacks your body through sickness, debility, weakening of the knees, and all the members. It dissipates the strength of soul and body."[72] The testimony of these activities comes to us in the form of narratives and short teaching sentences, or "sayings," of these desert fathers. Such sayings probably started circulating orally in the fourth century about spiritual feats of individuals living alone and in desert communities. Their influence was extensive.

The most popular early figure was Anthony, who sought isolation in the Egyptian desert. Inspired by Jesus's command in Matthew 19:21, "If you wish to be complete, go *and* sell your possessions and give to *the* poor, and you will have treasure in heaven; and come, follow Me" (NASB), Anthony obeyed by embracing a life of austerity and incessant prayer that led to regular reports of healings and spiritual warfare. Athanasius popularized Anthony as a spiritual hero in his work *Life of Anthony* that led other Christians, disillusioned with culture, to go to the desert to hear these heroes teach and disciple, and sometimes to follow similar lifestyles themselves.

These monastic movements helped to shape the culture of medieval Christendom. Niebuhr describes how the Rule of St. Benedict guided medieval monks and also influenced later monastic and mendicant

---

71. Lane, *Solace*, 37, 39.
72. Ehrman and Jacobs, *Christianity in Late Antiquity*, 302.

movements, as it "directed to the achievement of a Christian life, apart from civilization."[73] Monastic influence touched the church for generations, ranging from formal monasticism to later Mennonites and Friends with attitudes of community separation from the world and corresponding worldly things.

The second radical response was the church's adoption of an apocalyptic mentality. Apocalyptic responses sought to understand contemporary, difficult realities in light of future hopes. John H. Collins has concisely remarked: "Apocalypses are usually regarded as crisis literature."[74] Apocalypticism involves an adjustment of one's outlook on the present situation to allow for a more heavenly minded perspective in which future rewards and justice will be made actual. It comes primarily in the form of literature characterized by visions and angels that provide insight into the final actions of God's current relationship with his creation—actions involving tribulation of God's people followed by divine intervention in which justice is applied. Thus, the effect is one of hope in the present. Heavenly rewards help to justify earthly sacrifice.

The book of Revelation is our best biblical example of a comprehensive apocalyptic work. The milieu of the church at the time could have influenced the writing of the work, as well as both contemporary and later interpretations. For example, patristic writers often viewed the figure of antichrist in divergent manners, depending on the contemporary social circumstances in which they read the text.[75]

In the apocalyptic genre, final rewards are not always at the end of time, but the future can be made actual in order to offer hope to the present. In an apocalyptic moment, the African Christians at Scilla suffering imperial persecution cried, *Hodie martyres in caelis sumus,* "Today the martyrs are in heaven!"[76] Their hope of reward and final justice followed a sacrificial death that led to heaven. The historian Edward Gibbon described the Roman view of this sacrificial suffering: "[Christians are] animated by a contempt for present existence and by confidence in

---

73. Niebuhr, *Christ and Culture*, 56.

74. Collins, "Apocalyptic Literature," 74.

75. See McGinn, *Antichrist*.

76. Shelton, *Martyrdom from Exegesis*, 60; and Frend, *Martyrdom and Persecution*, 233.

Learning from Patristic Responses to Cultural Opposition

immortality."[77] Niebuhr responds: "The two-edged faith has baffled and angered glorifiers of modern civilization as well as defenders of Rome, radical revolutionaries as well as conservers of the old order, believers in continuing progress and desponding anticipators of the decline of culture.... Christianity seems to threaten culture at this point ... because Christ enables men to regard this disaster with a certain equanimity, directs their hopes toward another world, and so seems to deprive them of motivation to engage in the ceaseless labor of conserving a massive but insecure social heritage."[78]

At times the apocalyptic response was excessive, and there is evidence that apocalypticism fostered attitudes of false immediacy in the early church. Perhaps seeking to balance an otherworldly obsession, Hippolytus wrote seemingly to defray a disproportionate hope of the Parousia.[79] Under the strain of persecution, some may have hoped that Christ's return would interrupt their potential martyrdom. Congregations under persecution were not to redirect their hope falsely into a mysterious future, but to focus patiently and bravely on their service to Christ, even unto martyrdom: "What is the use, then, this inquisitive study about the time and this investigation about the day (of the Lord), when the Savior himself has concealed it from us? Tell me: do you know the day of your death, so as to worry thus about the end of the whole world?"[80] In his eschatological system, Hippolytus breaks with Irenaeus and postpones the Parousia almost three hundred years. In so doing, he "removes the element of the imminent rescue and forces his readers to focus on their calling to martyrdom."[81]

If left unchecked, an apocalyptic mentality can lead to an unhealthy detachment. Hippolytus tells the story of an embarrassing abuse of the apocalyptic mindset in his own day. A certain church leader did not understand the commands of the Lord about his return, and he persuaded

---

77. Gibbon, *History of the Decline and Fall*, 1:402 (cited in Niebuhr, *Christ and Culture*, 5).

78. Niebuhr, *Christ and Culture*, 5-6.

79. Shelton, *Martyrdom from Exegesis*, 108-12.

80. Hippolytus *Commentary on Daniel* 4.22.1-2. Translated material taken from Shelton, *Martyrdom from Exegesis*.

81. Shelton, *Martyrdom from Exegesis*, 111.

other believers to go to the desert to meet Christ upon his return. In this case, the governor ignored the matter in order to avoid provoking a general persecution, just before they returned to their cities in shame when Christ never returned.[82] D. H. Williams captures the contemporary problem: "The study of theology is denigrated by the 'end times' mindset as an unfortunate process of participating in a fallen system. Contemporary prophecy experts often parade the lack of academic credentials or absence of ecclesiastical affiliation as a strength and basis for the trustworthiness of the message." The problem for many evangelicals is compounded, Williams says, "by the privatization of faith and the interpretive license of every man or woman to expound the Bible with little other guidance than the subjective operation of the Spirit. . . . Any *essential* connection between the historical theology of the church and the Bible is thereby severed."[83]

However, the heavenly perspective that comes with apocalyptic mentality can be both biblical and valuable. Likewise, the attitude of the monastic heart can find biblical rationale for honoring God with all of one's strength. Both the apocalyptic and monastic movements seem to illustrate Niebuhr's models of Christ *against* culture and Christ *above* culture, although there are other characteristics of a Christ-*paradoxes*-culture paradigm. After all, in both of these positions of weakness—suffering tribulation in apocalypticism and deprecating the flesh in ascetic monasticism—there is strength and sanctification. Both demonstrate obedience to the words of 1 John 2:15–17: "Do not love the world nor the things in the world. . . . For all that is in the world, the lust of the flesh and the lust of the eyes and the boastful pride of life, is not from the Father, but is from the world. The world is passing away, and *also* its lusts; but the one who does the will of God lives forever" (NASB). Such perspective is imperative for a twenty-first century contemporary church.

---

82. Hippolytus *Commentary on Daniel* 4.18. The testimony is thought to be a description of Montanism, with which Hippolytus was familiar yet toward which he was unfavorable. See Shelton, *Martyrdom from Exegesis*, 141–42.

83. Williams, *Retrieving the Tradition*, 22–23.

Learning from Patristic Responses to Cultural Opposition

Dissociative Lessons for the Contemporary Church

The resistance efforts of the early church provide models for denunciation, depending on the circumstances that a contemporary church member might face. They also provide models that deserve to be avoided.

First, the early martyrs offer us a lesson in perspective. The American church has much to learn about suffering. As residents of a materialistic culture, we struggle to keep a healthy perspective on the social blessings that we possess. Unfortunately, even a multi-million dollar evangelical subculture buttresses our comfortable lifestyles in ways that can be unhealthy. A study of the persecuted early church can lead us to consider the extent of our current commitment to Christ. In fact, the church that suffers tends to be more pure as affliction helps to keep lives God-centered rather than self-centered. There are lessons in faithfulness to Christ among these stories. Just as the martyrs' stories inspired Christians in antiquity, so they can move evangelicals seeking greater purpose in their church attendance and personal Christian lives. These Christians can be presented as heroes of the faith and can shape the worldview of young believers who need to find models of spiritual disciplines, commitment to Christ's larger body, and humble, selfless service in the face of hostile Christ-*against*-culture situations. As we stand for Christ, we obey God's command to testify and be faithful for him. Describing the perseverance of Peter and John in Acts, I. Howard Marshall declares: "The church cannot obey orders to give up its most characteristic activity, witness to the risen Lord, although it must be prepared to pay the price of its refusal to keep quiet."[84]

Although non-Christians do not commonly persecute the American church physically, experiences of ridicule and social alienation are not foreign to many who suffer social persecution. Furthermore, Christians in the Middle East, North Africa, China, and central Asia live with social and physical threats to their lives. One can read the martyr stories and find inspiration to stand strong amidst any level of persecution. These ancient works can be inspirational reading, and their exhortations might even apply to contemporary situations: Tertullian's *To the Martyrs*, Origen's *Exhortation to Martyrdom*, Cyprian's *To Fortunatus*, Pseudo-

---

84. Marshall, *Acts*, 97.

Cyprian's *Glory of Martyrdom*, and Hippolytus' *Commentary on Daniel* all offer important insights into the value of suffering and the ultimate sacrifice of giving one's life for Christ.

Persecution seems to have united early Christians in a manner that the contemporary church should note. Schaff describes how they "were a closely united body, fresh, vigorous, hopeful, and daily increasing."[85] A horizontal success resulted from common persecution, as early Christians agreed together about their purpose, about their Scripture and the teachings of the apostles, and their call to obedience as followers of Christ. Protestant Christianity on the whole ought to remember the principle of unity amidst cultural diversity that more characterizes other branches of the faith.

The early church's *contra* approach provides an important posture for the contemporary church. To know one's theological enemies and to know how to respond to their positions was key to their legal responses and is key for the *contra* approach. The church directly engaged and rejected certain alternative theologies that were spiritually harmful. Irenaeus, Hippolytus, and Epiphanius in particular provided lists of theological opponents and set out to refute their individual points on a literary level. The church needs not only works against culture, but a restored practice of greater learning of the whole. A group of leading evangelicals appealed for this exact reform thirty years ago in the "Chicago Call," insisting that Christian colleges and seminaries ought to teach church history and historical theology more rigorously, evangelical publishing houses ought to publish good, solid reading material rather than easy-selling pop literature, and the local church ought to create a vision for fostering these important components of our faith.[86]

The patristic monastic efforts can also instruct the contemporary church. Evangelicals should beware of dismissing the pursuit of the desert fathers as a selfish and useless endeavor, a neglecting of the lost by pursuing seclusion. Although an extreme expression of devotion, their willingness to sacrifice and deny worldly pleasures is a lesson to comfortable American evangelicals surrounded by a subculture of church.

---

85. Schaff, *History of the Christian Church*, 22.
86. Webber and Bloesch, *Orthodox Evangelicals*, 37–38.

We have become experts at justifying our first-world lifestyle "unto the Lord," leading authors such as Ron Sider in *The Scandal of the Evangelical Conscience* to call for a more outward acting faith.[87] Noteworthy is how monastic service principles are finding expression in some evangelical circles, notably in a trend of "monastic evangelicalism."[88]

Furthermore, the monastics longed for something that many evangelicals have deemed lacking in their own churches. Just because Christian worship is a spiritual exercise does not mean we should strip it of all external and outward decoration, believing that the more primitive the worship, the more spiritual it is. Thomas Howard, an advocate for liturgical worship, argues that the physical dimensions of worship are extremely important to posture our attitude toward God. The desert fathers knew this. Howard remarks: "We see the unseen in the seen. The surface of things bespeaks what lies beneath."[89] Take, for example, a Christian in prayer: "The outward posture actually helps to create the inner attitude" that evangelical Christians so prioritize in worship. Our insistence that we are not required to kneel in prayer or to engage in any other outward act can lead to a tendency of "falling into the error of supposing that physical attitudes do not matter. It is once again to locate faith and piety in a disembodied realm. We know that this is false. Our innermost attitudes cry out for a shape. They long to be clothed in flesh."[90]

At the very least, the desert fathers surpass us in their efforts to face the suffering conducive to their own sanctification. This is no more evident than in materialistic cultures like ours, in which we buffer ourselves with extreme comfort and immediate satisfaction. These Christians' priority on the personal spiritual disciplines echoes evangelical value of such practices, but without the lifestyle distractions and without the priority on physical comfort.

A healthy doctrine of eschatology—both personal and corporate—could greatly benefit the existing church. The apocalyptic perspective and its literature can remind evangelicals of the importance of being heavenly

---

87. Sider, *Scandal of the Evangelical Conscience*.
88. Moll, "New Monasticism," 38–46.
89. Howard, *Evangelical Is Not Enough*, 27.
90. Ibid., 43–44.

minded. The church lacks a healthy, honest perspective of death. William Weinrich points out that our materialistic and distracted culture ignores death in the day-to-day: "At a time when in our own culture the reality of death is increasingly trivialized and made simply a matter of one's own choice, and at a time when the activist generation of the 1960's is entering into its 'golden' years, the question of 'what does it mean to die' comes more and more to center stage and, I suspect, will be a major focus of the church's proclamation in the next quarter century."[91]

On matters of corporate eschatology, the early church was less precise about identifying the signs of the times and more holistic in letting apocalyptic potential influence their circumstances. Val Sauer develops such a model when he cautions against two extremes, the "undue restraint" position and the "travelog eschatology" position. One pole maintains an attitude that eschatology does not matter, perhaps because it is difficult or seems irrelevant. The other pole overstates the specificity and chronology of events in a way that makes our understanding of the future look like a clear, detailed map that is simplistically self-evident.[92] This balanced perspective is instructive to many contemporary authors who disproportionately emphasize eschatological features in the life of the church.

Strategic dissociative responses must be applied rightly to the Christian confrontation with culture still today. As Kretschmar claims, "Faith needs to take shape in every culture," and its efforts are the work of the Holy Spirit.[93]

Conclusion

If Kretschmar is right, then as faith takes shape in every culture, the church ought to engage in a strategic and intentional decision-making process to know how to react. The wisdom to know whether to answer culture according to its folly may lie along the lines of answering a fool in Proverbs 26:4–5: do not answer culture according to its folly, lest you be like it (v. 4), but answer culture according to its folly, lest it be wise in

---

91. Weinrich, "Death and Martyrdom," 327.
92. Sauer, *Eschatology Handbook*, 3–12.
93. Kretschmar, "Early Church," 44.

its own eyes (v. 5). This essay has not critically evaluated the patristic engagement with culture in an exhaustive manner, but rather has described the diverse approaches among early Christians with the hope of prompting an evangelical recognition that spiritual preparation, thoughtful and biblical reflection, strategic response, and perseverance matter for the contemporary church.

Although we have seen models worth considering from the patristic response to persecution and cultural opposition, any type of response is really both engaging and resisting. A Christian philosopher who engages a Greek pagan thinker on philosophical grounds is still resisting something about his or her opponent's position. Plus, any strategically directed response against an enemy is an apologetic response. Likewise, a martyr who resists his captors by not denying Christ is offering a witness that engages something about his or her opponent's position. The radical Tertullian used the best Roman rhetorical training to argue against cultural Christianity, while Augustine, the great model of conversionism, watched his friend Alypius attend Roman games only to succumb to their thrilling excesses.[94] Still, there are several models worthy of consideration for each generation that must reconsider how Christ relates to culture.

The task of responding to cultural opposition begins with a Christian understanding of an ongoing paradigmatic shift in the church's relationship to culture. Lesslie Newbigin defines our project: "Christian theology is a form of rational discourse developed within the community which accepts the primacy of this story and seeks actively to live in the world in accordance with the story."[95] Just as the church can fall short by letting culture frame the discourse, it can also founder by "failing to understand and take seriously the world in which it is set, so that the gospel is not heard but remains incomprehensible because the Church has sought security in its own past instead of risking its life in a deep involvement in the world."[96] This is the lesson of the early Christian apologists, both integrative and dissociative.

---

94. Augustine *Confessions* 6.7–10 (*NPNF*1 1:94–98).
95. Newbigin, *Gospel in a Pluralist Society*, 152.
96. Ibid.

In the end, we know the fate of any culture that runs contrary to the will of the God who enabled it by divine common grace. With unparalleled confidence—almost buoyant optimism—Christ declared to the same disciples whom he warned of cultural opposition: "These things I have spoken to you, so that in Me you may have peace. In the world you have tribulation, but take courage; I have overcome the world" (John 16:33, NASB).

6

Learning from Patristic Preaching of Social Ethics

BRIAN J. MATZ

❊ THIS ESSAY argues for a sympathetic reading of early Christian social homilies within the evangelical movement of our day. Two such homilies will be studied in this essay with a concern to elucidate both the social ethics of each homily and the exegetical method of the homilist. Together with some brief remarks about the wider world of early Christian social preaching, the essay articulates several points of contact between that world and evangelicals today. These points of contact may well serve as trajectories for a change in the way evangelicals approach their own construction and articulation of social ethics.

An article within a volume of this sort ought to begin with some disclaimers by its author, for, as Hartog has noted in his introduction, there is no one bridge between the ancient world and the contemporary, evangelical scene. This is just as true because no two evangelicals bring to the table the same presuppositions or predispositions as it is because there was no one "early church" or one "patristic tradition." The history of early Christianity is far too complex to allow for generalizations of any helpful sort, and this should be a significant warning to any in the contemporary church who try to appropriate the early church's forms of worship or its teaching. There is just too much particularity in the reading of Christianity in late antiquity.

Thus, the construction of my own bridge between the two worlds begins by acknowledging some of my own predispositions. Most importantly, I have been formed spiritually within the evangelical Protestant tradition of the United States. Having been raised in a military family, regular moves about the country led to my engagement with a variety of "evangelical" churches across several denominations. I have always felt a sense of freedom within the evangelical movement to unite myself over time with communities that differ on their style of worship as well as their style of theology. One may conclude that I was bred—and here I steal a phrase from a Brethren church in Dallas of which I was a part for several years—"to keep the main thing the main thing" and leave everything else to Pauline liberty. Give me Trinitarianism, a full Christology, expository preaching, and a commitment to social justice—I'll be happy.

Another of my predispositions is that I am not a proponent of reading the Bible as a self-interpreting document. The Bible is a book that requires interpretation in every age, so evangelicals must be cognizant both of the cultural and of the theological lenses that they apply to their reading of the text. The differences between our lenses and those of the church fathers remind us that we cannot read the Bible today as they did. We do not live in their culture, we do not swim in their philosophical and rhetorical waters, and we do not accept many of their socio-cultural proclivities. Likewise, the fathers would probably be dismayed by what they would find in modern-day preaching and biblical teaching in evangelical churches. They would not understand our culture.

Preaching is, by definition, a task of contextualization. Pastors must interpret the Bible with a sensitivity to the signs of the times. What this means is that it is possible for our preaching and biblical teaching to be wrong, because we are influenced by our culture in how we read the Bible. There is no need to apologize for that. It is what Christians have always done, but we should at least accept that we do it and accept its associated limitations. One of those limitations is historical shortsightedness. For that reason, reading the fathers' homilies and commentaries on Scripture provides us a way out of our twenty-first-century, American-evangelical myopia. The fathers' preaching and teaching was not pristine teaching, but it is was different, and different is helpful to us in honing our ability both to read and to critique our culture well, and thus it is helpful for our ability to preach and to teach the Scriptures well.

With respect to the topic at hand, interpreting Scripture with our culture invites us to identify the poverty of our preaching and biblical teaching in the area of social ethics. I examine here two homilies from late antiquity, both of which are an interpretation of Jesus's parable in Luke 16 about the rich man and Lazarus. In late antiquity, the reading of this Gospel text in the Sunday liturgy was (more often than not) the occasion to preach about social ethics. The text's distinctions between heaven and hell are little more than placeholders for the characters in the story. In our modern evangelical context, Luke 16 is (more often than not) an occasion to affirm a belief that heaven and hell are real places and that there is no hope for the damned after death. The characters in the story are little more than placeholders for the destinies the story describes. There is a clear opportunity here to critique our reading of Scripture by opening ourselves to some different ways of preaching from the past. In doing so, evangelicals become more conscious that they already interpret Scripture in light of the signs of the times, that they ought to continue to do so, and how they might do so better in the future.

Before turning to the patristic homilies on Luke 16, some perspective on early Christian social preaching will be helpful. From the Greek and Latin Christian worlds, I have identified more than three hundred passages in which an author reflects on a socio-ethical theme. Fully one-fourth of that collection consists of full texts, including nearly fifty homilies. The homilies are of particular interest, for they tread the same biblical ground that today's preachers and social ethicists trod. There are homilies from well-known figures, including Gregory of Nyssa, Basil of Caesarea, John Chrysostom, Augustine, Ambrose, Jerome, and Gregory the Great. There are also many homilies from lesser-known figures: Asterius of Amasea, Peter of Alexandria, Peter Chrysologus, Theodoret of Cyrus, Maximus of Turin, and Salvian of Marseille.

Less diverse are the number of biblical passages that are the subject of these homilies. Social themes are often raised with expositions of Tobit, Psalm 14, Psalm 36, Luke 16, Matthew 25, and various other passages where almsgiving and fasting are mentioned. The latter are important because it seems that many of these homilies were given during

Lent, a season for thinking about self-sacrifice and about one's misuse or abuse of good gifts given by God. The homilies deal primarily with one or more of five themes: usury, disposition of private property, treatment of the poor, justice, and the common good. (In the widest collection of passages I have studied, other concerns may be found such as slavery, land rights, labor, war, and non-violence.)

There are some interesting features in these homilies that make clear they are from a different time and place. For example, they accept slavery as a fact of life, completely denounce the collection of interest on loans, build an argument for the universal destination of the earth's goods from the perspective of an agriculture-based economy, frame their arguments in eschatological terms, accept existing social class structures, and generally do not question the political status quo. Indeed, historians of Christianity in late antiquity arguably have their work cut out for them when inviting a contemporary, evangelical audience into a meaningful discussion. Having said that, we turn now to an examination of Asterius of Amasea's *Homily* 2 and then to Jerome's *Homily* 86.

Asterius of Amasea, Homily 2

We know very little about Asterius. He came of age in the mid fourth century and by the early 390s was preaching in Amasea, a city in the Pontus region (along the south-central coast of the Black Sea in modern-day Turkey). Sixteen homilies are attributed to him today, although some had earlier been misattributed and some additional homilies previously passed down under Asterius' name are now correctly assigned to others.[1] The highly rhetorical style of most of his homilies suggests he had some extensive education, and we should expect that he had some contact with other Cappadocian luminaries of the late fourth century. In any case, we consider here Asterius' second homily, entitled "The Rich Man and Lazarus." As with all but one of Asterius' homilies, we have nothing in this or other texts to help us identify a date for its delivery. Luke 16 was

---

1. The critical edition of the sixteen homilies is Datema, *Asterius of Amasea*. For some examination of the history of homilies that at one time or another passed under his name, see Datema's introduction and cf. Leemans et al., *Let Us Die that We May Live*, introduction to Asterius' *Hom*. 9.

Learning from Patristic Preaching of Social Ethics

a popular passage upon which to preach in late antiquity, and Asterius no doubt was aware that by doing so he was helping fulfill the government's mandate that Christian churches and clergy come to the aid of the poor with their resources in exchange for the various tax exemptions they received.[2]

Our concern with this homily (as well as Jerome's homily below) is both what Asterius had to say about social ethics and how he said it. On both fronts, the reader is challenged throughout the homily to match his or her words of Christian instruction with his or her deeds of service. This is itself an important, socio-ethical point insofar as our lives are to mimic the life of Christ. Asterius praises Christ for having taught both by commands and by stories of deeds. Words and deeds ought to go together, and this is no less true in how Jesus teaches us. Thus, Asterius sets himself to the task both of expositing what Jesus has done (i.e., uses words) and of expanding Jesus's teachings with additional stories or further details about the story (i.e., deeds).

From this starting point, the reader is then quickly drawn into the first socio-ethical lesson: "[Jesus] turns away from the overbearing and haughty man of wealth, and loves a kindly disposition, and poverty when united to righteousness."[3] To Asterius and most church fathers of his and earlier generations, the status of the wealthy person in the church is dubious. Most certainly, the "haughty" rich man is condemned. For the wealthy Christian, everything depends on his or her disposition toward wealth and, for that matter, toward those who are in need of their kindness. By the same token, the quote above also reminds the audience that the poor person is not automatically accepted as being more spiritual. Poverty is to be "united to righteousness." Asterius' homily will later declare that some poor people inappropriately rationalize acts of thievery with the excuse that it meets an immediate, financial need. For Asterius, poverty is not a good thing, but it certainly is to be borne with dignity by those whose lot in life it is.

2. Cf. Brown, *Poverty and Leadership*, 26–44, esp. 26–32.

3. Asterius *Hom.* 1.1 (Anderson and Goodspeed, *Ancient Sermons for Modern Times*, 19). ἀποστρέφεσθαι μὲν τὸν ὑπερήφανον καὶ ὑψαύχενα πλοῦτον, ἀγαπᾶν δὲ γνώμην φιλάνθρωπον καὶ τὴν μετὰ δικαιοσύνης πενίαν (Datema, *Homilies* I–XIV, 7).

Having said this as an introduction, Asterius then begins his exposition of Jesus's parable, and we are presented with a second socio-ethical argument: superfluous wealth is to be distributed to those with needs.[4] This is a remarkably far-reaching argument. To begin with, every person should ask himself or herself the question, "What do I need?" Sufficient wealth is what one needs to survive plus enough to be hospitable toward others.[5] The rich man in Jesus's parable indulged in unmeasured wastefulness with his resources, and this is to be contrasted with what should be the proper orientation of Christians: "It is the dwelling-place and nature of the ones taking hold of an ordered and frugal life to measure the need for the need of necessary things."[6]

To Asterius, one example of unmeasured wastefulness is the love of the wealthy for decorative clothing. Wealthy people spurn clothing fabrics from natural resources (flax and sheep's wool); instead, they demand threads drawn from Persian worms that have been dyed in colors made with the blood of shellfish. Then, as if love for the dyes was not enough damage to the wealthy person's soul, they require pictures be woven into or painted upon the fabrics. Christians who try to act piously by incorporating into their clothing pictures of biblical scenes or of the person of Jesus have only exposed their avarice all the more. Asterius replies to all of this by saying, "If they take my advice let them sell those clothes and honor the living image of God. Do not depict Christ [i.e., on your

---

4. It is the early third-century Clement of Alexandria to whom we look for the first, significant Christian exposition of this sufficiency argument. Cf. Robinson, *Clement of Alexandria*, 1–15.

5. Clement *Paedagogus* 2.3, had encouraged his followers to purchase goods for their use that had more than one purpose. For example, he would not have been a proponent of having chinaware in one's house reserved for special occasions in addition to everyday dishware. One set of dishes is sufficient; acquiring more would be a needless expense and a waste of financial resources better intended for the poor. Clement also identified a number of extravagances, including the possession of more than a handful of pieces of jewelry, makeup, decorative clothing, glass bowls, etc.

6. Asterius *Hom.* 1.2.1 (English translation is my own). Τῶν δὲ τὴν εὐπολίτευτον ζωὴν αἱρουμένων καὶ ἀπερίεργον οἰκεῖον καὶ φίλον τὸ τῇ χρείᾳ τῶν ἀναγκαίων τὴν χρῆσιν μετρεῖν (Datema, 7).

garments] ... but, bearing understanding, carry around the incorporeal Word upon your soul."⁷

Although this matter of clothing seems strange to us today (gawdy Christian T-shirts aside), there are at least two truths at stake in this for Asterius that have currency in our day. First, when people spurn natural fabrics for specialty fabrics and dyes, in effect they are denouncing God's gift of the natural world. Asterius wrote, "God created sheep with well-fleeced skins, abounding in wool. Take them, shear it off, and give it to a skilful weaver, ... But if you need for greater comfort lighter clothing in the time of summer, God has given the use of flax, and it is very easy for you to get from it a becoming covering, that at once clothes and refreshes you by its lightness."⁸

This goes back to the creation narrative. God had given to Adam and Eve the rest of the created realm to meet their physical needs. Sheep are one of the many universal gifts of God, and they are a renewable resource. Sheep are shorn for their wool to make clothing, and then the wool grows back to provide new clothing at a later time. Persian worms were made by God for purposes other than for providing silk threads. Shellfish were made by God for purposes other than for humans to kill them to extract their blood for fabric dyes. To think and to behave otherwise is, to Asterius, "to misuse life."⁹ God intended that we use the renewable resources that he has made available to all humans (other church fathers will point to God's provision of the sun, rain, arable land, and winds as other universal goods) to meet our physical needs.

The second truth at stake in this complaint about how wealthy Christians misuse their clothing goes back to Asterius' earlier distinction between words and deeds. The biblical images that wealthy Christians

---

7. Ibid., 1.4 (my translation). Ἐμὴν δὲ εἰ δέχονται συμβουλήν, ἐκεῖνα πωλήσαντες τὰς ζώσας εἰκόνας τοῦ Θεοῦ τιμησάτωσαν. Μὴ γράφε τὸν Κριστόν ... ἐπὶ δὲ τῆς ψυχῆς σου βαστάζων νοητῶς τὸν ἀσώματον Λόγον περίφερε (Datema, 9).

8. Ibid., 1.2 (Anderson and Goodspeed, 21). Πρόβατον ὁ Θεὸς ἔκτισεν εὔκομον τὴν δορὰν καὶ τοῖς μαλλοῖς εὐθηνούμενον· τοῦτο λαβὼν ἀπόκειρον καὶ δὸς ὑφαντικῇ τέχνῃ τὴν ὕλην, ... Εἰ δέ σοι καὶ κουφοτέρας ἐσθῆτος κρεία κατὰ τὴν ὥραν τοῦ θέρους, ἔδωκεν ὁ Θεὸς τοῦ λίνου τὴν χρῆσιν εἰς πλατυτέραν ἀπόλαυσιν· καί σοι ῥᾷστον ἐκεῖθεν κτήσασθαι σκέπην εὐσχήμονα ἀμφιεννύσαν ὁμοῦ καὶ ἀναψύχουσαν τῇ κουφότητι (Datema, 7–8).

9. Ibid., 1.3 (Anderson and Goodspeed, 38). παραχρώμενοι τῷ βίῳ (Datema, 8).

portray on their garments are merely "words," but deeds bring the words to life. If wealthy Christians would feed the hungry instead of picturing the baskets of bread left over from the miraculous feeding of the crowd, according to one of Asterius' examples, then their deeds would bring the "words" (i.e., the pictures) to life and tutor others in the faith. Asterius' social thought places a premium on deeds rather than words, for needy people require real help and not just the sympathy of those who pass by or are around them.

We have thus a fair amount of extension of the biblical parable in Asterius' preaching about the particular ways in which rich people live, in how they abuse the natural resources given by God, and in how they prefer words to deeds. Yet Asterius is not finished. Continuing with the theme of the problem of superfluous wealth, Asterius adds to his concerns about clothing a further concern with the ways in which rich people live. In Jesus's parable, the rich man ate sumptuously every day while Lazarus starved. Asterius extends this imagery to excoriate the wealthy for not only their sumptuous meals but also their jewel-encrusted houses, their finely decorated furniture, their dishware made with precious metals, and the expensive imported foods served upon them. There is no end to the luxuries rich people seek, and all of this comes at the expense of the widows, orphans, and poor people whose needs may otherwise have been met with these funds. Indeed, for Asterius, the "poor are robbed! ... orphans maltreated!"[10]

The only way the poor can be said to be robbed is if the rich are taking from the poor what belongs to them and spending it on themselves. Indeed, this is precisely Asterius' (and other church fathers') point. Superfluous wealth does not belong to the person now in possession of it, but it actually belongs to the needy person. Put another way, not only does Asterius require the wealthy to be concerned about the *just use* of their wealth, they must also be concerned about the *just ownership* of their wealth. Once a wealthy person has met his "needs," such a person actually ceases to be the owner of the additional wealth now in his or her possession. That wealth belongs instead to those with immediate financial or hunger needs. Now, Asterius does not believe the poor should go

---

10. Ibid., 1.5 (Anderson and Goodspeed, 17). πόσοι πένητες ἀδικοῦνται πόσοι δὲ ὀρφανοὶ κονδυλίζονται (Datema, 10).

Learning from Patristic Preaching of Social Ethics

and take by force what the wealthy refuse to give to them, but it hardly seems consistent to exclude that as one reasonable course of action. Apparently, many had done precisely this, for Asterius characterized such poor people as incorrigible. "[T]he poverty of those who are in extreme want, and have at the same time an unmanageable or incorrigible disposition, leads to many evil deeds of daring."[11] Far better, in his view, that the poor bear their hardships with a Stoic disposition. In Christian social thought today, this is very much a disputed question: just how far may the poor go in demanding that a rich person's superfluous resources be handed over to relieve their suffering? Wealthy Christians should never let matters reach that point of despair, but if they are unwilling to honor God and give their superfluous goods to the needy, what is a Christian poor person to do?

With that, we may turn now from this discussion of the problem of superfluous wealth—a remarkably broad and far-reaching concern—to another feature of Asterius' social ethic. Asterius placed the burden for social change upon the conscience of wealthy persons. To this way of thinking, wealthy persons control most of the cards, so justice may be achieved once they agree to change their ways, divest their superfluous wealth, and orient their lives toward service to the needy. If only the wealthy and powerful would change, life for the rest of us would improve. This becomes clear when, nearly halfway into the homily, Asterius turns his focus toward Lazarus. At least, that is what we are led to believe when he opens a new paragraph with the citation of the verse, "There was a certain beggar named Lazarus." Asterius mentions the details about Lazarus in the biblical text, but then informs us that Lazarus' place in the story is to serve as little more than a literary foil for the rich man. "And very carefully the beneficial aspects of the narrative on the final circumstances of the beggar [were written], in order that the hardness of the one who had no mercy might be recorded."[12] Indeed, it is the plight of the rich man,

---

11. Ibid., 1.10 (Anderson and Goodspeed, 38). Ἐπεὶ τοῖς ἀπορουμένοις ἁπλῶς, ἔχουσι δὲ τὸν τρόπον ἀπαιδαγώγητον ἢ ἀκατόρθωτον, ἐφόδιον γίνεται πολλῶν καὶ πονηρῶν τολμημάτων ἡ πρὸς ἀνάγκην ἀκτημοσύνη (Datema, 13).

12. Ibid., 1.6 (my translation). Καὶ λίαν ἐπιμελῶς τῇ διηγήσει τὰς συμφορὰς ἐπὶ τέλει ἐκτραγῳδεῖ τοῦ πτωχοῦ, ἵνα τὴν τοῦ μὴ ἐλεοῦντος στηλιτεύσῃ σκληρότητα (Datema, 10).

not that of Lazarus, that concerns Asterius. This is not unusual in early Christian social preaching; the poor are rarely the subject of any special inquiry. To be sure there is regular mention of "the poor" or "the needy," but in only a handful of cases does one actually get a glimpse into what life might be like for the poor person of late antiquity.[13] As noted above, Asterius did not deem poverty to be, on its own accord, a characteristic of a life of righteousness, and neither did the secular society give the poor people more than a passing glance. Understandably, Asterius probably believed keeping the focus on the wealthy and powerful individuals of Amasea would be the most expedient course of action toward social justice.

Such a way of thinking is attractive, but the important question today would be whether or not it can be scaled to larger, relational structures. Like Jesus's parable, Asterius limited his comments to the sphere of individuals. It made sense to do so in the context of a culture with limited mobility and few contacts outside the town or region in which one lived. Yet today we recognize that individual poor people are not oppressed by any single, individual rich person. Individual poor persons suffer at the hands of institutions, be they financial, industrial, political or transnational. Thus, evangelical pastors today are invited to preach this biblical passage with larger institutional structures of power in mind. Pastors ought to help their congregations understand the connections that exist between the decisions of our government and the effects those decisions have on poor people. Pastors ought to help their congregants understand the connections that exist between their decisions on what to buy and where to buy and the salaries paid to the laborers involved in the production and sale of those goods. So, too, pastors ought to help their congregants appreciate the complexities of global labor markets, of agricultural subsidies paid to farmers in the developed world, and of the financial instruments sold to developed nations by organizations like the World Bank, to name just a few. This does not dismiss the biblical challenge for those with superfluous wealth to transfer that to needy persons (e.g., via organizations like Compassion International and World Vision), but it does put the problems of the poor in wider perspective.

13. One thinks here of Gregory of Nazianzus *Oration* 14 or John Chrysostom *Sermons on Genesis* 5.

Learning from Patristic Preaching of Social Ethics

Having discoursed briefly on the life of Lazarus, Asterius turns in his final paragraphs to the disconcerting future facing those rich people who do not have a proper disposition toward the needy. Here, Asterius emphasizes two important points. First, whatever joys or pleasures are associated with wealth in this life are short-lived, and these things will be unavoidably exchanged for pain and torment without end in the next life. Second, and equally important, no amount of pleading for forgiveness in the next life will be met by God with the ability to leave that torment and enter heaven. The chasm of death is too wide to be overcome by pleas of repentance. This is Asterius' final, pastoral card. If the wealthy are moved to help the needy neither by appeals to their greed (i.e., God will reward you a hundred-fold for giving to the needy) nor by appeals to their soul (i.e., the dire life condition of needy persons) nor by appeals to their conscience (i.e., the wealthy are responsible for the plight of the needy), then perhaps they will be moved by appeals to their self-interest (i.e., do what you ought to do now before death makes it too late). Belief in the reality of punishment for the damned in the afterlife was a consistent theme in many early Christian social homilies. Early Christian pastors were not afraid of drawing on the entirety of Scripture's resources in calling their congregants to repentance.

To summarize, Asterius has walked us through a delightful forest of biblical and social ideas. One nearly forgets, in fact, that Asterius is preaching a *parable*, for the homily regularly treats the characters in Jesus's story as if the people and the events were real. For having done so, Asterius' audience—and we may include ourselves here as a part of the extended audience—comes to grip both with the dangers associated with luxurious living and the seriousness of a callous disregard for the plight of the poor.[14] The rich people Asterius condemns are those who misuse their superfluous wealth. They deny the goodness of God by misusing or appropriating for private use the goods God created and intended for use by all humans for the maintenance of life. Worse, they assume their wealth entitles them to a life free of entanglements with the needy. Moreover, they harbor a fundamental disdain for the truths of Scripture in that even after death they arrogantly demand that their pleas for

---

14. Mayer, "Audience(s) for Patristic Social Teaching."

forgiveness be met by God with mercy. Asterius has indeed covered a lot of ground with such a short biblical pericope. We turn now to Jerome's exposition and to his consideration of the socio-ethical issues at stake in preaching Luke 16.

Jerome, Homily on the Gospel of Luke

To pick up Jerome's *Homily* 86 is to be confronted immediately with the grand place he holds in Christian history—a leading, theological light of the Western world in the late fourth and early fifth century and a translator of the Bible into the vernacular of his day, Latin.[15] His service to the Christian church began in Rome as a member of the bishop's staff and continued during travels to Trier and Aquileia, until finally he settled in Bethlehem. There, he built a monastery and his travel companion and patron, Paula, also built there a convent.[16] Jerome remained in Bethlehem from 398 until his death in 419 or 420, although he occasionally traveled to visit other monasteries and to learn of their ways of life, including especially those of Pachomius in Egypt, but also monasteries at Caesarea and on the outskirts of Jerusalem. Nearly all Jerome's homilies were preached during his latter years, most probably after 400, after the founding of his monastery nearby the Church of the Nativity.

Jerome preached often at the Bethlehem church, usually on Sundays but at least once on a Wednesday (filling in for an ill priest).[17] Also, from

---

15. Morin, *S. Hieronymi presbyteri opera*, 507–16.

16. On the relationship between Jerome and Paula, see Jerome *Ep.* 45. It should be noted of importance that simply because one has chosen an ascetic life, that does not necessarily mean one has chosen to live an austere life. Paula was famously wealthy and donated generously throughout her life, suggesting that she did not suddenly divest herself of all wealth. For studies on the wealth of monasteries and the use of that wealth ostensibly for the benefit of the poor, see Goehring, "Monasticism in Byzantine Egypt"; Wipszycka, "Diaconia"; Serfass, "Wine for Widows."

17. On Jerome's life and his preaching in Bethlehem, see Ewald, *Homilies of Saint Jerome*, xvii–xxi; Kelly, *Jerome*, 116–40, esp. 134–38; and Morin, "Les monuments." Other secondary literature works on Jerome's life do not discuss his preaching, but they still are valuable as a context for Jerome's life in Bethlehem and his travels during the later decades of his life, particularly the Origenist and Pelagian controversies in which he was embroiled. See Grutzmacher, *Hieronymus* (see vol. 3 for Jerome's life after 400); Cavallera, *Saint Jérôme*, 1:123–29; Rebenich, *Jerome*, 41–59; and Booth, "Date of Jerome's Birth."

Learning from Patristic Preaching of Social Ethics

comments in some of his homilies, he occasionally was invited to preach alongside the bishop, John, in Jerusalem.[18] Every Sunday, the monks of Jerome's monastery and the nuns at Paula's neighboring convent were expected to be in attendance. Judging by the rough estimates given of the sizes of their respective communities, the two communities alone may have contributed nearly one hundred congregants for worship.[19] Naturally, one expects to find in Jerome's homilies—apparently all delivered extemporaneously—evidence of his concern to address their experiences.

Homily 86 offers hints in this direction, so one suspects it was one of those delivered to a predominantly monastic audience at the Church of the Nativity in Bethlehem. Assigning a year to the homily, however, is all but impossible. Jerome says in the homily only that he was delivering it during the early days of Lent, and that Psalm 103 was read together that Sunday with the Luke passage.[20]

This homily is a thorough reworking of the biblical text into a drama set as often in the fifth-century context of his audience as it is within the first-century context in which Jesus related it. Indeed, a first reading of the homily calls to mind the dramatic plays that often supplement or replace preaching in seeker-driven, evangelical churches today. Jerome frequently changed persona, alternately (1) speaking the words of the biblical text, (2) giving voice to the rich man's interior thoughts, (3) enjoining his audience to condemn the rich man, (4) playing the role of Abraham, (5) narrating with word pictures the scenes of Hades experienced by Lazarus and the rich man, and (6) pastorally exhorting his audience to avoid the sins of the rich man. Often the dialogue is short, presented in staccato fashion in the text, but it may not be that Jerome delivered it this way. Since he apparently taught *ex tempore*, what we have

---

18. Cf. Kelly, *Jerome*, 135–36.

19. Ibid., 131–33, where he cites Palladius' *Lausiac History* 41 (which reported fifty nuns as a part of Paula's convent), and where he also cites Epiphanius who reported "a multitude of dedicated brothers" in the monastery. If that "multitude" number could be seen as something at least the size of the convent, then at least one hundred monks and nuns were in the area of Bethlehem at the time in question.

20. Jerome *Hom.* 86.232–39 (Morin, *S. Hieronymi presbyteri opera*, 514).

today is what a scribe was able to record while Jerome spoke.[21] We have the *ipsissima vox* of Jerome, but probably not the *ipsissima verba*. Even so, the dramatic interpretation of the passage is vibrant and engaging. One can imagine the audience hanging on Jerome's every word.

In the course of the homily, Jerome makes at least three socio-ethical arguments. First and foremost, he promotes the right use of superfluous wealth. Like Asterius, Jerome believed that it is okay to have wealth so long as a person willingly distributes to the needy that which is superfluous to his or her needs. Jerome told his audience, "Why do you save what is superfluous to your pleasures? Give in alms to your own member what you waste. I am not telling you to throw away your wealth. What you throw out, the crumbs from your table, offer as alms."[22] To Jerome, the heart of the rich man's problem is pride, and this manifests itself in disdain for the lives and fortunes of others. Pride looks down on those who do not achieve similar or proportional levels of success. It disdains those who try to meet their needs in ways (e.g., by begging) other than the ways in which the rich person met his or her needs. Moreover, this disdain takes no account of the abilities or disabilities of those who are the objects of scorn. The rich man paid heed neither to Lazarus' hunger nor to his incapacitating illness, both of which surely prevented his ability to work. Besides all this, the social ideas at the time all but doomed beggars like Lazarus to an early death, and this fact alone probably comforted the rich man in knowing that he would not have to bear Lazarus' appeals for help for too long.

This is why Jerome put forward his second argument, that the antidote for pride is compassion. Addressing the rich man, Jerome said, "Most wretched of men, you see a member of your own body lying there outside at your gate, and have you no compassion?"[23] Jerome does not let

---

21. Oberhelman, *Rhetoric and Homiletics*, 86; Ewald, *Homilies of Saint Jerome*, xix. For a discussion of the art of speaking *ex tempore* and its training in Greco-Roman *paideia*, see Hammerstaedt and Terbuyken, "Improvisation."

22. Jerome *Hom. in Lucam XVI* (Ewald, *Homilies of Saint Jerome*, 201). "Quid servas in deliciis tuis quod superfluum est? Quod iactas, tribue in elemosinam membro tuo. Non dico ut auferas divitiis tuis: quod foras iactas, micas mensae tuae praebe in elemosinam membro tuo" (Morin, 508).

23. Ibid. (Ewald, 201). "Infelicissime hominum, partem corporis tui vides iacere ante ianuam, et non misereris?" (Morin, 508).

the rich man off the hook for suggesting he did not notice him or that no one made his presence known. The lack of compassion prevented the rich man from seeing those around him with needs.

Jerome's third socio-ethical argument in this homily is that the poor are obliged to suffer their indignities in this life. For whatever reason, God has seen fit to allow the events of this world to take their course. The rich seem to get richer at the expense of ever greater numbers of poor people. While oppressed people have to wait until the afterlife to find relief for their suffering, Jerome is satisfied that the proud will have their day in God's court soon enough. He wrote, "If ever we are sick, if we are beggars, if we are wasting away in sickness, if we are perishing from the cold, if there is no hospitality for us, let us be glad and rejoice; let us receive evil things in our lifetime. When the crushing weight of infirmity and sickness bears down upon us, let us think of Lazarus."[24]

There is a long-standing debate in liberation theology circles about just how far those who are oppressed may go to remove the yoke of their oppressors. It was safe for Jerome to preach that the poor and oppressed ought to look to Lazarus and to suffer their indignities with honor in this life. As well, it was certainly the case that the Christian church played a significant role in mitigating the suffering of many in late antiquity, but *mitigating* the suffering was all it was prepared (and perhaps able) to do. Jerome and others in his day trusted that God would restore the fortunes of the righteous poor in the afterlife.

It remains, finally, for us to consider some hermeneutical features of the homily that may enhance a dialogue between this early Christian homily and evangelicals. Indeed, there are a number of such features, but three deserve special mention. First and most interesting, Jerome's entire exposition is a fairly elaborate dialogue he has constructed between himself and the characters in the biblical story. Consider the following passage:

> "Send Lazarus to dip the tip of his finger in water." "Send Lazarus."
> You are mistaken, miserable man; Abraham cannot send, but he

24. Ibid. (Ewald, 204–5). "Si quando aegrotamus, si pauperes sumus, si aegrotatione conficimur, si frigore, si hospitium non habemus: laetemur, gaudeamus, accipiamus mala in vita nostra. Quando nos infirmitatis et aegrotationis magnitudo premit, Lazarum cogitemus" (Morin, 511).

can receive. "To dip the tip of his finger in water." Recall your lifetime, rich man; you did not condescend to see Lazarus and now you are longing for the tip of his finger. "Send Lazarus." You should have done that for him while he lived. "To dip the tip of his finger in water." See the conscience of the sinner; he does not dare ask for the whole finger. "Cool my tongue, for I am tormented in this flame." Cool my tongue, for it has uttered many a proud word. Where there is sin, there is also the penalty for sin. "To cool my tongue, for I am tormented in this flame." How evil the tongue can be, James has told us in his Letter: "The tongue also is a little member, but it boasts mightily." The more it has sinned, the more it is tortured. You long for water, who formerly were so fastidious at the mere sight of smeary and spattered dishes.[25]

We may reorganize the same passage into four columns: (1) Jerome's citation of the biblical passage, (2) Jerome's dialogue with the rich man, (3) Jerome pretending he is the rich man, and (4) Jerome's pastoral exhortations to his audience.

---

25. Jerome *Hom.* 86.110–24 (Ewald, 204). *Mitte Lazarum, ut intinguat extremum digiti sui in aquam.* Mitte Lazarum. Erras, miser. Abraham mittere non potest, sed suscipere potest. Ut intinguat extremum digiti sui in aquam. Recordare, dives, vitae tuae: Lazarum videre non dignabaris, et nunc digitum eius desideras. Mitte Lazarum. Hoc tu ei debueras facere, dum adviveret. Ut intinguat extremum digiti sui in aquam. Vide conscientiam peccatoris: non totum audet poscere digitum. Ut refrigeret linguam, quia crucior in hac flamma. Ut refrigeret linguam meam: multa enim superba locuta est. Ubi peccatrum, ibi et poena. Ut refrigeret linguam meam, quia crucior in hac flamma. Quanta mala lingua habet, Iacobus in epistula sua loquitur: 'Modicum quidem membrum est, sed magna exaltat'. Qua plurimum peccavit, amplius torquetur. Aquam desideras, qui delibutos cibos ante fastidiebas (Morin, 510–11).

Learning from Patristic Preaching of Social Ethics

(1)   (2)   (3)   (4)

(1) "Send Lazarus to dip the tip of his finger in water."

(1) "Send Lazarus."

    (2) You are mistaken, miserable man; Abraham cannot send, but he can receive.

(1) "To dip the tip of his finger in water."

    (2) Recall your lifetime, rich man; you did not condescend to see Lazarus and now you are longing for the tip of his finger.

(1) "Send Lazarus."

    (2) You should have done that for him while he lived.

    (2) "To dip the tip of his finger in water."

        (4) See the conscience of the sinner; he does not dare ask for the whole finger.

(1) "Cool my tongue, for I am tormented in this flame."

    (3) Cool my tongue, for it has uttered many a proud word.

        (4) Where there is sin, there is also the penalty for sin.

(1) "To cool my tongue, for I am tormented in this flame."

        (4) How evil the tongue can be, James has told us in his Letter: "The tongue also is a little member, but it boasts mightily." The more it has sinned, the more it is tortured.

    (2) You long for water, who formerly were so fastidious at the mere sight of smeary and spattered dishes.

Jerome has made a delightful play with the biblical text here. Not only has he recited the biblical text and consequently addressed his audience as their pastor, but he has also inserted himself into the story both as Abraham addressing the rich man and, most interesting of all, as the rich man himself(!) explaining why he had behaved so poorly in his earthly life. Elsewhere in the homily, Jerome plays the role of Lazarus, so we have yet a fifth persona in other passages. To wit, one can imagine Jerome constantly changing his stance as he shifts between the many roles in which he has cast himself for this homiletic play. The homiletic license Jerome takes here offers several openings to evangelicals today.

147

In Jerome's way of thinking, the biblical text is something of a cue card to an extemporaneous speech. In reading what Jerome writes, one is reminded of Paul Ricoeur's second stage of *mimesis*.[26] The biblical text's meaning is by no means fixed; the compactness of its narrative demands (nay, cries out for) an expansion into a dialogue with contemporary referents. Indeed, one may imagine something like the following:

(1)   (2)   (3)   (4)
(1) "Send Lazarus to dip the tip of his finger in water."
(1) "Send Lazarus."
       (2) Send Lazarus? Like pearls before swine, that would be like sending Mother Theresa to help Brittany Spears improve her image!
(1) "To dip the tip of his finger in water."
       (2) You want relief from pain? You should have shared your wealth with your family members when they got in over their heads on a home mortgage loan. You should have supported the local food bank when it made an appeal for contributions. You should have been more just with the salaries you paid to your workers.

We could go on, but the point is clear. One discovers in Jerome's homily an invitation to construct a play of our own with the characters in the biblical story. Their voices, their lines, can all be shifted around to create a new story worthy of a contemporary audience's sensibilities.

This passage from the homily reveals also another important feature sure to interest evangelicals today. Here I refer to Jerome's forgetting that four centuries had passed since the time of Jesus in his reworking of several of the story's time elements. He does this while explaining one of the key metaphors of Luke 16, that of a chasm that separates sinners and saints in the netherworld. Consider this passage, in which Jerome first quotes the relevant biblical text then exposits it, saying, "'Besides all that, between us and you a great gulf is fixed.' It cannot be bridged, removed, or leveled. We can see it but cannot cross it. We see what we have escaped;

---

26. Ricoeur, *Time and Narrative*, 64–70.

you see what you have lost. Our joy and happiness multiply your torments; your torments augment our happiness."[27] Notice Jerome's change of the "we" of Lazarus and Abraham in Luke 16 to the "we" and "our" of himself and his audience. As could Lazarus and Abraham, so too Jerome and his audience could see that the damned are tormented, and that, even if they wish to help, the nature of the afterlife is such that they cannot. Indeed, that Jerome and his audience have escaped torments is all the more reason for joy! To Jerome, since his own experience in the afterlife and that of his audience will be that of Lazarus and Abraham, there is no reason not to anticipate what that will be like by imagining himself and them in Lazarus' place in the story.[28]

Another occasion for Jerome to play with the biblical text and to rewrite some of its prescriptions surrounds the chasm metaphor. In many evangelical churches, Jesus's chasm metaphor is a prooftext for the existence of a literal, eternal hell. Once in hell, there is no possibility of redemption, so the best course of action is to align oneself with God in the present life. Not unlike such churches, Jerome plays with the metaphor in much the same way. Consider, for example, that whereas in Luke 16 the rich man arguably is portrayed as penitent, even if to no avail, Jerome portrays him as opportunistic. Jerome declared, "Torments, not the disposition of your soul, force you to repent."[29] This is a very interesting point, since it reveals that, to Jerome, this chasm is more than just an unbridgeable divide. It is also a way both of *marking* and *blurring* the boundary lines separating this life and the next.

---

27. Jerome *Hom. in Lucam XVI* (Ewald, *Homilies of Saint Jerome*, 205). "Et in his omnibus inter nos et vos chaos magnum firmatum est. Dissolui non potest, non potest agitari et concuti. Videre possumus, transire non possumus: et nos videmus quid fugerimus, et vos videtis quid perdideritis (Morin, 511).

28. Yet, if we push this pastoral move by Jerome very far, we end up exposing a contradiction in his thought. Recall earlier that Jerome had insisted these events were taking place at the time Jesus was speaking and that, according to a footnote above, this was so because Jerome believed Jesus's crucifixion and resurrection would lead to the opening of the doors from the netherworld into heaven. Since that event in Jesus's life has since happened, there should no longer be a netherworld to which Jerome and his fellow believers will descend. They should pass immediately to the day of judgment and then enter heaven. Jerome has now been caught up fully in the web of his own constrained exegesis.

29. Jerome *Hom. in Lucam XVI* (Ewald, 203). "Tormenta te cogunt agere paenitentiam, non mentis affectus" (Morin, 510).

On the one hand, the chasm reminds one that death is the time limit for repentance, but, on the other hand, the dispositions of one's soul continue from this life to the next. The reason one cannot be reformed in the afterlife is because one cannot be repentant for any of the right reasons. Torments cloud the soul in the afterlife much as greed or pride clouded it in the life on earth.

In sum, we have seen that Jerome shares with Asterius a deep disdain for the corruption of the soul, the profligate lifestyle, and the neglect of the poor associated with superfluous wealth. Since pride lay at the root of this problem, compassion is the necessary antidote. Also like Asterius, Jerome encouraged the poor to bear their burden with dignity and to await God's restoration in the afterlife. We also encountered three features of Jerome's exposition that are helpful to the construction of a dialogue between this early Christian homilist and evangelicals. Jerome's play with elements of time in the parable seemed to justify his free construction of a new dialogue between the characters of the story, inserting himself and his audience into the mix. Also, we encountered Jerome's play with the chasm metaphor that both *refined* and *blurred* this imaginary line separating saints and sinners. Insofar as the chasm cannot be crossed in the afterlife, Jerome's call for his audience to get right with God now suggests the chasm separates also the present life and the afterlife. Moreover, the reason the chasm is a chasm at all is because the disposition of a human soul remains fixed once crossing into the afterlife. The torments of the afterlife keep the unrepentant soul in a state of wishing to repent, but for all the wrong reasons.

Perhaps we may even add another point to the discussion: Jerome's homily constructed a world we today may imagine inhabiting. The rich man's groanings, yearnings, wailings and pains all resonate with our own search for rest in God. From an evangelical reader's perspective, one draws from them both admonition and consolation, reminders about the fragility of life and encouragement to be faithful.

Contours for Evangelical Ressourcement

What precisely should be the evangelical *ressourcement* of this world of Asterius and Jerome and their social homilies? I propose five ways in which evangelicals, especially pastors, may connect their communities to what we have been evaluating. To begin with, it should not be overlooked that Asterius and Jerome once traveled the same road of Christian faith that we now tread. For this reason alone, their voices are a light for the path still ahead of us, and we would do well to listen to what they have to say. As pastors, gifted as they were by the Holy Spirit for this office, the ways in which they addressed social problems may be of some benefit since, we must admit, most of the same problems continue in our day. In this regard, one of the chief contributions by Asterius and Jerome to our modern discourse is their challenge to the notion that wealth belongs to the possessor of wealth. Wealth may reside in the hands of select individuals, but it *belongs* to any who have needs. Pastorally, the task of Asterius and Jerome (as it is the task of pastors today) was to reshape the mentalities of those with wealth, to help the rich live in accordance with biblical instruction regarding their use of wealth.

Second, and related to the first, evangelicals may renew the link they once cherished between caring for the poor and preaching the gospel. Before the Social Gospel movement and before Dorothy Day and the Catholic Worker movement, there were in the late nineteenth and early twentieth centuries evangelical Protestants championing issues for the common good such as free access to public education, the suffrage movement, worker protections in view of the industrial revolution, and relief for the urban poor. Few are the evangelical Protestants in movements for social justice today.[30] Asterius and Jerome unabashedly proclaimed God's preference for the righteous poor. Evangelicals ought to take strength from their example in reclaiming the mantle of social justice. Preachers need to be bold in declaring God's preference for the oppressed, including preference for those who are not paid a living wage, those who are underemployed, those who are without healthcare, single parents, low-skill laborers, those held back by racism, and on the list could go. The bottom line is that to preach God's love for the oppressed is to proclaim

---

30. In the global context, members of the Latin American Theological Fraternity (made up of scholars like Samuel Escobar, Renee Padilla, and Orlando Costas) have taken seriously the needs raised by liberationists like Gustavo Gutiérrez and have argued for the "whole gospel"—proclamation and social justice.

the gospel's teaching of the love of Jesus for all of his creatures in greater clarity.

Perhaps one caveat of this study worth remembering is that Jerome and Asterius neglected social sin in favor of treating in their homilies the obligations of individual rich persons toward individual poor persons. If they were aware of the role of social institutions in oppressing the poor, they did not reveal this. The class structure of Roman society, the tax policies, the legal system and even the monetary system with its distinction between bronze coins for commerce and gold coins for tax payments, all contributed to the plight of the working poor and the lowest of the poor. Evangelicals today should pay more attention than did Jerome and Asterius in their day to the social institutions that oppress people and the tacit or non-tacit role everyone plays in maintaining them. Sin is as much a problem of societies at large as it is of individuals, and evangelicals would do well to learn from the oversight of Jerome and Asterius and to allow this to figure prominently in their own socio-ethical framework.

Third, evangelicals may recover the strength of expository preaching. On the positive side, evangelicals share with Asterius and Jerome a commitment to biblical fidelity. For Asterius and Jerome, no detail of the biblical story was without meaning. Each verse deserved an exposition, and each verse was respected as a contributor to the whole of the pericope. Moreover, both of our authors understood that Luke 16 had a wider, theological context—the entire biblical canon. From that wider canon, our authors found connections between this story and the stories of creation, of Abraham, of Christ's crucifixion, between this and biblical references to Sheol or Hades, to prophetic language about God's preference for the oppressed, and to our Christian, eschatological hope. In addition, our authors were careful to exposit the biblical passage using stories of their own making that amplified the message of the biblical text. Asterius spoke of the lives and livelihoods of the rich and famous, including their lavish parties and their decorative clothing. Jerome created conversations taking place in Hades between the rich man and his own audience. It was important for Asterius and Jerome to have done so, since their audiences were nearly four hundred years removed from the time of Jesus! No less, evangelicals today are concerned to bridge the historical gaps between the biblical time and our time, and they do so by creating stories that by analogy help modern audiences comprehend the deeper meaning of the biblical texts.

Thus, in various ways one discovers that Asterius and Jerome were as concerned as evangelicals today to exposit the biblical text with integrity. Moreover, Asterius and Jerome remind us that expository preaching need not be cast from a mold of social irrelevancy. Every biblical text, when read theologically through the lens of the entire canon, confronts us with the socially transforming power of Jesus Christ. To our own community's detriment, evangelical preachers try too hard either to keep their exegesis tied to a single text or to refrain from exposition at all. In doing so they miss the opportunity of every biblical text to connect our community to the power of Jesus Christ that aims to transform individuals for the common good.

Fourth, evangelicals may find the resolve to reprove oppressors and sinners. Evangelical churches that attempt to recast their ministries as friendly to seekers too often shy away from sincere reproof and correction. This approach has required those with long lives of faith to endure worship services that praise youthfulness, trivialize sin, and dwell interminably on themes considered culturally relevant. Talk of and accountability for sin has been delegated to "accountability groups," small groups of believers who gather ostensibly for Bible study and accountability, but their real aim is to function as social outlets so that seekers do not feel overwhelmed by the anonymity of larger worship services.

Asterius and Jerome would probably not know what to do in such an evangelical church. They would be asking why the preacher is not pointing out directly who are the sinners—naming names if one must—in the culture.[31] They would be shocked at the lack of conviction that grips the audience following the closing of the service. They would be surprised at the level of biblical illiteracy among the congregation and the concomitant limitation that such illiteracy places on the preacher's ability to draw on the entire Bible during a biblical exposition. Asterius and Jerome reproved and corrected their audiences. They saw this as their pastoral duty. They did not care if their congregants liked them. To

---

31. Cf. Gregory of Nyssa's *Against the Usurers*, in which he asks his audience to remember the usurious man from their community who had recently died and whose children now resent even the mention of their father's name.

be ordained is to be set apart from the community. Pastors should never try to limit their reproofs so as to maximize their friendships. Such is not the life of an ordained person, irrespective of the time or culture.

Fifth, evangelicals may embrace the creation of new stories and images around their biblical expositions. Although Jerome more than Asterius, both of our early homilists recast the biblical story and its injunctions in new stories and images taken from their own culture. To their way of thinking, the biblical text was pliable, meant to be reshaped into a story meaningful to their congregants. Evangelicals may welcome the freedom this gives to biblical exposition—now a task not about articulating the ancient context but about articulating the biblical theme in a modern garb. The simplicity and, indeed, compactness of any biblical narrative belie its theological and social complexity, a complexity which offers ever-expanding horizons of meaning from which evangelicals may draw to communicate anew God's love for his creation.

Conclusion

This paper has argued that both social preaching and social ethics in the early Christian world provide trajectories for a re-evaluation of social ethics in the modern, evangelical context. Certainly, evangelicals share with Jerome and Asterius a concern to exposit fully and faithfully the biblical text. As well, in earlier days, evangelicals also shared the patristic authors' particular concern for the poor and the oppressed. Yet the patristic homilies invite evangelicals both to strengthen their resolve to continue a forceful preaching tradition, including recognition that a preference for the poor is a constitutive element of evangelism, and to declare unreservedly their commitment to social justice.

7

Learning from Patristic Christology

Francis X. Gumerlock

❃ Christ, the Article on *Which the Church Stands or Falls*

According to Lutheran teaching the church stands or falls on the article of justification.[1] As much as I love the Pauline teaching of justification, that we are clothed with and stand in the imputed righteousness of Christ, I think a case can be made from Jesus' own lips that Christology, not justification, is the article upon which the church stands or falls. The Lord asked Peter, "But who do you say that I am?" In response to the confession of Peter, that he was "the Christ, the Son of the living God," Jesus said, "Upon this rock I will build My church" (Matt 16:15–18, NASB). The beloved disciple John also recognized that Christology was of the utmost importance, saying, "Whoever denies the Son does not have the Father; the one who confesses the Son has the Father also." And later, "He who has the Son has the life; he who does not have the Son of God does not have the life" (1 John 2:23; 5:12, NASB). What is the place of orthodox Christology in evangelicalism today? How can patristic Christology inform our faith?

In the late twentieth century, as liberals were debating over whether the Jesus of the Gospels was the Jesus of history, evangelicalism was

---

1. Martin Luther, *Exposition on Psalm* 130:4: ". . . quia isto articulo stante stat Ecclesia, ruente ruit Ecclesia" (Anderson et al., *Justification by Faith*, 320 n. 51). See also the Lutheran *Smalcald Articles* 2.1 and *Book of Concord* 292, in which justification is called the "first and chief article" (as cited in *Joint Declaration*, 9).

experiencing its own christological debacles. Presidents of three major evangelical universities and seminaries were teaching views about Christ similar to errors condemned by the early church. One declared that Jesus was nine hundred feet tall, that the Holy Spirit is Christ in another form, and that in the crucifixion the devil destroyed Jesus' body, but "never got the real Christ."[2] Another president was denying the eternal Sonship of Christ.[3] And still another wrote that Christ has only one will, not two, a view historically known as "monothelitism," from the Greek words meaning "one" and "will."[4] In such a context, calls for reform included an engagement with the ancient faith of our fathers.

   2. Oral Roberts, who was president of Oral Roberts University, which grants master's degrees in theology. On the 900-foot Jesus, see Muck, "God and Oral," 17; Brown, "Oral Roberts," 450–52; Brown, "Oral Tradition," 278–79. Interestingly, the Elchasaites of the early church alleged that the Son of God was 96 miles wide. Cf. Hippolytus of Rome *Refutation of All Heresies* 9.12 (*ANF* 5:131–32). On Roberts's confusion of the Son with the Holy Spirit, see Roberts, *How to Get Through*, 171: "He [the Father] sent Him [Jesus] back in the invisible, unlimited form of the Holy Spirit to be in us—both with us and in us. It is through the invisible, unlimited Christ, the form in which God sends the other Comforter, that the Holy Spirit fills my spirit." Also: "And God raised Him [Jesus] from the dead, giving Him a new form that is unlimited and invisible ... Jesus has come back in the invisible, unlimited form of the Holy Spirit to be in us, as well as to be with us" (ibid., 240). Roberts, *Miracles of Christ*, 37: "Now, as I said, the Holy Spirit is Jesus' Other Self." On the devil not getting the real Christ, see Roberts, "Gifts of the Spirit," 36–37.

   3. John MacArthur, the president of The Master's Seminary, in *Hebrews*, 27–28: "As was noted, Son is an incarnational title of Christ. Though His sonship was anticipated in the Old Testament (Prov 30:4), He did not become a Son until He was begotten into time. Prior to time and His incarnation He was eternal God with God. The term Son has only to do with Jesus Christ in His incarnation ... The Bible nowhere speaks of the eternal sonship of Christ ... He was always God, but He became Son ... Christ was not Son until His incarnation." Also, see the paper written by him and distributed by him, "Sonship of Christ." Works directed against his position include Zeller and Showers, *Eternal Sonship of Christ*; and Ross, *Trinity and the Eternal Sonship of Christ*. In 1999 MacArthur retracted his teaching and affirmed the eternal Sonship of Christ in a paper entitled "Re-examining the Eternal Sonship of Christ."

   4. John F. Walvoord, the former president of Dallas Theological Seminary, in *Jesus Christ Our Lord*, 119–20: "The Relation of the Two Natures to the Will of Christ. In view of the complete divine and human natures in Christ, the question has been raised whether each nature had its corresponding will. The problem is occasioned by ambiguity in the word 'will.' If by will is meant desire, it is clear that there could be conflicting desires in the divine and human natures of Christ. If by will, however, is meant that resulting moral decision, one person can have only one will. In the case of Christ, this will was

Learning from Patristic Christology

Today, in the early twenty-first century, a new generation of evangelical professors has arisen. Trained not only in Scripture but also in historical theology, they have found the study of the early church a tremendous help in the attempt to promote orthodox Christology. This essay will reflect upon four ways that studying patristics helped my faith and will elaborate on two scriptural truths that the early church taught about Christ.

How the Study of Patristics Has Helped My Christian Faith

Study of early Christian theology has aided my faith in many ways. It has helped me to be more discerning of true and false interpretations of Scripture and has broadened my understanding of Scripture, especially when tackling difficult passages. Investigating early Christianity has also given me a sense of historical connectedness, and has led to the discovery of texts of which the church, for the most part, had not been previously aware.

Discernment

My first exposure to early Christianity occurred in the context of problems that were besetting our Christian fellowship on my college campus in New Jersey. Some people were telling us that we were not saved if we had been baptized in the name of the Father, Son, and Holy Spirit, and that we needed to be re-baptized in the name of Jesus only. In response to this difficulty, our campus minister flew in his friend from Dallas to teach us classes on the Trinity, Christology, and apologetics during one of our breaks. We loved it, found it refreshing, and felt that we had some protection against those who were trying to upset our faith.

---

always the will of God ... It is therefore no more proper to speak of two sovereign wills in Christ than it is of two wills in an ordinary believer who has both a sin nature and a new nature." It is unfortunate that Walvoord in this discussion did not interact with the patristic controversy on the number of wills in Christ, especially canons 10–18 of the Lateran Council of 649 against monothelitism and the statement on the wills of Christ against monothelitism issued by the Third Council of Constantinople in 681, also called the Sixth Ecumenical Council. For these statements, see Denzinger, *Sources of Catholic Dogma*, 103–5; and Clarkson et al., *Church Teaches*, 187–88.

We learned that Oneness Pentecostalism, the religion from which those "Jesus only" beliefs had come, started about a century ago through a vision that John Scheppe had one evening tarrying in prayer, which told him that there was only one member of the Godhead, and that was Jesus.[5] Moreover, it was our drawing back upon patristic Trinitarianism that caused us to understand that the distinctions in the Trinity are eternal, and that the modalism of the Oneness Pentecostals had been condemned some seventeen hundred years ago. Modalism (or "Sabellianism," named after one of its leading proponents) taught that God was only one person, not three, who revealed himself in three modes at different times. We looked at the Scriptures that show that the three persons in the Trinity are not simply temporal manifestations. Seeing that the early church had problems similar to ours as well as learning what the early church believed fortified my Christian faith against present dangers.

Next, we had members of our college Christian fellowship who, influenced by the "Word of Faith" teachings of Kenneth Hagin, believed that Jesus was "born again" at the resurrection.[6] We knew it did not sound right, but through our engagement with patristic Christology we saw that such teaching had affinity with the condemned gnostic teaching of a redeemed redeemer and with the heresy of adoptionism.

Learning about past errors helped me recognize present manifestations of them, not for the purpose of "heresy hunting"—which I do not believe is a fruit of the Spirit, but more often seems to be a deed of the flesh (cf. Gal 5:20)—but for discernment and for keeping me from repeating earlier mistakes. Now when I hear a theory of the *kenosis* in Philippians 2 that conveys a Jesus that is emptied of deity, I know it is wrong. For, the church fathers debated long and hard and showed from Scripture that the incarnation did not involve a mutation from divinity to humanity, but rather an assumption of humanity by the second person of the Trinity, with all of the properties of divinity still intact.

---

5. Robeck, "Schaepe, John G.," 768–69; and Hollenweger, *Pentecostals*, 31–32.

6. Hagin, *Present Day Ministry of Jesus*, 7. See also Crenshaw, *Man as God*, 317–19 (directed against E. W. Kenyon and Kenneth Copeland, who also preached a born-again Jesus); Hux, "Is He 'Another Jesus'?," 16–17; Rosenbladt, "Who Do Televangelists Say That I Am?," 117–19; and McConnell, *Different Gospel*, 119–21.

Learning from Patristic Christology

Christology, as it was hammered out in the early centuries, gave me better discernment.

Help with Biblical Difficulties

As a Christian, it is my loving service to him who first loved me to understand his Word, and most of all to become a doer of it. But some things in the Bible are very difficult to understand. What did Jesus mean when he said that the Father was greater than he (cf. John 14:28)? What did Paul mean when he wrote that those who speak in tongues speak not to man but to God (1 Cor 14:2)? And when John depicted a reign of the saints for a thousand years (Rev 20:1–6), did he mean an earthly reign between the second coming and the new heaven and new earth? How should we interpret Jesus' Olivet Discourse (Matt 24–25), as already fulfilled or awaiting fulfillment? In these and similar questions, I have found the writings of the early church to be extremely helpful; for they often bridge the geographical, cultural, and linguistic gaps that stand between these first-century authors and us in the twenty-first century.

Regarding the first question, both Augustine and the Eleventh Council of Toledo taught that the Son is equal to the Father by virtue of his deity, and less than the Father because of his humanity.[7] It had nothing to do with any eternal subordination within the Godhead.

Regarding tongues, I found that many writers of the early church touched upon the subject, and all understood the miracle of tongues to be a supernatural deposit of a known human language, not a secret prayer language that only the believer and the Holy Spirit know.[8]

Concerning the thousand year reign, some in the early church held to a literal thousand-year earthly reign of the saints on earth after the second coming, while others believed the thousand years to be figurative

---

7. Augustine Sermon 91.3 (Hill, *Sermons (51–94)*, 49): "[I]n the form of man he is less than the Father, in the form of God equal to the Father." Canons of the Eleventh Council of Toledo, in Neuner and Dupuis, *Christian Faith*, 170–71: "Similarly, by the fact that He is God, He is equal to the Father; by the fact that He is man, He is less than the Father . . ."

8. For a dossier of early Christian writers on the subject of tongues, see Gumerlock, "Tongues in the Church Fathers," 123–38. On medieval understandings of the gift of interpretation of tongues, see Gumerlock, "Interpretation of Tongues in the Middle Ages," 160–68.

of either the present reign of the saints in the church age or the reign of believing souls who are now with Christ after their death before they receive their glorified bodies at his second coming.[9] While today we argue over the interpretation of the thousand years to the point of even excluding from teaching in our seminaries people who have a different view of Revelation 20:1–6 than ourselves, I found it interesting that the early church councils neither affirmed nor condemned chiliasm.[10] The approach of both Jerome and Augustine was to construct arguments for their own position but also to be tolerant of opposing views on the matter.[11]

While interpreting the Olivet Discourse, the church fathers pointed out that Jesus was answering several questions raised by the disciples: one about when the buildings of Jerusalem would be toppled and another about the sign of his coming and the end of the world. The early Christians overwhelmingly took a "now and not yet" approach in their interpretations of Matthew 24–25. They generally held that the prophecies of false Christs and the flight to the mountains were fulfilled in connection with the Roman siege of AD 68–70. But the coming of the Son of Man in the clouds, the gathering of the elect from the four corners of the earth, and the judgment of the sheep and goats, they saw as not having been fulfilled in their time, but as references to future events associated with the coming of Christ at the end of the world. The church fathers said other prophecies, such as the abomination of desolation, have a double reference. First, it pointed to the placing of an idol in the temple by a Roman emperor, and then an act of an end-time antichrist

---

9. The chiliast writers are listed and quoted in Zuck, *Basic Bible Interpretation*, 233–35. The non-chiliasts are listed and quoted in a draft of my "Amillennialism in the Early Church."

10. Although it is often said that the Second Council of Constantinople condemned chiliasm, this was not the case. See my "Millennialism and the Early Church Councils," 83–95. See also the research of Michael J. Svigel, who countered the assertion that the Council of Ephesus condemned chiliasm, in "Phantom Heresy," 105–12.

11. Jerome *Commentary on Jeremiah*, on Jer 19:10–11 (Alcañiz, *Ecclesia Patristica*, 212–13): "[W]e are not able to condemn them [chiliast views] because many men and martyrs of the church spoke these things. Let each person abound in his own understanding, and all things will be reserved for the judgment of the Lord". Cf. *Augustine City of God* 20.7.1.

who will come before the consummation of all things. How does this inform evangelicals today? According to most church fathers, both the preterist approach and classical dispensational approaches to the Olivet Discourse are wrong. It was not fulfilled in its entirety, nor is the entirety of it awaiting fulfillment in the great tribulation.[12]

To summarize, when attempting to solve a biblical difficulty, I gain tremendously from the opinions of those who lived in closer temporal, geographical, and cultural proximity to the biblical authors; and I trust this is the experience of many who are currently engaged with patristic theology.

A Sense of Historical Connectedness

Christians today, especially those from non-confessional backgrounds, want to understand the relationship of the present to the past. In fact, one of the main reasons that evangelicals cite for converting to Roman Catholicism is that their new community gives them a sense of historical connectedness that they did not find in evangelicalism.[13] Oh, we hear little tidbits in sermons from time to time about John Wycliffe or John Hus, John Wesley or Jonathan Edwards, Charles Finney or Charles Spurgeon, Smith Wigglesworth or Kathryn Kuhlman. But many evangelicals do not have a big picture of how the church journeyed from the time of the Apostles to the present. But they are seeing a need for it. Why? Because they know that they are organically united in the body of Christ with the church of the previous twenty centuries. Consequently more and more evangelical seminaries are offering majors in historical theology. Much more, however, needs to be done to strengthen these departments if they want to draw the evangelicals interested in church history, many of whom currently choose non-evangelical schools for their historical training.

First, the seminaries need to invest in the historical theology sections of their libraries, purchasing the series of primary patristic works,

---

12. On the interpretation of the early part of the Olivet Discourse by writers of ancient and medieval Christianity in relationship to the Roman-Judean war, see my "Olivet Discourse."

13. McKnight, "Wheaton to Rome," 463–66.

not only the English translations but also the Latin and Greek editions, as well as the extensive periodical and secondary literature coming off of the presses. Secondly, seminaries need to adjust their curricula and hire appropriate professors so that students learn to read primary sources in Latin and Greek, and eventually Syriac, Coptic, and Arabic, the languages in which many patristic texts are preserved.

Those evangelicals who have turned on to church history are also rejecting the older evangelical frameworks of history that promoted a lack of connection with the thousand years of Christianity from the fourth through sixteenth centuries. Those frameworks which do a hop, skip, and a jump over the Middle Ages, from the radical Landmark position to the more moderate Constantine conspiracy view, are no longer in vogue. Landmarkism says that very shortly after the Apostles, the church by and large disappeared. But because Jesus said that "the gates of hell shall not prevail against it" (Matt 16:18, KJV), a remnant was saved throughout the Middle Ages. Those true remnant churches were the Novatianists and Donatists, and groups like the Paulicians, Cathari, and Albigenses.[14] The problem with this approach is that most of the groups the Landmarkers portray as their forefathers were heretics. But the only other option is to admit that medieval Catholicism was the church, and to them such a thought is untenable.

Twenty-first-century evangelicals are also discarding the notion that says that the ante-Nicene fathers can be helpful, but once the emperor Constantine became a so-called Christian, the end was near; the end, that is, of anything worth learning about. They no longer buy into the tale that with the conversion of Constantine, Christianity became almost completely apostate overnight and that the marriage of church and state, baptism of infants, and rejection of premillennialism are evidences for that.[15]

---

14. The classic work for this view of church history is Carroll, *Trail of Blood*, which in 1987 was in its 59th printing and had sold almost two million copies. Other books include Everts, *Church in the Wilderness*; Stovall, *Baptist History and Succession*; and Jarrel, *Baptist Church Perpetuity*. Critical of this concept of church history are McGoldrick, *Baptist Successionism*; Ross, *Old Landmarkism and the Baptist*; and Patterson, *Baptist Successionism*.

15. Such views have been strong in various Anabaptist and Baptist traditions. Sebastian Franck, a sixteenth-century Anabaptist, said of Ambrose, Augustine, Jerome, and

Learning from Patristic Christology

To evangelicals today, the Dark Ages are not so dark. They want to know about the church between Constantine and Luther, and many are majoring, researching, and writing on the theology of late antiquity and the Middle Ages, and are finding a wealth of material beneficial to their faith. Interestingly, the Patristics Study Group of the Evangelical Theological Society changed its name to the Patristics and Medieval History Section in 2007.

Evangelicals are finding that studying early Christianity provides them with a sense of historical connection. And part of this has been their rediscovery of what had been lost, or rather of what had been denied them, namely, the richness of Christianity after Constantine, the faith of Jerome and Augustine, Leo the Great and Gregory the Great, Fulgentius of Ruspe and Caesarius of Arles, Basil of Caesarea and Gregory of Nazianzus, Cyril and Justinian, Chrysostom and Epiphanius, John Maxentius and John of Damascus.

New Discoveries

Finally, the study of the early church has caused me to make new discoveries that broaden my understanding of the faith once delivered unto the saints. I do not mean new in the sense of additional revelation, but rather different viewpoints on the interpretation of Scriptures that I never before heard or considered. For example, hearing patristic interpretations of the 144,000 of Revelation 7 as the first-fruits of the Jews who had believed in Christ in the first century, or as the number of Jews who fled the siege of the Romans, was fascinating.[16] I never came across these viewpoints except when examining patristic texts.

Sometimes the writings of the early church have a striking affinity with or correlation to contemporary positions or answers to today's theological problems. For example, reading the commentary of the students of Cassiodorus on the Pauline Epistles was eye-opening. They interpreted the "all" in 1 Timothy 2:4 (God "desires all men to be saved and

---

Gregory that "not even one knew Christ, nor was sent by God to teach. But rather all were and shall remain the apostles of Antichrist." Quoted in McGrath, *Reformation Thought*, 205.

16. These were the views of Ecumenius of Tricca and Andrew of Caesarea in Cappadocia. See Weinrich, *Ancient Christian Commentary*, 105, 108.

to come to the knowledge of the truth," NASB) as a figure of synecdoche, a whole term placed for a part. In other words, they taught that God does not want to save absolutely everyone, but the elect from all classes and stations of humanity.[17] Regardless of whether or not this interpretation is exegetically correct, it certainly has the ring of familiarity with modern Reformed interpretations that understand the passage in light of the doctrines of unconditional election and particular redemption.

When Christians argue over theistic evolution because it has death existing before the fall of Adam, they often are brought to passages in Romans that link death to sin. But patristic anthropology can add breadth to the discussion. For the Council of Carthage in 411 condemned the proposition of Celestius the Pelagian that Adam was created mortal (i.e., that Adam's death was not a result of sin but part of the natural created order).[18]

And when certain Calvinists, who may be called "Hyper-Calvinists," quote Isaiah 45:7 in support of the teaching that God created evil, I think of the church father nicknamed "Golden-mouth" (Chrysostom) because of his excellent preaching, who interpreted "evil" in that passage not as moral evil but as calamity, namely, the captivity and servitude that Israel was experiencing.[19]

Of course, these interpretations are not new to the body of Christ, but were new to me. Once in awhile, however, students of patristics have the privilege of finding truly lost treasures. That is, they come upon something about which the church by and large is unaware. The theory that J. N. Darby was the inventor of the teaching of a pre-tribulation rapture is rather common in evangelical circles. However, earlier this decade I found what looks like a rapture of the saints, occurring quite some time before the final coming of Christ in judgment, in both a patristic apocalyptic text and a fourteenth-century historical treatise.[20]

---

17. Pseudo-Primasius *Commentary on the Epistles of Saint Paul* (PL 68:663).

18. Thomas M. Sennott also made the connection between contemporary theistic evolution and the Pelagian heresy in his *On Exonerating Pelagius*.

19. Hill, *St. John Chrysostom*, 38–39. Curt Daniel defined Hyper-Calvinism as "Calvinism carried to illogical conclusions." Daniel, *History and Theology of Calvinism*, 89.

20. See my "Rapture in the *Apocalypse of Elijah*"; "Rapture Citation in the Fourteenth Century," 349–62; "Before Darby"; and *Day and the Hour*, 80, 91–92.

Learning from Patristic Christology

Similarly, in 2002 or 2003, while researching at the Vatican Film Library at Saint Louis University, by accident I came across a fifth-century text in which the name of the emperor Nero was clearly being used to interpret the number of the beast in Revelation 13:18.[21] This is significant because the identification of the name Nero with the number of the beast is generally thought to be a nineteenth-century theory of German theologians. This text pushes that theory back historically some 1400 years.[22]

Discoveries like these make the study of patristic theology not just helpful but exciting. For the church historian, coming across "new" informative texts can be as thrilling as the creation of a new technology for an engineer, the unearthing of a new cure to the medical community, or the purchase of the ossuary (allegedly) of James "brother of Jesus" by an archeologist.

Scriptural Truths about Christ That I Learned from the Early Church

I have learned much from the early church about the deity and humanity of our Lord Jesus Christ, and the unity of his two natures in one person. The Word was a person and not an "it" before the incarnation, contrary to what Marcellus of Ancyra in the early church thought and Kenneth Copeland teaches today.[23] There was never a time when the Son did not exist, in contrast with the Arians. Our Lord is the natural Son of God, not an adopted Son, contrary to the Adoptionists. Our Lord is one person with two natures, human and divine. He has all of the properties of each nature. Whatever can be said about one nature of Christ can be said about his person, under any title, human or divine, contrary to the Nestorians. It was not just a human who died on the cross as the later Nestorians asserted, but a member of the Trinity was crucified in the flesh, as the Council of Constantinople affirmed in 553. Among the many things I learned from patristic Christology, I would like to elaborate in

---

21. See also Aune, *Revelation 6–16*, 770–71.

22. The text is cited and translated in my "Nero Antichrist," 347–60.

23. On Marcellus of Ancyra's view, see Sample, "Christology of the Council of Antioch," 18–26 at 23. For Copeland's view, see Copeland, *Power of the Tongue*, 4–10.

some detail on two aspects of Christology, his true humanity and his eternal Sonship.

The True Humanity of Our Lord

The incarnation, along with what theologians call his humiliation (i.e., his temptation), his earthly ministry, and his death on the cross, is the most important event in all of human history. The Word becoming flesh, the Son of God taking on humanity, means that Christ was born from the seed of a woman. He was truly the son of Mary and received his genetic makeup from her side of the family. He probably looked like his uncles and grandfather on her side. The early gnostics denied that Christ was truly flesh, because they believed that matter was synonymous with moral evil. But the Lord is truly human and not just a divine idea. The way our churches can affirm the true humanity of our Lord is by weekly readings from the Gospels, by celebrating the Lord's Supper frequently, by recitations of creeds that profess the Son becoming man "for us men and for our salvation" and being "crucified under Pontius Pilate," and by displays of crosses in our churches, something that non-confessional Protestants avert as ritualistic and "the tradition of men" (Mark 7:8).

Unfortunately, certain Anabaptists, who tended to be non-creedal, did not start out with a clear affirmation of our Lord's true humanity. Some like Menno Simons erred in saying that Christ brought his flesh down from heaven with him. Misunderstanding Hebrew 10:5, they taught that Christ received nothing from Mary, and that her womb merely acted as an incubator for the Lord. Perhaps a better understanding of patristic Christology on their part, namely, the church fathers' affirmation of the true humanity of Christ against the gnostics, would have kept these Anabaptists from repeating a similar error.

Christ's full humanity entails the insistence that he truly suffered. Scripture tells us that he experienced hunger, thirst, and weariness (Matt 4:2; 8:24; Luke 8:23; John 4:6–7; 19:28). Nevertheless, a group called the Aphthartodocetae "conceived the humanity of Christ not only as sinless but as having been completely alien to the consequences of the sin of Adam."[24] To them, the body of Christ was like that of Adam before the

---

24. Meyendorff, *Christ in Eastern Christian Thought*, 165. The favorite passages of the

Learning from Patristic Christology

fall, not like the bodies of fallen men. Their error was in making Christ like Superman. His body was incorruptible, they said, since death and corruption were a result of sin, and Christ never sinned. The orthodox position was that the body of Christ was "passible," capable of suffering and sharing in the influences of the elements in a fallen world. These are not incompatible with Christ's moral perfection. The orthodox said that Christ's body was destructible, his death being the result of the violence of men (Rom 8:3; Heb 2:14-17; 1 Pet 2:21). Christ's incorruptibility was not manifested in the incarnation, but awaited the glorification of the resurrection, when that which was corruptible and mortal took on incorruption and immortality (Acts 2:27; 1 Cor 15:42-43, 52-53).[25]

Affirming Christ's true humanity also entails believing that he will come again visibly in his body with the clouds. The angels said to the disciples at the ascension that Jesus would return in the same way that he left (Acts 1:11). To the church fathers this meant not only in the clouds but also bodily. Christ will not return invisibly, in spirit, or separate from his humanity. Rather, the Son of Man shall come in his majesty, sit on his throne of glory, and render judgment to everyone (Matt 25:31-32; John 5:27). Unfortunately, there are many ways that people in the evangelical tradition deny this. One is when the Seventh-Day Adventists, or at least those who belong to the General Conference of Seventh-Day Adventists, claim that the Son of Man came with the clouds in 1844. However, the reason no one saw him is because he came to the heavenly sanctuary where he is now doing an "investigative judgment" before he returns visibly and bodily.[26] Another is any theory of the rapture that has Jesus returning to earth and quickly leaving with many people never seeing him, but only seeing the effects of that return such as cars without driv-

---

Aphthartodocetae were those which said that he voluntarily submitted to death, such as John 10:15, 18; Phil 2:8; and Acts 2:24.

25. John of Damascus *Exposition on the Orthodox Faith* 3.28 (*NPNF2* 9:72); Photius, *Bibliotheca*, 162. On the controversy, see Esbroeck, "Aphthartodocetic Edict of Justinian," 578–85; Meyendorff, *Christ in Eastern Christian Thought*, 166–67; Vailhé, "Corrupticoles"; Draguet, *Julien d'Halicarnasse*; Wigram, *Separation of the Monophysites*, 121–22, 151–55; Luce, *Monophysitism*, 76–77; and Dorner, *History of the Development*, 128–31.

26. *Seventh-Day Adventists Believe*, 321–24. I recognize that many evangelicals do not consider Seventh-Day Adventists as within the evangelical fold because of their views on soul sleep, annihilation, and Old Testament law-keeping.

ers, lawnmowers running with no one pushing them, and piles of clothes left behind on previously occupied chairs. A third way in which the true humanity of our Lord is unwittingly weakened is in the teaching that the second coming of Christ was an invisible coming that occurred in AD 70. Of course, all three of these theories have the redeeming quality of affirming that our Lord will eventually come in bodily form, in addition to returning invisibly either in AD 70,[27] in 1844, or seven years before his final descent.[28]

Some of the church fathers who taught that Christ's return to earth will be both bodily and visible included Gregory of Nazianzus, Chrysostom, and Augustine. Gregory wrote, "[H]e will come with his body—so I have learned—such as he was seen by his disciples in the mount."[29] Chrysostom declared, "'As the lightning' ([Matt 24] ver. 27), He says, shall He come; not concealed in any corner, but shining everywhere. It requires no one to point it out, so splendid will it be, even as the lightning needs no one to point it out."[30] Likewise Augustine: "What's *will come in the same way* (Acts 1:11)? Will come in that same form, in order to fulfill what was written, *They will see the one whom they pierced* (Zech 12:10). That's how he will come. He will come to men, he will come, a man; but it is God who will come as a man. He will come as true man and God . . ."[31] Furthermore, a council at Constantinople in 754 anathematized anyone who "does not confess that Christ is seated with God the Father in body and soul, and so will come to judge."[32] Perhaps patristic training on the ramifications of Christ's humanity in his current session at the right hand of the Father and in his second coming can prevent any further theories of an invisible second coming

---

27. Partial preterists tend to believe in both a coming of Christ in AD 70 and a final bodily coming at the end of time. Full preterists reject the tenet of a future bodily coming of Christ.

28. To be fair, some of the church fathers did allow for a non-bodily "coming" of Christ into people's hearts and to receive their souls at the moment of death. See my "Olivet Discourse," 98–103.

29. Gregory of Nazianzus *Ep. ad Cled.* (*NPNF2* 7:440).

30. John Chrysostom *Homilies Thessalonians* 1 (*NPNF1* 13:379).

31. Augustine *Sermon 265 on the Ascension of the Lord* (Hill, Sermons [51–94], 236).

32. "Epitome of the Definition of the Iconoclastic Conciliabulum, Held in Constantinople, A.D. 754" (*NPNF2* 14:545).

Learning from Patristic Christology

rather than the true visible, bodily coming of the Lord Jesus Christ who is forever the God-man.

For our Lord to be truly human also means that he had a true human soul. Unfortunately, when Apollinaris (d. 390), who was otherwise a respected teacher, tried to explain how Christ was both God and man, he erred in saying that just as a person is made up of body and soul, so Christ is made up of body and Logos. In other words, the Logos took the place of the human soul in Christ. Scripture, however, teaches that Christ had not only a human body but a human soul (Isa 53:3; Matt 11:29; Acts 2:30–31). The Council of Chalcedon affirmed this in 451, saying that Christ is truly God and truly man, with a rational soul and body.

Part of the faculty of a human soul is a human mind. Christ grew in wisdom (Luke 2:52) and learned obedience (Heb 5:8). Nevertheless, these facts do not negate Paul's teaching that "in him are all the treasures of wisdom and knowledge" (Col 3:2, NASB). Somehow they are both true. His omniscience does not cancel out the human development of his mind and soul, nor does Christ's ignorance mean that the God-man was not all-knowing, just as his local presence did not mean that he was not omnipresent. For the incarnation was not an exchange of deity for humanity, but the one person of our Lord Jesus Christ possessed all of the properties of both humanity and divinity. The church fathers spilled much ink on the subject of the Lord's statement that he did not know the day or the hour of his coming (cf. Mark 13:32), and they interpreted it in various ways. What they agreed upon was that the Lord's omniscience was not minimized through the incarnation, contrary to the position of the "Agnotae," who denied the omniscience of our Lord Jesus Christ. And against the Nestorians, the fathers stated that the Lord's human mind did not receive divine knowledge in increments, as the prophets of old did. For if that were the case, then he was not the God-man but just a man who participated in the divinity.[33]

Another faculty of a rational human soul is volition. Our Lord Jesus also possesses a true human will (Luke 22:42; John 6:38), which was always submissive to the divine will. This scriptural truth of two wills in Christ, a human will and a divine will, was affirmed against the

---

33. For a fuller discussion of the problem and issues, see Gumerlock, "Mark 13:32," 205–13.

Monothelites who denied that there was a human will in Christ and said that there was in him only a divine will. Monothelitism robs Christ of true humanity.

The Eternal Generation of the Son

1 John 5:18 states, "He who was born of God keeps him, and the evil one does not touch him" (NASB). In this passage Jesus is called "He who was born of God." The doctrine of eternal generation answers the question of whether that birth took place at some point in time or is a timeless, eternal generation. If God the Father brought forth God the Son at a specific point in time, then the Son would be a creature who had a beginning, and therefore not truly God. The truth of the matter is that the Father is God and the Son is God. The Father, Son, and Holy Spirit always existed. There was never a time when God was not Father and when the Son did not exist. This birth, begetting, or generation of the Son from the Father, talked about in Scripture, is therefore timeless. It is an eternal generation. The teaching is defined as "the doctrine that the Logos or Son of God is 'eternally generated' by the Father, that is, the Son is co-eternal with the Father but the Father is eternally the source of the Son."[34] Scriptural support for the eternal Sonship of Christ is found in Matt 14:22–33; Mark 12:1–9; John 1:14, 18; 3:16; 5:17–18; 16:28; 20:21; Rom 8:3; Gal 2:20; 4:4; Heb 1:1–3; 5:8; 7:3; 1 John 1:1–3; 4:10, 14.[35]

In the late second and early third centuries of Christian history, some of the apologists like Justin Martyr and Tertullian did not articulate the doctrine of eternal generation. Irenaeus, however, in the late second century wrote of "the Son, eternally co-existing with the Father, from of old, yea from the beginning."[36] And in the early third century, Origen in a homily on Jeremiah taught the doctrine of eternal generation. He wrote:

---

34. Need, *Truly Divine and Truly Human*, 165.

35. The best dcriptural defense I have read is J. C. Philpot's *True, Proper, and Eternal Sonship*.

36. Irenaeus *Against Heresies* 2.30.9 (ANF 1:406). Other hints of eternal generation in Irenaeus include his statement in *Against Heresies* 2.28.6: "[I]f anyone, therefore, says to us, 'How then was the Son produced by the Father? we reply to him, that no man understands that production or generation . . . but the Father only who begat, and the Son who was begotten." For views of certain pre-Nicene apologists like Justin Martyr and

> If then I shall make clear to you that in the case of the Saviour the Father did not once beget the Son, and then His Father released Him from this relationship, but that He continually begets Him ... He is the brightness of His glory (Heb 1:3). It is not that the brightness of His glory was once for all generated and is now generated no more, but so long as light produces brightness, so long is the brightness of God's glory generated ... then the Saviour is continually being generated, that is the reason for His saying, "Before all the hills He begets me." It is not, "Before all the hills He has begotten me," but, "Before all the hills He begets me," and the Saviour is continually begotten of the Father.[37]

Around 320, when a cleric in the church at Alexandria named Arius began to teach that there was a time when the Son did not exist, the church saw the danger of such statements, and the scriptural doctrine of the Son's eternal generation came to the forefront of Christian thinking. For Arius, when the Scriptures spoke of the Son being "begotten" by the Father, it meant "created" or "made" by the Father. For Arius, the Son was a creature made by the Father. According to his treatise *Thalia*, "God was not eternally a father. There was [a time] when God was all alone, and was not yet father; only later did he become a father. The Son did not always exist." The treatise went on to say that the Son came into being by the Father's will and "was born in the order of time."[38] In a letter to Eusebius of Nicomedia, Arius said that he and his party were being persecuted because he taught that the Son had a beginning.[39]

In opposition to Arius' teaching, Athanasius and other Christians affirmed that the Son always existed, being eternally generated from the Father. At the Council of Nicaea in 325, the orthodox stated that the Son is "begotten not made" and anathematized those who said that "There was [a time] when he was not" and "Before he was begotten, he was not." The bishops at the Council affirmed the scriptural teaching that Christ

---

Tertullian who did not articulate a doctrine of eternal generation, see Fortman, *Triune God*, 45–46; 110–11.

37. Origen *Homily on Jeremiah* 9.4 (Tollinton, *Selections from the Commentaries*, 23–24). In other writings, however, Origen did not escape subordinationism.

38. Arius *Thalia* (Williams, *Arius*, 100, 102). On Arius, see Böhm, "Arius", 49; Simonetti, "Arius-Arians-Arianism"; and Hanson, *Search for the Christian Doctrine of God*.

39. Arius *Letter to Eusebius of Nicomedia* (Nichols, *For Us*, 95).

"is the only begotten Son who is eternally begotten and who has the same substance or essence of God."[40] However, it took decades before Arian teaching was expunged in the East, and in the West forms of Arianism captivated the Goths and Vandals well into the sixth century.[41]

The issue of the Son's generation was of major importance to the churches that experienced the Arian crisis. In fact, according to Robert Gregg and Dennis Groh, "There is no sharper contrast to be found between Arian and orthodox thinkers than the manner in which these parties construe language of 'begetting.'"[42]

Selected Church Fathers on Eternal Generation

The following words of prominent Christians of late antiquity from Christian communities in Alexandria, Rome, Milan, North Africa, Scythia and elsewhere illustrate the significance of the doctrine of eternal generation in their faith.

> Athanasius (c. 357): "It is right to call the Son the eternal offspring of the Father. For the substance of the Father was never imperfect, so that what belonged to it might be added later. To beget in time is characteristic of man: for man's nature is incomplete; God's offspring is eternal, for his nature is always perfect."[43]

> Hilary of Poitiers (c. 360): "And so we confess that God Only-begotten was born, but born before times eternal: since we must make our confession within such limits as the express preaching of Apostles and Prophets assigns to us; though at the same time human thought cannot grasp any intelligible idea of birth out of time . . . [T]he belief that He was born before times eternal is not only the reasonable conclusion of human intelligence, but the confession of thoughtful faith."[44]

---

40. Need, *Truly Divine and Truly Human*, 53–55. See also Toon, *Yesterday, Today and Forever*, 86–87.

41. On Arianism, see Gwynn, *Eusebians*; Gregg, *Arianism*; McGuckin, "Arianism," 29–30; Williams, "Arianism"; Barnes and Williams, *Arianism After Arius*; Vaggione, *Eunomius*; and Kopecek, *History of Neo-Arianism*.

42. Gregg and Groh, *Early Arianism*, 84.

43. Athanasius *Against the Arians* 1.14 (Bettenson, *Early Christian Fathers*, 276).

44. Hilary of Poitiers *On the Trinity* 12.26 (*NPNF2* 9:224–25).

Ambrose of Milan (c. 378): "The devout spirit affirms a generation that is not in time and so declares Father and Son to be co-eternal."[45]

Ambrosiaster (c. 380): "Christ is the Son of God from eternity."[46]

Augustine (c. 393): "He was begotten before all time, before all ages. 'Begotten before.' Before what, since there is no before with Him? Absolutely do not think of any time before that nativity of Christ whereby He was begotten of the Father ... Do not suppose that in this nativity there was a beginning of time; do not imagine any interval or period of eternity when the Father was and the Son was not ... The Father has always been without beginning, the Son, always without beginning."[47]

Victor of Vita (c. 484): "Therefore, we acknowledge that the Father has everlastingly begotten the Son from himself in an indescribable way."[48]

John Maxentius (c. 521): "If anyone does not confess two births in the one Son of God: God the Word before all ages indeed born of the Father, and in these last times the same born of a mother, let him be anathema."[49]

Fulgentius of Ruspe (d. 533): "On the Birth of the Lord. Concerning the Dual Nativity of Christ, One Eternal from the Father, the Other Temporal from the Virgin ... [This birth] is not transitory but eternal, not made but begotten from God the father, not only begotten but also only-begotten."[50]

---

45. Ambrose of Milan *On the Christian Faith* 1.9.60 (*NPNF2* 10:211).

46. Ambrosiaster *127 Questions on the Old and New Testament*, q. 54 (Souter, *Pseudo-Augustini quaestiones*, 99): "Christus dei filius ex aeterno est ..."

47. Augustine *Creed* 3.8 (Ewald, *Treatises on Marriage*, 295).

48. Victor of Vita, *History of the Vandal Persecution*, 66 (Moorhead, *Victor of Vita*, 48).

49. John Maxentius *Chapters against the Nestorians and Pelagians* 8 (Glorie, *Maxentii aliorumque Scytharum*, 30): "Si quis non confitetur duas nativitates in uno filio dei: deo verbo ante saecula quidem nato de patre, in novissimis autem temporibus eodem de matre genitor, anathema sit."

50. Fulgentius of Ruspe *Sermon 2 on the Birth of the Lord* 1 (Fraipont, *Sancti Fulgentii*,

The Contemporary Church and the Early Chruch

Early Creedal Statements on Eternal Generation

Besides the words of influential Christian writers of the early church, creedal formulations are also a valuable tool for assessing the faith of their adherents. The creedal statements below, gathered from communities in the East and the West, illustrate the importance of the doctrine of the Son's eternal generation for Christians of late antiquity.

> Baptismal Creed of Jerusalem (348): "... in one Lord Jesus Christ, the only begotten Son of God, who was begotten from the Father as true God before all ages."

> Syrian Creed (4th c.): "And in our Lord Jesus Christ, His only-begotten Son, the first-begotten of all creation; Who before ages was born, not created ..."

> Creed of Mopsuestia (383): "And in one Lord Jesus Christ the only-begotten Son of God, the first-begotten of all creation, Who was begotten from His Father before all ages, not made, true God from true God, of one substance with His Father."

> Creed of Antioch (430): "And in our Lord Jesus Christ His only-begotten Son and first-begotten of all creation, born from Him before the ages and not made."[51]

> Athanasian Creed (5th cent.): "The Father is eternal, the Son is eternal, and the Holy Spirit is eternal ... As God He was begotten of the substance of the Father before time; as man He was born in time of the substance of His mother."[52]

> Gallic Creed (500): "[T]he Father is he who begot, and the Son is he who is begotten; the Holy Spirit in truth is neither begotten nor unbegotten, neither created nor made, but proceeding from the Father and the Son, coeternal and coequal and the cooperator with the Father and the Son ... The Father begot the Son, not by

---

899): "IN NATALE DOMINI DE DUPLICI NATIVITATE CHRISTI UNA AETERNA EX PATRE ALTERA TEMPORALI EX VIRGINE ... non transitorium sed aeternum; non factum a Deo Patre sed genitum; nec solum genitum sed etiam unigenitum."

51. Kelly, *Early Christian Creeds*, 183–84, 186–87.
52. "Athanasian Creed" (Fortman, *Triune God*, 159).

will, nor by necessity, but by nature. The Son in the fullness of time came down from the Father to save us..."[53]

Creed of Arles (503-43): "And I believe in Jesus Christ, his only begotten eternal Son."[54]

Early Church Councils on Eternal Generation

Statements of faith formulated by church councils are also a means by which one can ascertain the common faith of Christians. Below are statements on the subject of eternal generation issued by various councils, some regional and some ecumenical, convened in late antiquity.

Council of Constantinople (381): "We believe in . . . one Lord Jesus Christ only begotten Son of God, begotten from the Father before all time."[55]

Council of Rome (382): "Anyone who denies that the Father is always, the Son is always, and the Holy Spirit is always, is a heretic. Anyone who denies that the Son is born of the Father, that is of His divine substance, is a heretic."[56]

Council of Toledo (447): "Therefore this Son of God, God, born of the Father entirely before every beginning, has sanctified the womb of the Blessed Mary Virgin, and from her has assumed true man..."[57]

Council of Chalcedon (451): "Before time began he was begotten of the Father in respect to his deity, and now in these 'last days,' for us and on behalf of our salvation, this selfsame one was born of Mary the virgin... Thus have the prophets of old testified; thus the Lord Jesus Christ himself taught us; thus the Symbol of the fathers has handed down to us."

---

53. The so-called *Faith of Damasus* (Denzinger, *Sources of Catholic Dogma*, 10-11).

54. Kelly, *Early Christian Creeds*, 179: "Credo et in Iesum Christum filium eius unigenitum sempiterum."

55. Leith, *Creeds of the Churches*, 33.

56. Neuner and Dupuis, *Christian Faith*, 100.

57. Denzinger, *Sources of Catholic Dogma*, 13.

Second Council of Constantinople (553): "If anyone does not confess that God the Word was twice begotten, the first before all time from the Father, non-temporal and bodiless, the other in the last days when he came down from the heavens and was incarnate by the holy, glorious, *theotokos*, ever-virgin Mary, and born of her, let him be anathema."[58]

Lateran Council (649): "If anyone does not, according to the holy Fathers, confess truly and properly two births of the one our Lord Jesus Christ Himself, one incorporeal and eternal from God the Father before all ages, the other, corporeal and in the last age, from holy Mary . . . let him be condemned."

Council of Toledo (675): "We also confess that the Son of God was born of the substance of the Father, before all ages, without beginning . . . However the Son is completely equal to God the Father because his birth has not begun in time and has not ceased . . . We must believe that the Son is begotten or born from the womb of the Father, that is, from his very substance. Therefore the Father is eternal and the Son is eternal. If He was always Father, He always had a Son, whose Father He was, and therefore we confess that the Son was born from the Father without beginning . . . Between the Father who generates and the Son who is generated or the Holy Spirit who proceeds, there has not been an interval of time in which the one who generates would precede the one who is generated."[59]

Eternal Generation: The Faith of Our Fathers

Scripture teaches that the Son is co-eternal with the Father. The Son, the brightness of the Father's glory, shared that glory with the Father before the world began. In time, the Father sent the Son into the world to save the lost. In the fourth century, Arius denied the eternality of the Son. In reaction, orthodox bishops, local creeds, regional synods, and ecumenical councils affirmed the biblical doctrine of the Son's eternal generation from the Father. Despite this testimony of so great a cloud of witnesses,

---

58. Leith, *Creeds of the Churches*, 36, 46.
59. Neuner and Dupuis, *Christian Faith*, 103, 166.

Learning from Patristic Christology

some associated with evangelicalism think that the expression of the Son of God as eternally begotten is erroneous.

In the early twentieth century, the Brethren churches experienced division after some in their ranks denied the eternality of the Sonship of Christ. In the 1920s and 1930s the controversy centered on James Taylor of New York who, following the views of F. E. Raven (d. 1903), taught a "temporal Sonship" of Christ. James Taylor Jr. carried the teaching into the mid twentieth century, which among Brethren was confined mainly to those known as Taylor Exclusive Brethren. However, in the 1970s and 1980s many Brethren congregations were beset with people seeking to fellowship who had been influenced by the Taylors' teaching. This resulted in no small output of literature by Brethren publishers defending the eternal Sonship of our Lord.[60]

In the 1990s the denial of Christ's eternal Sonship by John MacArthur caused a major division in the Independent Fundamental Churches of America to which he belongs.[61] Several regional associations issued resolutions upholding the doctrine of eternal Sonship, a critique of McArthur's booklet "The Sonship of Christ" was presented to their National Executive Committee in 1991, and many churches left the association over it.[62] By 1993, several evangelical authors had published books countering MacArthur's view of "incarnational Sonship" and defending our Lord's eternal Sonship.[63] Thankfully, in 1999, MacArthur issued a retraction of his former teaching and affirmed Christ's eternal Sonship in a paper entitled "Reexamining the Eternal Sonship of Christ."[64]

More recently, in the Reformed community, Robert Reymond (an Orthodox Presbyterian pastor, author of numerous books, and professor emeritus of Knox Theological Seminary) denied the doctrine of

---

60. Hocking, *Son of His Love*, a reprint of his papers from the early twentieth century; Ouweneel, *What Is the Sonship of Christ?*; Huebner, *F. E. Raven's Evil Doctrines*; and Dronsfield, *Eternal Son of the Father*.

61. Now simply called the IFCA International.

62. Zeller, "Critique of John MacArthur's Booklet"; and Zeller, "Doctrinal Crisis."

63. Zeller and Showers, *Eternal Sonship of Christ*; and Ross, *Trinity and the Eternal Sonship of Christ*.

64. MacArthur, "Reexamining the Eternal Sonship of Christ."

eternal generation.⁶⁵ Several authors have written articles against this new attack.⁶⁶ The controversy is significant enough that the president of Northwest Theological Seminary in 2007 addressed the issue at the seminary's annual conference, defending the eternal Sonship of Christ from Scripture and nine different Reformed confessions.⁶⁷

While Scripture is the ultimate authority in matters of faith, church history plays a significant role in discerning orthodox from heterodox theology. Of course, the mere presence of a teaching in church history does not make it true. But examining the history of a particular interpretation of Scripture can be helpful. Does the interpretation have a time-honored history, or is it a historical novelty? What were the views of the revered doctors of the church, whom the Holy Spirit illuminated no less than he illuminates us today? Was the interpretation ever formally affirmed or condemned at a church council? These are all valid and useful questions.

While various pre-Nicene fathers of the church did not articulate the doctrine of eternal generation, Christ's eternal Sonship was the faith of the orthodox after Nicaea. It was the faith of Athanasius and Augustine, Ambrose and Hilary, Maxentius and Fulgentius. The eternal generation of the Son was part of the creedal profession of baptizands in orthodox churches all over the inhabited world. In addition, regional and ecumenical councils of bishops representing the entire Christian world affirmed it and anathematized its detractors. The doctrine of Christ's eternal Sonship is not only scriptural; it is the historic faith of our fathers.

---

65. Reymond, *New Systematic Theology*, 341: "[The] two additional propositions that the Son's essence is eternally generated by the Father and that the Spirit eternally and essentially proceeds from the Father and the Son . . . [are] beyond the deliverances of Scripture . . . these last two propositions should not be made elements of Trinitarian orthodoxy."

66. Owen, "Examination of Robert Reymond's Understanding of the Trinity," 262–81; and Bain, "Robert Reymond's Attack." For more on this most recent controversy, see "Eternal Generation of the Son."

67. Dennison, "Remarks on the Current Rejection of the Eternal Generation of the Son."

Engaging with Patristic Christology

During the first several centuries of the Christian era, God's people wrestled with understanding the God-man, our Lord Jesus Christ. When heresies twisted the Scriptures about him, the faithful devoted themselves to explication of the true teaching of Christ revealed to the apostles in Holy Writ. Through the illumination of the Holy Spirit, the same gift that contemporary biblical exegetes possess, they painstakingly explained and defended him who gave his life for them, against demonic counterfeits. It is my hope that an engagement by evangelicals with the Christology of the early church, especially the post-Constantinian church, will strengthen the feeble knees upon which evangelicalism of the late twentieth century was tottering with respect to its Christology.

From my conversion as a college freshman to my current teaching ministry, patristic Christology has aided my faith. It has helped me to be more discerning of Scripture truths about our Lord, has assisted me in solving biblical difficulties, has given me a sense of historical connectedness, and has stirred me with zeal when I have encountered interpretations of Scripture that are available only in patristic texts. In addition it has reaffirmed my faith in the doctrine of the eternal Sonship of Christ. It has caused me to see the ramifications of the scriptural truth that the Word became flesh; for example, that his sufferings were real, that he will come again visibly in the body, and that like us he has a human soul with reason and volition. I am very thankful for the opportunity to study the early Christian writers, especially for the ways they have pointed me to the Lord of glory.

8

Evangelicals and the Quest for the Historical Church —A Lutheran Response

GLEN L. THOMPSON

❦ THERE IS no doubt that in the past two decades, *some* evangelicals have in *some* ways discovered the fathers. Speaking from "the evangelical underground," Tom Oden gave a keynote address to the Evangelical Theological Society (ETS) in 1990 calling more evangelicals to study the post-apostolic and pre-Reformation fathers. The existence of an ETS study group, and indeed this volume, bears witness that the call was heeded by some. Jeff Bingham's plenary address at the ETS annual meeting several years ago would indicate that there are evangelical leaders who are also sympathetic to this endeavor.[1] And each year witnesses an increasing number of publications and papers authored by evangelicals that deal with the fathers—whether in biblical exegesis, church life, or systematic theology.

In the publishing world, the last decade has witnessed a significant evangelical involvement in and appreciation for Oden's *Ancient Christian Commentary on Scripture*.[2] There was also a call to a historical reconnec-

1. In fact, the overall theme of that annual meeting of the Evangelical Theological Society (2005) was "Christianity in the Early Centuries."

2. The series, published by InterVarsity Press, was completed in 2008 and has fourteen volumes for each of the two testaments. Parts have already been published in numerous other European and Asian languages as well.

tion with the early church and its teachings, even if this meant learning from Catholic scholars, as exhibited by Eerdman's substantial series entitled Ressourcement: Retrieval and Renewal in Catholic Thought. This in turn spurred Dan Williams and Baker to produce their own thoughtful series in our present decade, Evangelical Ressourcement: Ancient Sources for the Church's Future. The subtitle of that series evoked the terminology of Robert Webber, an evangelical scholar who stimulated vigorous debate with his calls for a liturgical and meditative reconnection with the early church and its practices.

Thus, it might seem that this volume is merely a matter of celebrating what has occurred, commenting on its highpoints, and calling for more of the same. However, as most of the essayists have indicated, there is still no agreement in evangelical circles whether the patristic Holy Grail has yet been found, whether it can be, and even whether it is important to do so. And for evangelicals, and in particular the members of ETS, it is noteworthy that Oden, Williams, and Webber, while often writing for evangelicals, never became leading figures in ETS. In fact, any number of scholars who began their lives in evangelical ministry and then "found the fathers" ended in non-evangelical denominations. As a result, on some evangelical fronts the fathers are viewed as sirens luring believers to the rocks of Canterbury, Constantinople, or Rome.

The contributions in this volume have included personal testimonies concerning how the fathers have enriched the theology, spirituality, and practice of the authors. The present writer is an evangelical Lutheran who has been a regular participant in ETS for the past two decades and has seen the growing interest in patristics mentioned above.[3] At the same time, while always warmly received within the ETS family, as a confessional Lutheran I have always been somewhat of an outsider, unable to connect with many of the debates and tensions that have washed over the ETS and the conservative free churches in

---

3. As long as Bebbington's four characteristics of evangelicals (cf. Hartog above, p. 8) are not interpreted through glasses too colored with Arminian theology, evangelical Lutherans can truly qualify as evangelicals. However, their biblical centeredness would include the sacraments, the Word made visible; their central theology of the cross would not exclude the importance of the active righteousness of Christ; and their stress on personal conversion would center on the revivification by the Spirit to the exclusion of a synergistic contribution by the sinner.

America. In response to this fine set of papers, I will attempt to use that view from the fringe to take another look at the issue of the current and future evangelical church and the early fathers. In order to provide this panoramic view, the details will of necessity be sketchy. My presentation will look at the search for the apostolic church, the question of what exactly has been handed down to us, the proper attitudes and skills necessary for proper use of the church's tradition, and finally problems that are particular to the evangelical church in properly appropriating the wisdom of the early church.

In Search of the Apostolic Church

Πιστεύομεν ... εἰς μίαν ἁγίαν καθολικὴν καὶ ἀποστολικὴν ἐκκλησίαν. "We believe ... in one holy, universal, and apostolic Church."[4] I would hope that all evangelicals would agree with this venerable statement from the Nicene Creed. From one point of view, the history of the church has been a debate over the proper interpretation of these words and, in particular, over what exactly the *apostolic* church is. Many evangelical churches, and especially non-denominational congregations, advertise that they are New Testament churches. By doing so they are indicating, often intentionally, that they find little positive to learn from the history of the church. By directly accessing the New Testament scriptures without any input from the last two millennia of interpretation, and by imitating New Testament congregational practices, they claim to be the pure "apostolic church." While this idea appeared among the Waldensians and other medieval groups, and although its modern incarnation can be traced to the Anabaptists and other non-conformist churches of the sixteenth and seventeenth centuries, its blossoming in America during the last century was energized by the high value placed on individualism, self-sufficiency, and visible success in gathering the harvest.

One result of this burgeoning movement has been to put the Reformation churches on the defensive. Since the sixteenth century,

---

4. Transliterating the Greek word as "catholic" is both confusing and anachronistic. The word meant "general," or "universal," and was used in the fourth-century church to distinguish the church from its smaller break-off groups—Montanists, Novatians, Donatists, Arians, etc.

Lutherans, Anglicans and Episcopalians, Presbyterians and the Reformed churches have all seen *themselves* as embodying the "apostolic church." They threw off the traditions each identified as being harmful accruals to the Western church during the previous millennium. Most, however, retained some of the inheritance of the early churches—creeds, doctrinal formulations, and some rites and practices. The Reformers, moreover, avidly studied and quoted the fathers both for their own study of Scripture and in order to demonstrate that their teachings were not innovations, but merely a return to the teachings of the early church, as Hartog has pointed out.[5] However, soon the Reformers and their chief disciples themselves became *fathers* of their respective movements, and *they* were increasingly cited rather than the earlier post-canonical fathers. This in turn led to new generations of believers who were ignorant of the writings and practices of the post-apostolic church, leaving the latter as the exclusive domain of Roman Catholics and the Eastern Orthodox. Thus, illogically and unintentionally, the early fathers were labeled as less than useful reading, a sort of concomitant guilt by association.

If we as evangelical patristics scholars are calling for a return *ad fontes*, one of the first realities that we need to face is that every such call is itself shaped by a particular view of the early church. Williams writes long and hard to dispel the idea of a fourth-century "fall" of the church, and if he is right, study of the sixth-century fathers should be as useful as reading the third-century writers.[6] Everett Ferguson, as cited approvingly by Hartog, stresses the importance of the second-century fathers, and in so doing, seems to imply some sort of third-century fall. Such views more likely depend on an individual's view of the growing power and importance of certain ecclesiological structures than scholarly evaluations of the doctrinal formulations of a specific period. In other words, each person's ideal conception of the "apostolic church" is formed, at least initially, by his or her church background and upbringing as much as by an examination of early church history. Thus, as evangelical patristics scholars, we must help produce an accurate and comprehensive (i.e., theological, ecclesiological, and historical) picture of the church's development and

5. See Hartog above, pp. 4–5.

6. See especially Williams, *Retrieving the Tradition*, ch. 4 (101–31); Litfin also questions such a fall in his *Getting to Know the Church Fathers*, 24–28.

the role played by the primitive church. In so far as we can agree on that picture, we will have a basis for developing a more consistent evangelical agreement on the development of the true apostolic church.

What Has Been Handed Down

The situation can also be approached from the viewpoint of that loaded term "tradition." This word stirs up emotions amid evangelicals as strongly as they stirred up Tevye in *Fiddler on the Roof*. We would all agree with Paul when he tells Timothy, "The things which you have heard from me in the presence of many witnesses, entrust these to faithful men who will be able to teach others also" (2 Tim 2:2, NASB). But how are we today to ascertain which are the authentic "things handed down"?

Evangelicals, and Protestants in general, have to a great extent restricted the "things handed down" to the canonical Scriptures. Logically this would result, at least in theory, in restricting points of discussion to matters of textual criticism and textual interpretation. If this is so, of what value is the primitive Rule of Faith that is described above so cogently by Bryan Litfin? Does it merely encapsulate or summarize the teachings of Scripture, or does it also *expound* the faith? Roman Catholics and Eastern Orthodox alike consider additional teachings and customs to be "handed down"—traditions that they see as complementary to, even if they are not specifically mentioned in, Holy Scripture.[7] Can evangelicals allow for logical extensions of biblical teaching?[8] And although evangelicals agree on the principle of *sola Scriptura* in matters of doctrine, what about matters of practice? The early church demonstrates widespread use of baptismal creeds, the "Te Deum" and other liturgical rites, penitential practices, formal and public excommunication of those supporting deviant moral and doctrinal positions, reverence for and liturgical remembrance of

---

7. For a Protestant equivalent, see n. 27 below on the concept of *norma normata*.

8. Evangelical Lutherans view the Reformed teaching of predestination to hell as such a logical extension of the biblical teaching of predestination to salvation, but view this as contradictory to the clear teaching that God wants all to be saved. This is just one example of how evangelicals who share a commitment to the principle of *sola Scriptura* have still had trouble agreeing on what is scriptural and what is not.

martyrs and the like. Since these are largely "post-biblical" witnesses to the faith, are they to be ignored, studied, or imitated?[9]

And what about the things that have *not* been handed down? Although arguments from silence are innately problematic, is it possible for us to learn also from the fathers' silence on certain matters? For example, Matz has pointed out that the fathers seemed to be unaware of institutional patterns of oppression, or at least concentrated all their efforts on changing individual rather than corporate behavior in regards to slavery and poverty.[10] It would appear to me that such silence may not be due to the accidents of preservation of our source material, but rather may well reflect a *theological position*. While not denying the existence of corporate or institutionalized patterns of behavior that are evil, this silence rather reflects a deep-seated biblical understanding that the church's sole focus is the conversion of souls rather than the conversion of systems, and that it relies on those converted souls to then change or dismantle the ungodly systems to the best of their ability.

This in turn leads to the even more vexing question of authority—who gets to decide? The New Testament does not clearly and specifically set up one binding form of church administration and decision-making. So where does this authority lie? Is it *totally* up to each individual, or to majority vote—the alternatives most favored in our own Western cultural tradition? Many of the most common evangelical responses to such questions appear to be radical reactions to the position of "the enemy"—a Catholicism which has too often claimed antiquity for less-than-ancient practices and teachings, and which has restricted the decision-making process to a very limited hierarchy. Can a study of the fathers help us to make more "biblical" decisions about what is allowable and beneficial for the church and its faith life? Can the fathers help us take another look at what Hartog has properly identified as this "nagging question of authority"?[11]

---

9. In this area, Hartog's distinction between extra-apostolic and anti-apostolic practices is useful (see Hartog above, p. 18).

10. Matz above, pp. 140, 152.

11. Hartog above, p. 19.

Finding Allies or Learning from the Faithful?

This leads us to the question of methodology in using the fathers. What sort of groundedness and historical perspective will the fathers give us if we only listen to them in some matters and ignore them in others? The preceding essays have demonstrated that there is much gold to be found in the vast mines carved out by the fathers. But how does one know what gold is genuine and what is merely fool's gold? What objective criteria have we developed for distinguishing the pearls of great price? Or, to change the metaphor to our great American commercial tradition, have the fathers become a mall where we spend a few minutes window shopping at one establishment before browsing in the next shop, looking for something that catches our eye, something that complements our personal or denominational theological décor?

If so, I would argue that the fathers would be horrified. This type of cafeteria approach—choosing what we want and like, and bypassing the rest—is totally inimical to the tradition that "*all* Scripture is given for our learning." Does not such an approach lead its practitioners into becoming ecclesiastical, dogmatic, and/or hermeneutical Marcionites, people who reject whole sections of early church faith and practice while keeping those that agree with their own theological presuppositions? Are we historical Marys or Marthas? Do we sit at the feet of the fathers, or do we merely busy ourselves seeking new patristic condiments to spice up the meal we had already prepared? Are we searching for new allies or are we seeking also to discover new insights from our elders in the faith? The use of the fathers for our own apologetic purposes may reacquaint the modern church with the names of the fathers whom we quote or footnote, but this will not have a significant impact on the church or provide any real *ressourcement*. On the other hand, a disciplined, systematic, and devotional yet critical interaction with the fathers might provide a significant impulse toward church renewal on a variety of fronts. This is the critical appropriation for which Hartog cogently argues.[12]

The Council of Trent was a total victory for the scholastic or Thomist version of doctrine, practice, and culture in the Roman church. This entailed the loss of the more evangelical, Augustinian, and mysti-

---

12. Ibid., pp. 24–26.

cal components of late medieval theology. The Catholic *ressourcement* movement of the twentieth century, by reconnecting with the fathers, has to some degree allowed those latter voices to be heard again. In the same way, a true evangelical reconnection with the fathers could help us overcome denominational (or non-denominational) doctrinal and cultural conceits that may be historical accruals, and open our eyes to other possibilities. Of course, as evangelicals, we will test those new ideas in the refining fires of Holy Scripture. But rather than having only our own new ideas, we will also have the ideas of generations of devout men of God, many of whom spoke the language of the New Testament as their native tongue, lived in a culture very similar to the cultures of the Old and New Testaments, and often had their faith tested in ways we cannot imagine. Should we not use such men as more than mere allies, but also as mentors? If so, the ETS and its Patristics and Medieval History Section could be one of the places where not only a systematic rationale but also evangelical guidelines for the use of the fathers could be hammered out and presented to the evangelical community in volumes subsequent to this one.

Counting the Cost

If we are in agreement that this "quest for the historical church"[13] would be of value to our modern evangelical church, we must finally ask: What will it take to do this? Do we have the human and spiritual resources to undertake such a quest? If the church itself becomes convinced of the necessity for it, the God of the church will certainly provide the gifts necessary. Let me, however, mention just three areas where a specific effort will be needed to achieve this goal.

First of all, accessing the fathers is hard work. A serious interaction with the fathers must be led by skilled evangelical scholars. This requires scholars with a thorough theological training, not just in the biblical languages, but in addition a thorough acquaintance with the fathers themselves and the historical world (religiously, economically, politically, socially, and linguistically) in which the fathers lived and worked. Without this the fathers themselves can be too easily misinter-

13. See Rowan Williams, *Why Study the Past? The Quest for the Historical Church.*

preted. This will itself take academic time, effort, and discipline. It will require institutions and donor individuals willing to support this kind of effort, which until now has not been viewed as of very high importance in the evangelical community. Also, it will require scholars adept not only at Greek and Latin, but also at Coptic and Syriac, and a few who can also work in Armenian, Georgian, Ethiopian, and the like. We will need evangelical scholars to read about these fathers in studies, translations, and commentaries written in German, French, Italian and other modern languages.[14] Only then will we be able to interact with the entire tradition of the fathers. The writers in this present volume are the "firstfruits" (both chronologically and in ability) in this evangelical effort, and the number of younger evangelical scholars interested in this field has risen from almost nil to several dozen, thanks to the efforts of those such as Jeff Bingham.[15] So a good start has been made, and this must be continued and followed up by institutional funding and academic positions for such scholars and by new programs at evangelical institutions of higher learning that will supply high-level training for future evangelical patrologists. And since the areas of expertise are so numerous and specialized, evangelical patristics scholars should increasingly think in terms of teamwork in tackling the projects that await us. Thanks to the Internet and other modern communication options, such joint projects are more feasible than ever before.[16]

---

14. Nowhere is the evangelical absence from patristic studies more evident than in the bibliography of editions and secondary studies of the fathers during the past two centuries. A few Anglican scholars have made outstanding contributions to the field, most notably M. J. Routh with his five-volume *Reliquae sacrae*, J. B. Lightfoot with his classic *Apostolic Fathers*, and the editors and translators of *Ante-Nicene Fathers* and *Nicene and Post-Nicene Fathers*, which ran to 38 vols. in its American edition. However, excepting the contributions of American Catholic scholars, there has been a dearth of English language publications in the field. This makes the ability to access other European-language studies more critical than in most other fields of theological scholarship.

15. The essays in this volume do demonstrate, however, how our current evangelical scholars are for the most part still limited to a study of the Greek and Latin fathers.

16. For an example, see this author's www.fourthcentury.com Web site. Note that it is intended to be a clearing house for scholarship. An online patristic bibliography, and online versions of *Clavis Patrum Latinorum* and *Clavis Patrum Graecorum* (as well as Syriac and Coptic equivalents) could easily be organized and constantly updated for the benefit of the entire scholarly world. It is feared, however, that the current copyrights will

A second area that requires serious change is much more difficult for many evangelicals to comprehend. Evangelicals must learn to better distinguish between evangelical teaching and practice and revivalist and other evangelical cultural forms. With our long interest in cross-cultural mission work, one would not expect this to be a major issue. However, from my seat on the fringe, this is a most pressing problem. We will never be able to sit at the feet of the fathers in a useful way if we can only picture them as primitive versions of Pat Robertson or Bill Hybels. We cannot expect altar calls in the sermons of John Chrysostom, or simplistically interpret early house churches in light of modern cell groups.[17] We must first be able to accurately put ourselves into the intellectual and religious situation of second-century paganism and then listen to what Justin Martyr (or another father) is telling us.[18] Once we

continue to make free access the exception. Publishing houses such as Brill have been involved in digitizing many patristic Christian texts and tools, but their prices have assured that they will only be accessible in major research libraries. The best way to lobby those involved for more open access to digital resources and to move forward on new projects would be for the North American Patristics Society to take up the cause and develop and give long-term support to such projects.

17. See Butler above, p. 70. Home groups of megachurches may actually be closer to what the New Testament house churches were like than other types of house churches, at least in one basic sense. There must have been many house churches in a large Greco-Roman metropolis, but the apostles and apostolic fathers stress the importance of all the Christians in an area meeting together on the Lord's Day (i.e., in bigger groups). This may be the meaning of Heb 10:25; see also Ignatius *Ephesians* 5:3, 13:1, and 20:2; Ignatius *Polycarp* 4.2; Justin *1 Apol.* 67; and *Canons of Elvira* 21. If we remember that literacy and texts were scarce, it is doubtful that "Bible study" could have taken place in the smaller groups, and hence they functioned more as support and prayer groups in contrast to the larger teaching assembly. The fathers warn about the "largely self-organizing groups" mentioned by Butler, and insist on their connection to and participation in other larger Christian bodies (local, national, and international).

18. Smither's discussion above of early evangelism is somewhat confusing due to his use of modern categories. Thus when he speaks of "official, full-time evangelists" as preaching publicly (p. 31), of bishops and others who were part-time evangelists, and of lay evangelists who were "anonymous" (pp. 32–34), it would seem more accurate and helpful to speak of "appointed" leaders who were charged with evangelism as part of their official church duties, and Christians who evangelized as members of the universal priesthood, even though they were not officially appointed to do so in the name of the church. People in both categories may have done so full-time or part-time (and the same person may have done both, depending on seasonal work and weather cycles), and neither were probably paid, except in kind, or in donations for future ministry. In fact it was

hear in their original contexts what the fathers stressed in their addresses to the unchurched and in their sermons to believers, then we can think through how our contemporary messages and practices might be shaped or improved upon today. Thus we will avoid the simplistic "primitivism" and "restorationism" of which Hartog warned.[19]

For example, Smither notes that "articulated" or "recorded testimonies" were one component of early evangelism.[20] While it is true that Paul did recount his testimony on several occasions, it is interesting to note that these tended to be in settings where he was being attacked physically or legally. And Augustine's great *Confessions* is so well-known at least in part because its genre is so unique. Most early "recorded testimonies," as Smither shows a few pages later, were recorded by Christians who told the stories of their own heroes of faith (martyrs, bishops, monks); they did not tell their own stories. Thus the roots of the modern custom of formal and informal "personal testimonies" as part of church services or evangelistic crusades does not readily seem to appear in the earliest centuries. However, such comparisons can and should be investigated, but in a thorough and scholarly way. Indeed, as we strip ourselves of our own cultural assumptions in order to transport ourselves accurately into the ancient world, we should be able to see more accurately which parts of our faith life are cultural and what parts belong to the core Christian worldview. That is why a study of the fathers must be historically based and not merely theologically based. Such an exercise could have stun-

---

said that heretics could be easily identified because they accepted money for preaching the Word! Early Christians were to be found at every social and economic level, and most reached out primarily to those on their own level in the course of their daily lives. Thus the use of modern terms such as full- and part-time, official and anonymous are more confusing than helpful.

19. Hartog above pp. 15–18. Matz mentions the 400-year gap between society in Jesus's time and that of Jerome and Asterius (p. 152). The conservatism of ancient life and culture made such a time span less critical than a half-century period in our day. In many cases it was not necessary for ancient preachers to contextualize New Testament stories much at all for their audiences. However, they still needed to apply the message to their hearers. I would emphasize more than he does the help that the fathers can provide us in properly understanding the historical and cultural situation.

20. Smither above, p. 35.

ning implications for evangelicalism as it reinvents itself in the face of our postmodern age.

Thirdly, we must learn to listen to all the voices. The old adage is most certainly true: it is much easier to be a good speaker than a good listener. If we are going to learn from the fathers, we must learn to be good listeners—and that means listening to all the voices. Not that all voices are of equal value, nor will we listen uncritically, but we must know all the voices if we are going to understand the context of the fathers and be able to hear their message accurately.

Good listeners also often rephrase and play back what they have heard to make sure they understand what was said—"So you are saying that . . ." We must do the same with the fathers— in our ETS patristics study group, and when we participate in the wider world of the North American Patristics Society and other scholarly venues. This is another crucial aspect of papers and volumes like this one: they are a check on our own understanding of what the fathers are saying. Only when we have ascertained what the fathers are really saying can we then proceed to evaluate and learn from them.

Listening to all the voices also requires linguistic capabilities. As mentioned earlier, we must also listen to those speaking Syriac and Coptic, Armenian and Georgian. It is no accident that the French Catholic *ressourcement* movement of the twentieth century led to the magnificent Sources Chrétiennes series of some two hundred volumes and counting—volumes that have the original text with a facing-page French translation. Do we need a similar series for evangelicals today? The nineteenth-century Nicene and Post-Nicene Fathers series can still whet appetites, but it no longer captures the interest of twenty-first-century audiences, and certainly does not reflect the current state of scholarship. Can we count on evangelicals to go to Paulist Press to read the Ancient Christian Writers volumes or Catholic University of America Press to find the Fathers of the Church or Library of Early Christianity series? While the Ancient Christian Commentary on Scripture is a wonderful resource in its own right, it is crucial that we also read whole texts so that we do not simply use the fathers for their interpretational gems or for prooftexting our previous interpretations. And yet selecting key texts for translation can also contribute to silencing other voices. There is no easy answer to this problem, and it is not unique to the evangelical world.[21] Perhaps for the present we can at least agree to acknowledge the issue and strive to hear the often unheard voices.[22]

One final thought that applies to the study of the fathers concerns the wider context. The patristic record shows us how the Hebrew Scriptures and the message of the Jewish carpenter and his Jewish disciples were incarnated into Greco-Roman and Middle Eastern cultures. In many ways the variety of modern Christian practice reflects a variety of opinion on whether this early incarnation is normative for modern Christians or merely appropriate for its own day. Should we return to early ecclesiological and liturgical practices, adapt them, or merely observe what they were and apply certain principles to our own situations? Patristics scholars should be in the forefront of this conversation. And if it is to bear fruit, it must again be based on an accurate understanding of the wider historical context of the ancient world.[23]

---

21. Lucifer of Cagliari and Marcellus of Ancyra are good examples of fourth-century fathers whose marginalization began in their own day but has continued until the present in part because of a lack of the preservation and translation of their works. And have we yet heard Nestorius' voice, or only what he is supposed to have said and taught through the voice of Cyril and his other opponents, or in the minutes of a hostile council? Despite recent re-evaluations of his theology, no English translation of his entire surviving corpus has yet appeared.

22. Oden's recent *How Africa Shaped the Christian Mind* is a good example of seeking to see the fathers more honestly and contextually, in this case from a more African point of view. His book, however, also illustrates the dangers of over-correction and over-statement. Patristics does not need to replace *Black Athena* with a "Black Tertullian"! However, the source for much of what Oden says about Tertullian, Wilhite's *Tertullian the African*, does give reason for a serious reconsideration of how this father has been read.

23. This task must begin with biblical exegesis. Unfortunately, we have yet to develop a consistent evangelical methodology for distinguishing what is cultural and what is normative in the biblical text. For an evangelical call for the proper reading of Old Testament prophecy, see Sandy, *Plowshares & Pruning Hooks*. For an attempt to delineate a larger methodology, cf. Webb, *Slaves, Women & Homosexuals*. While Webb's work has received mixed reviews at best, I am unaware of any subsequent yet equally broad attempt in this area.

Evangelical Problems

None of the problems just mentioned—committing time, resources, and academic rigor to the study of the fathers, dealing with our own cultural baggage, and listening to all the voices—are uniquely evangelical problems. They face all those who would sit at the feet of the fathers. I will conclude with a few areas where evangelicals face especially challenging issues in becoming properly connected with the early church.

First of all, even notoriously independent evangelicals often join forces in order to publicly acknowledge and impact important issues that face them. Yet, not only does the evangelical community not have a single voice, but it almost always speaks with competing voices in such matters. In fact, it is hard even to agree on who is an evangelical and who is not. In a few key matters, however, evangelicals coalesce around an issue—the Lausanne Committee in response to ecumenism, the recent Evangelical Manifesto, etc. Who will coalesce around a proper reconnection with the fathers? Robert Webber, Dan Williams, and several others put out "The Call to an Ancient-Evangelical Future" in 2006, and it has been followed up by an annual conference in Chicago, but this has not received the broad attention it deserves within the evangelical community.[24] The more recent 2008 Evangelical Manifesto did acknowledge "the 'universality' of the Christian church across the centuries," and claimed to look "equally to both the past and the future," but one will look in vain for specific encouragement that the study of the fathers can be a tool in reclaiming our evangelical identity and mandate.[25]

Another special issue for evangelicals is their suspicion of authority. The premise that Scripture alone is authoritative has led many to the conclusion that this allows for no other authority. While the Reformers subscribed to extra-canonical summaries and explanations of their teaching and practice (Westminster Confession, Augsburg Confession, Thirty-Nine Articles, etc.), evangelicals cannot even agree on subscribing to *Christianity Today*![26] In fact, even the three ecumenical creeds are

---

24. Webber, "Call to an Ancient-Evangelical Future."

25. "Evangelical Manifesto," 4, 6.

26. The General Baptist Orthodox Creed of 1678, mentioned above by Hartog (above, p. 5), could be added to this list to show that such documents are not even outside the "free church" tradition!

viewed with suspicion or simply ignored by some. This tendency to avoid giving authority to any non-canonical writing is distinctly modern. Perhaps it should be viewed as an evangelical version of postmodernism. If we are no longer willing to accept the teachings of Luther, Calvin, Knox, or Wesley as anything more than our own individual preferences, how will we possibly find a study of the fathers useful?[27]

Another post-Reformation trait of much evangelicalism is shallowness of teaching. At least in part this has been inherited from Protestant fundamentalism in the narrow sense. The importance of and stress on some core doctrines has led to dismissing or at least minimizing the importance of many others. Since other teachings are less fundamental, i.e., less important, they are not as thoroughly studied and, as a result, are often less thoroughly understood.[28] In fact, since they can be viewed as less important, many evangelicals further conclude that there is no need for Christians to be agreed on these teachings at all. Thus varieties of belief on baptism, the Lord's Supper, and the end of the world are tolerated within the same group, or simply not discussed in depth.[29] The disagreements on such teachings in turn lead some to view Scripture as being nebulous in its teaching, and so modern expositors can either avoid taking a position at all, or present their own as mere informed opinion. All the Reformers (and most fathers) would have decried such an approach, but it has become widespread, fueling the non-denominational movement, and often leading to very superficial preaching and exposi-

---

27. In this discussion it might be useful to begin with the sixteenth-century distinction between Scripture as the *norma normans* (the norm that norms all else) and the *norma normata* (norms that are such because they conform to the ultimate norm of Scripture).

28. One can see this influence also in pastoral training or the lack thereof. If the scriptural message can be boiled down to a few core fundamentals that must be shared with all nations, why bother learning Greek and Hebrew—or learning about church history or reading the fathers?

29. This has also led to a total dismissal of the early church's concept of fellowship and the need to break fellowship or excommunicate those who were not in agreement in all doctrinal points. Note the early church's use of "letters of communication" given to traveling Christians, positively identifying them as being of the true faith and thus eligible to partake in worship and the Lord's Supper in other congregations.

tion of many biblical texts.[30] People who know the fundamentals and need nothing else will certainly not be interested in reading the fathers, either devotionally or for instruction. Thus, in many parts of the broader evangelical spectrum, this attitude needs to be urgently addressed and should be of concern even to those with no interest in the fathers. And many evangelical patristics scholars, from a variety of traditions, will not agree with Matz that holding on to "Trinitarianism, a full Christology, expository preaching and a commitment to social justice" is a sufficient inheritance for us Christians to appropriate after 2000 years![31]

A third issue among evangelicals is what might be termed a tendency *toward bibliolotry*. I do not say this lightly. My own brand of Lutheranism (WELS) has been accused of bibliolotry by others within the Lutheran Church. Evangelical Christians by definition should be able to subscribe to the ETS statement: "The Bible alone, and the Bible in its entirety, is the Word of God written and is therefore inerrant in the autographs." But evangelicals should also acknowledge that the Word enters a person's heart and accomplishes its life-giving work through the *preaching* of that written message. Evangelicals should agree that Scripture is not life-giving in some magical way. We do not chant the syllables in Greek or Hebrew like some magician with his wand. And therefore, we acknowledge that throughout history God has raised up *people* to plant the seed of the Word through preaching and teaching, and that the Spirit has then produced fruit on that planted and watered seed.

However, within evangelical circles Christians at times have taken this proper teaching of Scripture as the "Word of God written," and drawn improper conclusions from it. Because it alone is inspired, it is the only book we need read. Thus, why read the fathers when we can read the Book itself? Why? For the same reason that we still go to church on Sunday and hear the Word "preached" to us rather than merely recited. Preaching has its place. But what gives a modern megachurch preacher the right to claim his message is what I need, while that of the great Augustine is not worth my time? One can argue that there is an ephem-

30. This is also partly due to the "paranoia" of creedal Christianity that Williams describes. See Williams, *Tradition, Scripture, and Interpretation*, 18, cited by Hartog above, p. 19.

31. Cf. Matz above, p. 132.

eral nature to much of modern hymnody, liturgical practice and preaching, while the works of the fathers, as the later Reformers, have stood the test of time. However, this is an argument that needs more public exploration, and Webber and Williams have already begun this in several of their books.[32] We must learn that there can be study of the fathers, use of the creeds, and subscription to Reformation confessions without denying or undercutting our allegiance to Holy Scripture. This would have been vehemently supported by the fathers, the Reformers, and the councils that produced our creeds. And it is a matter that evangelicals must seriously and prayerfully confront today.

Several times I have mentioned the individualistic impulse of modern evangelicalism. This impulse to just "do my own thing" has significant theological implications. The church has always been identified as the "gathering of believers." We might say, therefore, that the church is more than the sum of its individual believers, or individual congregations. Although the Reformers believed that the Nicene Creed's "*one holy, universal, and apostolic church*" may only be revealed in its true form and membership in heaven, they also felt compelled to imitate that heavenly gathering as closely as possible here on earth—creating local, regional, national, and international denominations of those like-minded in their beliefs. They did this with the full knowledge and confession that, unlike Rome's claim, their denominations did not consist of *all* the saved; nor did they believe that all within their particular denominations were saved. But to go to the other extreme, to forget about earthly groupings of Christians who did their best to imitate Christ in doctrine and practice was also seen as totally unacceptable. Many forms of non-denominationalism, however, have gone much further than the Reformers in minimizing the importance of Christian interconnectedness beyond the congregational level, or at least limiting that interconnectedness to commonality in prayer and friendship. On the other end, some evangelicals have been caught up in the ecumenical movement and have either returned to the fold of Roman Catholicism or the Eastern Orthodox Church, or helped craft statements of commonality between the latter churches and evangelicals.

32. See in particular, Williams, *Retrieving the Tradition*; as well as Webber, *Ancient-Future Faith*.

I believe a proper and comprehensive interaction with the fathers can prevent improper reactions at both ends of the spectrum. The fathers will remind us that the early church followed Paul in seeking to connect Christians not only locally, but regionally and internationally. On the other hand, the fathers also model for us proper Christian separation—"loving the Lord" could mean many things and was not in and of itself reason for common ecclesiastical support and activity. Councils were held which not only confirmed beliefs via creedal statements, but which also added anathemas—statements about what teachings and practices were fatal to faith, fellowship, and ultimately salvation.[33] These models can be instructive to the modern evangelical church as well, so that it will both be willing to dialogue with those of other traditions, but also so that this will not lead to a sellout of true biblical theology. The early controversies can help us not only learn how Christians conducted such a debate, but remind us that we must deal with past disagreements first, and that "starting from scratch" is normally a way of avoiding or minimizing disagreements rather than addressing and overcoming them.

Conclusion—or Beginning?

In the first half of the seventeenth century, the Strasbourg cleric John Georg Dorsch (1597–1654) coined the term *consensus quinque saecularis* (i.e., a consensus of the first five centuries) to denote the teachings of the church before its medieval corruption. A few years later, the Lutheran theologian George Calixt built on this idea, if not the term itself, in his quest for an outward unity for the church.[34] Some sections of the modern

---

33. Unfortunately, the creedal anathemas are almost totally unknown today. The Nicene anathemas were dropped after the defeat of Arianism, probably because they seemed irrelevant. While we may not wish to reintroduce them in the liturgy, they might well be reintroduced in other ways. Theologically they would be beneficial in our age of superficial and confused Christology, and they would also serve as a good example that doctrinal discussions need to include more than positive statements of agreement.

34. See Piepkorn, "Calixt(us), George," 350. It is important to note that Calixtus spoke of agreement on the fundamental articles. He sought "das Wesen des Christentums in das katholische Fundament," which was based on the narrower *Fundamentalen oder Heilsnotwendigen* (cf. Schüssler, *Georg Calixt*, 41–46). Though even his fundamentals were defined more broadly than those of twentieth-century fundamentalism, the outcome still was to privilege some teachings as more important than others. On Calixtus and

ecumenical movement have used this same idea as a tool in their quest, and people with evangelical beliefs such as Tom Oden might be numbered in this group.[35] However, delineating such a consensus has proven elusive for its proponents, leaving it up to the individual in many cases to determine what the consensus was on some points. In addition, there is still the very real question of whether this will end in a substantially diminished body of doctrine.

Thus we evangelical scholars are firmly planted on the horns of a patristic dilemma. On the one hand, the more we study the patristic sources and listen to all the voices, the more evident it is that unanimity never did exist among all Christians on all teachings and practices at any time after the Apostles. On the other hand, it is equally obvious to us evangelicals that there is no foundation to the widespread modern assertion that Pauline Christianity was *essentially* different from Johannine or Matthean Christianity, or that what became orthodoxy was just one of many equally valid first- and second-century versions of Christianity.

So the fact remains that, while the Apostle Paul's opponents are easily judged heretical by all evangelicals, there has been much less agreement in our evaluation of some teachings and practices of the church fathers. Aspects of baptism, the Lord's Supper, and the end of the world, are just a few of the teachings over which some early fathers disagree, as the Reformation fathers realized and attested, and about which consensus still has not been reached except along traditional denominational lines. So the question remains: how can continued study of disagreeing early fathers help us reach agreement today? At the same time, it is even

---

later proponents of this approach see also Mueller, "Molanus," 197–218, esp. 198. Werner Elert faults Calixt's use of Vincent of Lerin's famous dictum because Calixt emphasized *universality* and *antiquity* and minimized the importance of *agreement*. Elert, Structure of Lutheranism, 287.

35. Oden put together a detailed study of doctrine in three volumes (*Living God; Word of Life;* and *Life in the Spirit*) which expounded the Christian doctrine "upon which there has generally been substantial agreement between the traditions of East and West, including Catholic, Protestant, and Orthodox," thus finding a "deeper, ecumenical consensus." *Living God,* ix. In so doing, he admits openly that this has led him to seek consensus positions, and disregard differences (xii). But he does not spell out in detail how much agreement he needed to find to declare consensus on an issue. And how does one deal with positions such as "semi-Pelagianism" that became consensus positions in large parts of the church over many centuries?

more questionable that progress on these key questions (What is meant by the apostolic church? What did it teach? Who are its current heirs?) can be made without a serious study of the early fathers. Here we have perhaps the ultimate *raison d'être* for our study group. Could we seek to work out a more nuanced approach to evaluating the teachings and practices of the fathers, one that remains evangelical and christocentric, brutally honest and yet reverent and inclusive in its use of the sources? Might we be able to do what textual critics have done in their field— delineate a nuanced yet consistent *methodology* with guidelines for properly evaluating the fathers?[36] And if that is a worthy goal, who could do it better than this group, which approaches the subject from a variety of denominational perspectives and yet has both an unwavering belief in the sacred scriptural texts and a profound respect for the patristic legacy that grew from them? Again, this could start with the foundation laid by the Reformation fathers and their careful examination of the relation between their own understanding of *sola Scriptura*, their embracing of the early creeds, and their firm adherence to sixteenth-century statements of faith.[37] It is doubtful to the present writer whether even the

36. It should be noted that the twentieth-century "canons" of biblical textual criticism (especially in regard to the New Testament) have increasingly come under fire with the development of postmodern approaches to the field and the new dominance of *reasoned eclecticism* in the field. Most scholars, however, still find the traditional rules extremely useful in the day-to-day task of evaluating variant readings. And even Bart Ehrman did not jettison the traditional criteria for evaluating variants when revising Bruce Metzger's classic work. See Metzger and Ehrman, *Text of the New Testament*, 300–315.

37. See the study of Elert in *Structure of Lutheranism*. He distinguishes between the early Lutheran fathers' *obeying* Scripture while *embracing* the old creeds. This allowed them to access "the great stream of theological thinking which, after all, did not have its beginning in Wittenberg" and yet at the same time kept them from "running wild" (208). Thus patristic writings did not have a "formal authority" for the entire church, but were to be taken "seriously—subject to criticism in detail on the basis of the authority of Scripture—and thinking it out anew from the standpoint of reformational knowledge"; in this way "one subjected oneself to the high discipline of the dogmatic thought which distinguished the theology of the ancient church" thus confirming the Lutheran "claim to genuine catholicity" (ibid.). For the Lutherans, however, catholicity was dependent on adherence to the teachings of Scripture, not on antiquity or perpetuity, which, according to Elert, made a mockery of the Reformation (209; see the larger discussion in 200–210). He criticizes Calixt (see n. 32 above) for his "antireformational romanticism," not because he sought a catholicity in the early fathers, but because he was willing to give up the teachings of the Augsburg Confession in the process. From a dogmatic viewpoint, however,

most ambitious attempts to do so would result in total agreement among all participants. That will never occur as long as sin continues to cloud our minds, motives, and methods. But any exercise that brings us even a step closer to grasping and applying the entire truth of divine teaching would be worthwhile, and a step in the right direction for evangelicals.

The essayists in this volume have with their testimonies and their scholarship advanced the argument for patristic study in the evangelical church. They are models of how this enriches the church as well as enriches one's own faith. They also have demonstrated that this need not lead the scholar to part from his or her own roots—just as it should not lead one to part from one's Savior and faith. However, the Savior's call to "Follow me" does also apply to this part of one's journey. If larger segments of the evangelical movement become reconnected properly with the works of the early Christian fathers, and with the Reformers, this type of *ressourcement* can only bless the church, and perhaps, be part of its *semper reformanda* and its re-pristination.

---

the writings of the fathers and the Reformation confessions were both to be evaluated on the basis of Scripture, treasured for their exposition of Scripture, yet distinguished from Scripture because they were "merely a testimony of those living at that time" (210). On the Lutheran church's claim to "catholicity," see Elert, *Structure of Lutheranism*, 274–91. Robert Preus in his study of the Lutheran fathers, *Theology of Post-Reformation Lutheranism*, cites the distinctions made by Leonard Hutter (1563–1616) and Abraham Calov (1612–1686). Hutter, he explains, said that Scripture is "the infallible rule of faith" and all confessions must therefore be "based on and judged by Scripture"; that Scripture must be "the judge in all controversy in the church" and that the Lutheran Confessions are "only a witness to this judge"; and thirdly that Scripture is "self-authenticating," while all other writings are to be believed "only insofar as they agree with Scripture." Preus summarizes Calov's distinctions as follows: the Scriptures "come to us immediately from God by virtue of their inspiration," while the Confessions come from God "mediately, based as they are on Scripture"; the Scriptures represent "the thought and mind of God," while the Confessions are "the consensus of the church"; Scripture is "the source of divine truth" while "symbols contain conclusions that are based on Scripture"; and finally that Scripture is "the rule and norm of faith," while the Confessions are "a witness of the faith of the church." Preus, 38–39.

9

Evangelicals and the Tensions of Ressourcement —A Baptist Response

Paul A. Hartog

❦ I wish to thank the diverse panelists for their participation in this discussion forum. Along the way, we have been reminded of famous episodes, such as the conversion of Augustine. We have also been re-introduced to forgotten friends, such as Asterius of Amasia. As one may expect in such an academic panel setting, one finds differing emphases, perspectives, conclusions, and approaches among the participants and respondents. Glen Thompson has addressed his response from a confessional Lutheran perspective.[1] I will now close with my own final remarks from a Baptist perspective, as I respond to and critique the forms of evangelical ressourcement exemplified in this forum.[2]

---

1. One notes how the Lutheran "two kingdoms" approach seems to inform Thompson's discussion of the church's role in the transformation of political-economic systems; and the Lutheran-Reformed divide over "the regulative principle" may help elucidate his reference to "logical extensions of biblical teaching" in "matters of practice" (above, pp. 184–85). See Ritchie, *Regulative Principle of Worship*, 9–13.

2. On *ressourcement*, see also Husbands, "Introduction," 10–23. "One of the principle [*sic*] aims of *ressourcement* theology is to examine the ancient sources of the Christian faith in order to draw out their significance for revitalization of the contemporary church" (Husbands, "Introduction," 16).

Can I Get a Witness?

In 1993, long before the term "emerging" church had ever fallen upon my ears, I was a fumbling master's degree student in history at Iowa State University. While trying to find a thesis topic, I came upon Everett Ferguson's introductory essay to the debut volume of *Second Century: A Journal of Early Christian Studies*.[3] Ferguson declared, "In spite of its importance, the second century is a period of time inadequately understood in its own right. It might even be said to have been a neglected period."[4] "The difficulty created by this situation," he continued, "is our opportunity."[5] I took the bait, and I was hooked. The historical awareness among laypeople in the churches of my growing-up years often seemed to jump from the New Testament to Martin Luther.[6] The early church was a vast ocean of unchartered waters, and I set out to explore *terra incognita*.[7] Having set my hand to the plow, I have not turned back.

I am now a professor who teaches patristic courses (among other offerings) at a small, Baptist college and seminary.[8] Some may marvel at such a situation. I believe it is a calling. There are encouraging signs of historical awareness among my students, such as a renewed interest in the Reformers and the Puritans.[9] Notwithstanding, every year I receive undergraduate term papers that refer to the three "parts" of the Godhead. And I still have students who, when directly questioned, deny

---

3. The periodical eventually merged with the *Journal of Early Christian Studies*.

4. Ferguson, "New Journal," 4.

5. Ferguson, "New Journal," 4.

6. Cf. D. H. Williams' discussion of "an ahistorical jump from the apostles to the sixteenth century" (Williams, *Retrieving the Tradition*, 27).

7. "For others, the church fathers represent a vast unknown, unexplored territory" (Hall, *Reading Scripture with the Church Fathers*, 12). Williams refers to "a huge gap in the historical consciousness of the Free church" (Williams, *Retrieving the Tradition*, 5).

8. In this manner, like Thompson, I take my own "seat on the fringe" (above, p. 189). To assist my response from "the fringe," I will refer to the insights of my fellow seat-mate, Kevin Bauder.

9. This desire for historical rootedness "should come as no surprise," when one considers "this younger generation, with no strong ethnic roots, no firm religious upbringing, frequent changes of residence for jobs or education, and shoddy historical instruction" (Mammana, "Orthodox Twenty-Somethings," 50). One could add the prevalent breakdown of the nuclear family to this litany of rootlessness.

that Jesus had a human soul along with a human body. Such examples merely confirm the importance of my vocation. In my own experience, one simply cannot take the patristic foundation for granted. One may end up with Apollinarian students who cannot provide an orthodox explanation of the Trinity![10] If one "aims to be doctrinally orthodox," one "cannot do so without recourse to and integration of the foundational tradition of the early church."[11] On the other hand, it is wondrous to witness someone comprehend, for the very first time, the full implications of the Cappadocian maxim: "What the Son did not assume, He cannot redeem."[12]

As a Baptist "by conviction," I espouse a "free church" ecclesiology.[13] Believers within the "free church" tradition have their own roots. "For example," explains Nathan Finn, "when most Baptists come to Scripture, it is with a generally Chalcedonian understanding of Christological texts, a Reformational understanding of those texts related to soteriology, and later Baptist and Free Church interpretations of those texts related to ecclesiology."[14] Some might balk at those with a congregational polity borrowing from the Trinitarian and Christological insights of hierarchical bishops, or at a movement which has been typified by "simplicity of worship" learning from the moral lessons of a period characterized by increasing liturgical ornamentation.[15]

---

10. "Too often we assume potential church members already know the fundamentals of their faith, whereas in reality they are usually incapable of explaining the basics of 'the pattern of sound teaching' (2 Tim. 1:13)." Therefore, "ecclesiastical leadership must not shirk from the critical and time-consuming job of imparting Christian truth or catechizing those who profess to be Christian" (Williams, *Tradition, Scripture, and Interpretation*, 38).

11. Williams, *Retrieving the Tradition*, 18.

12. In other words, if humans in their entirety are to be saved, Jesus must have assumed full humanity, including a human soul.

13. The "free church" is "based upon the conviction that the church is not an institution on account of its structure or external rites, but exists only when it is voluntarily composed of the faithful" (Williams, *Retrieving the Tradition*, 2). The term "free church" appears among English Puritans typified by Nonconformist tendencies. They believed the church was to be "a community of personal believers of the regenerate, and only these" (ibid.). Early English Baptists emerged from English Separatist movements.

14. Finn, Review.

15. Baptists tend to see more of a New Testament pattern for church polity and decision-making than many others do.

But if necessity is the mother of invention, then theological tension is the mother of critical appropriation. What is needed is "not simply a rote imitation or repetition of the tradition as it was embodied centuries earlier," but a *re*-appropriation.[16] Those who are self-consciously indebted to the early traditions without naively romanticizing them often demonstrate an ideal mix of sympathy and critique. "In this respect," states Joel Scandrett, "we may heartily endorse the venerable understanding of *ecclesia semper reformanda*, the 'church always reforming,' which perhaps better than any other dictum expresses the idea of the critical reception of the Christian Tradition."[17] A faithful community should be characterized by reception, reformation, restoration, revival, and even resistance ("earnestly contending for the faith").[18]

In 1999, D. H. Williams noted that "There are very few scholars from the Free Church communions in the United States who are conversant with the literature of the fathers, though the growing number of graduate students specializing in patristics would indicate that their number is on the rise."[19] Williams insisted that one should not have to leave the "free church" in order "to be nourished by the substantial resources available in ancient (or patristic) Christianity."[20] He vowed, "I myself am planted within the free church tradition and intend to stay there."[21]

I am not implying that the "free church" tradition and evangelicalism are coterminous—μὴ γένοιτο.[22] I am simply acknowledging that a special set of problems accompany a "free church" *ressourcement*.

---

16. See Clapp, *Border Crossings*, 98.

17. Scandrett, "Trouble with Tradition," 14. Cf. Wellum, "Standing on the Shoulders," 2.

18. Jude 3. Thompson rightly implies that a robust sense of "orthodoxy" leads to a practice of "proper Christian separation," and the fathers developed both (above, p. 197). See Bauder, "Thinking about the Gospel."

19. Williams, *Retrieving the Tradition*, 129. In 1999, Williams declared that the integration of "the serious study of patristics" into "current theological reflections" within the free churches was "very much in its infancy" (ibid., 4–5).

20. Williams, *Retrieving the Tradition*, 31; Williams, *Evangelicals and Tradition*, 12.

21. Williams, *Evangelicals and Tradition*, 177. Williams continues, "Of course, some free church Christians end up taking a 'high church' route, but that is not what I am advocating here" (ibid.). See also the chapter entitled "What Keeps You from Becoming a Catholic?" in Harmon, *Towards Baptist Catholicity*, 193–213.

22. E. Glenn Hinson wishes to keep the evangelical tradition and the "free church" tradition patently distinct (Hinson, "Word," 580).

Furthermore, I do not share this personal narrative in order to portray my experience as normative for all those engaged in patristic scholarship. Quite the opposite—I simply wish to demonstrate the complexity and variety inherent within "*the*" recent discovery of the early church. More than one door leads to the great banquet hall where a patristic feast awaits. In today's climate, some incorrectly assume that an interest in the early church is a telltale sign of "emerging" weaknesses or of an inevitable return to Rome. Perhaps my description of the complexity and diversity may serve as my own *Apologia Pro Vita Sua*, or—more accurately—an apology for the broader importance of my academic field.

R. Kent Hughes warns, "to deny ourselves the wealth of the accumulated saints of the centuries is to consciously embrace spiritual anorexia."[23] There are plenty of chairs at this ancient table, and although the fathers are not flawless chefs, they consistently serve flavorful fare that nourishes the hungry and strengthens the weak. For these, and all other gifts of Providence, may the Lord make us truly grateful.

Squaring my Response with the "Quadrilateral"

I will not delineate all of my own differences or disagreements with all of the essays, but I will rather structure my response around "Bebbington's Quadrilateral," as described in my introductory article.[24] David Bebbington's four emphases that form the quadrilateral are "biblicism," "crucicentrism," "conversionism," and "activism." Along the way, I will attempt to apply some historically grounded insights to the pertinent discussions.[25] Therefore, I will frequently stress a "diachronic" approach that broadly encompasses various developments within ecclesiastical history.

---

23. Hughes, *Disciplines of a Godly Man*, 78.

24. At the same time, one is reminded that my essays use "evangelical" in a classic, expansive sense, going back historically to the inclusion of the Reformers (contrast Bebbington). See above, p. 1 n. 1; p. 8 n. 42.

25. I concur with Thompson's reminder that patristic study "must be historically based and not merely theologically based" (above, p. 190).

"Biblicism"

According to Bebbington, "biblicism" is a commitment to the authority of Scripture. Yet one immediately faces complexities as one adopts a diachronic approach to "biblicism" in the early church. The exact nature of "a commitment to the authority of Scripture" would look different in the year AD 80 than it would in the year 180, and different yet again in the year 380. Scholarly reconstructions place the composition of some documents now in the New Testament after the year 80. By the year 180, Irenaeus was arguing for the authority of the four Gospels and was quoting various "New Testament" documents as "Scripture." Nevertheless, although Irenaeus had a definite sense of what was "apostolic," he did not hold a precisely defined New Testament canon of twenty-seven books as we think of it today. The year 380 would find the discussion situated after Athanasius' famous "Easter Letter" of 367, which exactly listed (for the first time in undisputed, extant literature) the contents of the New Testament canon as accepted today.[26] In the same year of 380, however, one would still be awaiting the first conciliar delineation of this New Testament canon, which came at the Synod of Hippo in 393, shortly followed by the Synod of Carthage in 397.[27] All evangelical scholars realize the complexity of this diachronic outline as applied to the question of Scriptural authority in the early church. Many argue that the basic building blocks of the New Testament canonical structure ("Gospel" and "apostle") were already in place quite early, and I would agree with such assessments.[28] Nevertheless, a diachronic awareness clearly complicates the issue of "the authority of Scripture" in the early church, since the patristic period witnessed the recognition of the New Testament canon itself.

Another complication of "biblicism" implicitly weaving its way throughout these essays is the issue of "tradition," including (but not limited to) the diachronic development of "historical theology." Evangelicals

---

26. See Ferguson, *Early Christians Speak*, vol. 2, 50 (on Origen). For a discussion of Athanasius' listing of "Jeremiah with Baruch, Lamentations, and the epistle, one book" in the Old Testament canon, see ibid., 33.

27. Moreover, the Synods of Hippo and Carthage recognized "deuterocanonical" ("apocryphal") books in the Old Testament canon.

28. See Hartog, "Polycarp, Ephesians, and 'Scripture.'"

are becoming more aware that a "traditionless" religious movement is an oxymoron. While religious movements cannot be reduced to the communal transmitting of values and beliefs, they at least include this axiological and theological transmission. By definition, then, churches inculcate "traditions." Kevin Bauder explains, "Baptists find that some reliance upon tradition is virtually inescapable. With all orthodox Christians, Baptists are indebted to tradition, not as a doctrinal authority, but as a source of theological insight.... The fact is that virtually every aspect of our theology and methodology relies heavily upon something that we have received from the Christian past.... None of us has time within a single life to rethink every aspect of the Christian faith. None of us wishes to waste time reinventing the wheel. Our dependence upon tradition is precisely what makes doctrinal progress possible."[29]

Bauder adds,

> Some churches pride themselves upon being non- or even anti-traditional. This attitude is facile. Every church without exception works from some sort of a tradition. Churches that will not accept the living tradition of the Christian past will be forced to invent some tradition of their own. They invariably invent their own liturgies and contrive their own definitions of piety, worship, fellowship, and reverence.... The problem is not that these churches lack a tradition. The problem is that the tradition by which they guide themselves is one of recent invention, usually one that they or their immediate predecessors have made up themselves. Typically, they accommodate the forms of their Christianity to whatever else they are doing in their lives. And their tradition is transparent to them: they are blissfully unaware that they have exchanged the gold of the Christian past for a stubble of their own reaping.[30]

Moreover, the attempt to "throw away all traditions" leads to death by the self-inflicted wound of a new tradition of alleged traditionlessness. Some evangelicals have abandoned themselves to an endless attempt to continually re-invent "a new kind of Christian."[31] Instead of the "old-time

---

29. Bauder, "Understanding Conservative Christianity: Another Digression."
30. Bauder, "Understanding Conservative Christianity: A Digression."
31. Contrast Brian McLaren's willingness to categorize the Virgin Birth as negotia-

religion" one is left with a continuously changing, formless specter. Soon the loose "spiderwebbing" of Christian elements devolves into a postmodern smorgasbord of traditioned elements that tickle one's aesthetic fancy. As Jeff Bingham has reminded us, we must lament the fact that the "memory hard drive" of much of evangelicalism has been erased, leading to a woeful "loss of language."[32]

The Christian conversation precedes each and every one of us. We are situated in a Tradition grounded upon Scripture. We must hitch our wagons to the star of Scripture, even as we listen to the insights of "a multitude of counselors," including those godly trailblazers who have gone before and have left us their example and succor. "Others have walked the paths we so want to tread. They have chronicled the pitfalls and posted warnings along the way. They have also given us descriptions of spiritual delights which will draw us onward and upward."[33] The patristic authors, as able docents, would point us to the guiding light of Scripture. The fathers gladly serve as ministerial counselors to the magisterial authority of Scripture.[34]

Evangelical scholars recognize the important role of the proclamation of the "kerygma" before (and after) the composition of the New Testament documents. Many are becoming more aware of the role and nature of the *regula fidei* in the early church as well, and much can be

---

ble with Bryan Litfin's view: "the Virgin Birth is not up for debate. It is part of the received deposit of the faith." Therefore, I do not concur with McLaren's broad intent in his assumption that "there are possibilities at many points among the many various positions" in various theological matters (as cited in Shelton above, p. 113), since McLaren may classify fundamental doctrines as "secondary" matters.

32. From Jeff Bingham's "Response" at the 2008 ETS annual meeting, Patristics and Medieval History Section. Bingham insisted that evangelicals are "playing games" until the evangelical culture is reconnected to the classical Christian tradition. The very fact that such a reconnection is necessary is an evidence of contemporary conditions, lamented Bingham, even as the cause of the French *ressourcement* of the mid-twentieth century was the "dead" condition of society.

33. Hughes, *Disciplines of a Godly Man*, 78–79.

34. "The crucial criterion for evaluating the authenticity of a development, it seems to me, is whether the development faithfully, wisely and coherently expresses the truth found in Scripture. The apostolic teaching contained in the canonical Scriptures is the norm by which all developments must be tested" (Hall, "Tradition, Authority, Magisterium," 41).

gleaned from such studies.[35] Scholarship is indebted to Bryan Litfin for his masterful compilation of *regula fidei* materials. At the same time, an "evangelical" theology will insist upon the regnant authority of Scripture (even as Litfin has stated)—the supreme authority in faith and practice.[36] A firm "biblicism," a commitment to the supreme authority of Scripture, must not be sacrificed upon the altar of a misunderstanding of "Tradition." In this regard, insights from the Reformers may serve as helpful signposts along this journey, such as the differentiation between *sola Scriptura* and *nuda Scriptura* and the distinctions between *norma normans* and *norma normata*, as briefly described by Thompson.[37]

One must proceed with caution. Before one follows a path too far into the woods, one should pause for a respite of healthy reflection. If the *regula fidei* becomes the hermeneutical key that unlocks Scripture, but Scripture itself may be interpreted contrary to the authorial intentions of the original writers, where does the *de facto* authority lie?[38] Contemporary evangelical scholars need to think carefully through the interconnected nature of scriptural authority, hermeneutics, and learning from the fathers.[39] As Christopher Hall declares, "To argue for the

---

35. For my own guarded take on lessons from the patristic use of the "rule of faith," see Hartog, "'Rule of Faith' and Patristic Biblical Exegesis."

36. Historically, Baptist confessions of faith have referred to the "final," "supreme," or "ultimate" authority of Scripture.

37. I agree with Thompson that Patristic *ressourcement* must be done in a manner that does not deny or undercut allegiance to Scripture (above, p. 196).

38. David Wells warns against the (understandable) "longing for a tradition that will make sense of our evangelical tower of Babel, the recoil from self-serving exegesis, and the dissatisfaction with the miserable and stultifying parochialism of much evangelicalism" (Wells, "Nature and Function of Theology," 185). A qualitative difference exists between the deciphering of subjective or objective genitives and Augustine's acquiescence to any interpretation of a biblical text that yields love of God or neighbor (Augustine, *On Christian Doctrine* 1.36.40; cf. Augustine, *Expositions of the Psalms* 74.12).

39. See Wells, "Reservations about Catholic Renewal," 216–17. "Yet there are questions which a christic approach must face. Is the biblical text not itself a statement of truth, or is it only a pointer to some more central message? If it is a pointer, how does one avoid a subjectivism in the application of such a *sensus plenior* to Scripture? That is, what criterion for judgment is used in discovering Christ as the central message of each of the Bible's books? Why, for example, should we continue to spiritualize the Song of Songs? How is the authority of the text—of all the biblical text—maintained?" (Johnston, "Introduction," 12–13). I believe that opposing "a tendency toward bibliolatry" and an

richness and sensitivity of patristic exegesis, however, is not to posit its infallibility."[40]

"Crucicentrism"

Bebbington describes "crucicentrism" as a soteriological focus on the atoning work of Jesus Christ on the cross. A diachronic examination of this focus reveals complexities beneath the surface here, too. While the Reformers accentuated a penal substitutionary model of the atonement, patristic authors tended to portray the atonement in an array of models.[41] Many fathers vividly emphasized a *Christus Victor* approach to Christ's work in the cross and empty tomb. The New Testament documents themselves declare that Christ defeated both death and the Devil. Nevertheless, one must not lose sight of the essential and fundamental role of Christ's substitutionary sacrifice. For instance, the author of Hebrews describes Jesus' victorious cross-work (Heb 2:14–15), yet grounds the victory of the cross in the all-sufficiency of its sacrificial import (Heb 9–10).[42]

As one reads the divergent essays in this volume, the focus of "crucicentrism" raises other questions as well. If one's theology is centered in the cross, in the grace of God manifested in the Gospel, how important or how peripheral are other doctrinal considerations?[43] Bryan Litfin, af-

---

insistence that the Bible is not "a self-interpreting document" can be potentially misleading (due to the charge of "bibliolatry" in "modernist" debates in the former case, and due to possible philosophical-theological frameworks in the latter). In a similar manner, I am uncomfortable with a support of "eisegesis." At the same time, I recognize the impossibility of presupposition-less readings and the importance of Christological approaches to Scripture.

40. Hall, "Tradition, Authority, Magisterium," 40. In order "to exposit the biblical text with integrity," one might distinguish between interpreting a text, expanding upon the import of a text, and applying a text. The purported lack of a "fixed" meaning of the biblical text leads toward hermeneutical confusion. At the same time, I agree with Matz that "expository preaching need not be cast from a mold of social irrelevancy" (above, p. 153).

41. For a brief overview, see Bartlett, "Redemption."

42. See Kistemaker, "Atonement in Hebrews."

43. Gumerlock states, "The incarnation, along with what theologians call his humiliation, i.e. his temptation, earthly ministry, and death on the cross, is the most important event in all of human history" (above, p. 166). Both the New Testament documents and the patristic writings would encourage us to highlight the resurrection along with the crucifixion in the "Gospel" (1 Cor 15:1–5).

ter greatly benefiting future scholarship by collecting thirteen examples of the "rule of faith," rightly explains that the "rule of faith" focused upon God's actions in history. Litfin notes that the early examples of the *regula fidei* barely touched upon ecclesiology and eschatology, and they did not explain how salvation in Christ is applied to individuals. For this reason, both the Reformers and the Roman Catholics of the sixteenth century could still structure catechesis around the Apostles' Creed but yet differ in soteriology.

Yet a diachronic approach that encompasses the whole of ecclesiastical history recognizes that not all theological issues have been addressed with the same degree of fervency or urgency in every era. Some doctrines may remain behind the scenes in one period but may be forced to center stage as the drama of historical theology unfolds. As Litfin notes, one cannot expect early confessions to discuss bibliology in a twenty-first-century manner, since the early church itself was in the midst of the canonical recognition of the New Testament. One should not expect third-century confessions to defend biblical authority against "modernist" opponents. And one does not expect soteriological questions to be answered in fourth-century documents to the extent they are addressed in the sixteenth century.

I appreciated Francis Gumerlock's emphasis upon the humanity as well as deity of Christ, and we are indebted to him for his original research concerning the eternal Sonship of Christ. Gumerlock wears his intellectual passion for these topics upon his shirtsleeves.[44] Yet in cases such as "monotheletism," perhaps a diachronic unfolding of patristic Christological development would place early, deficient Christologies in a more empathetic light.[45] A diachronic understanding reminds us that not all ante-Chalcedonian fathers espoused the Chalcedonian definitions as hammered out in 451. Athanasius, for all his orthodox tenacity, did not delineate a fully Chalcedonian Christology. Scholars still debate whether

---

44. One might add another example to Gumerlock's historiography: the formation of the Gospel Standard Strict Baptists resulting from controversies concerning the doctrine of eternal generation among Strict and Particular Baptists in the 1830s and 1840s. See Toon, "English Strict Baptists."

45. Gumerlock's essay could also take into account more recent evaluations of so-called "Nestorianism." Cf. Thompson above, p. 192 n. 21.

the Alexandrian bishop taught a "Logos-Sarx Christology," since modern interpreters are left seeking more precise formulations to issues he handed on to future generations. According to D. H. Williams, "When it comes to acknowledging the foundational creeds, therefore, we are faced with viewing them not merely as doctrinal touchstones but as diachronic statements of faith whose theological and polemical contexts are just as important as the words of the creeds."[46] Not all deficient Christologies, such as "monothelitism," are necessarily "demonically" inspired.[47]

Along the way, Gumerlock positively reminds us that Jesus Christ himself lies at the heart of the Gospel. The minute one begins to centralize and hierarchicalize doctrines (as implied in the very term "crucicentrism"), tensions may arise, however. Thompson notes that various doctrines may be facilely abrogated to the periphery. "The disagreements on such teachings in turn can lead some to view Scripture as being nebulous in its teaching, and so modern expositors can either avoid taking a position at all, or present their own as mere informed opinion."[48] Thompson lays the blame, at least in part, upon "Protestant fundamentalism in the narrow sense."[49] My reading of history may differ, in that a reductionistic simplification of Protestantism came not necessarily with the historic fundamentalists, at least not those with a dual emphasis upon cardinal doctrines *and* "the whole counsel of God," but with various newer evangelicals who seemed to take "the fundamentals" for the entirety of the story rather than as the non-negotiables of the foundational plot.[50]

I do agree with Thompson that although one may hierarchicalize doctrines (as in a "crucicentric" or "Gospel-centered" manner), one does not simply cast aside those doctrines that do not seem to rest within the

---

46. Williams, "*Similis et Dissimilis*," 78.

47. Gumerlock grants that "some of the apologists like Justin Martyr and Tertullian did not articulate the doctrine of eternal generation" (above, p. 170). Gumerlock also notes that "Origen did not escape subordinationism" (p. 171 n. 37).

48. Thompson above, p. 194. Cf. Litfin above, p. 98.

49. Thompson above, p. 194.

50. See Nettleton, "Limited Message or a Limited Fellowship." Many of the "younger evangelicals" are now beyond the "new evangelical" movement of the 1940s. As Thompson notes, with tongue-in-cheek, "evangelicals cannot even agree on subscribing to *Christianity Today!*" (above, p. 193).

core of the Gospel. For example, as a Baptist, I believe that one's view of baptism is important, although it remains distinct from "the Gospel" itself (cf. 1 Cor 1:17). Moreover, I do not believe that patristic study necessarily teaches us that eschatology must remain a labyrinthine maze only to be unlocked by the *eschaton* itself. Herein lies the irony: the amillennial Lutheran and the premillennial Baptist agree that eschatology is worth studying and discussing, in its proper place![51] As a realist, I further agree with Thompson that "even the most ambitious attempts" would probably never "result in total agreement among all participants" of this forum. In fact, this forum may have highlighted our distinctive approaches even more clearly.

My response has been billed as a Baptist "free church" response, and Baptist theologians, churches, and fellowships have differed among themselves regarding eschatology. The Baptist movement has included amillennial, postmillennial, "dispensational" premillennial, and "classical" premillennial theologians.[52] Since my essay has been advanced as a "Baptist" response, I do not wish to bog down in an eschatological morass. But, if I may, I would like to shed one ray of light upon the topic of eschatology as raised in these essays.[53] All should agree that theological debates are not aided by the distortion of patristic evidence—or of

---

51. I find it interesting that Thompson asserts (with a sense of critique), "Thus varieties of belief on . . . the end of the world are tolerated within the same group, or simply not discussed in depth" (above, p. 194); while Gumerlock laments, ". . . today we argue over the interpretation of the thousand years to the point of even excluding from teaching in our seminaries people who have a different view of Rev 20:1-6 than ourselves" (above, p. 160). Gumerlock refers to situations "today," but various Reformers drew lines *against* "millennialism," even in confessional documents. See the *Augsburg Confession* 17; and Cranmer's additional article to what became the *Thirty-Nine Articles* ("Heretics Called 'Millenarians'"), published in 1553. For recent works that use patristic evidence to argue for amillennialism or premillennialism, see those by Charles E. Hill (amillennial) and Donald Fairburn (premillennial): Hill, *Regnum Caelorum*; Fairburn, "Contemporary Millennial/Tribulational Debates."

52. For example, A. H. Strong was a postmillennialist, Ray Summers was an amillennialist, and Millard Erickson is a premillennialist. Most of the smaller Baptist fellowships formed in the twentieth century are premillennialist. I thank George Houghton for his assistance with these materials.

53. I was intrigued by the freqeuent appearance of eschatology in these essays. Cf. Daley, *Hope of the Early Church*.

modern theologians and systems.[54] There are those, for example, who misrepresent specific premillennial fathers as if they taught the system of "dispensational" premillennialism, when they did not. Such interpreters seem to peer down into the well and see a reflection of themselves.[55] In the same manner, the call to accurately represent others reaches beyond figures of the distant past to those of more recent vintage (including, in turn, "dispensational" premillennialists and others).[56] Simplified generalizations and caricatures do not seem to move conversations forward. Although I oppose sensationalized eschatology, systematized eschatology should not become a whipping boy.[57]

The virtues of fairness and candor array the historian in fine attire, whatever theological system he or she may hold. For instance, Rex Butler's essay recognized the sacramental nature of baptism in various fathers, although he acknowledged his own non-sacramental theology in the conclusion. His work exemplified the tensions inherent in this forum,

---

54. As Thompson insists, we must produce "an accurate and comprehensive" picture (above, p. 183). Premillennial historians should not distort the evidence of amillennial fathers, and vice versa. In the final analysis, both are called to build their cases upon Scriptural support.

55. Other historians of a dispensational bent have acknowledged this fact and have simply examined rudimentary theological features without distorting the historical evidence or creating the fathers in their own image. See, for example, Crutchfield, "Rudiments of Dispensationalism in the Ante-Nicene Period."

56. Gumerlock counters "any theory of the rapture which has Jesus returning to earth [sic] and quickly leaving with many people never seeing him." In my understanding, the reason that early pretribulational theologians referred to the "secret" or "invisible" rapture of the church was because they divided (unlike most others throughout church history) the Second Coming into two phases, the earlier rapture of the saints to the clouds and the later advent "to earth." Gumerlock further implies that pretribulational theologians weaken the bodily return of Christ, therefore assaulting his true humanity (although he acknowledges the "redeeming quality that our Lord will eventually come in bodily form" seven years later). Ironically, early dispensationalists emphasized his bodily return, in the "first phase" (in their view) of the rapture to the clouds as well as the "second phase" of the earthly advent. Consider but one example of a classical dispensationalist: "First, this coming will be a *bodily* return" (McClain, *Greatness of the Kingdom*, 374; italics original). Gumerlock also generalizes that "classical" dispensationalists project the fulfillment of all of the Olivet Discourse into the eschatological future. But cf. Toussaint, *Behold the King*, 267–68.

57. See Bauder, "Those Pesky Premillennialists." Shelton notes that aspects of the "apocalyptic mentality" "can be both biblical and valuable" (above, p. 124).

as a non-sacramental theologian attempted to learn from the community formation and maintenance found in the patristic period, as taught by more sacramental theologians. "As we encounter interpretive traditions other than our own," explains Christopher Hall, "we can expect to experience theological cognitive dissonance, especially if we treat other's perspectives fairly."[58] Such commendable candor raises difficult corollary questions concerning the possible depth of a "free church" *ressourcement* of patristic theology. Nevertheless, I agree with various examples Butler brings forward.[59] One may, for example, be sharpened by the patristic emphasis upon church discipline (and the heinousness of sin) without adopting a penitential system.[60]

"Conversionism"

The third leg of Bebbington's evangelical table emphasizes the belief that individuals need to be personally converted. A diachronic awareness of the whole cloth of church history demonstrates the fallacy of equating personal conversion with "walking an aisle" or "saying the sinner's prayer," as popularly understood in various modern movements. Nevertheless, it does not logically follow that one is therefore forced to abandon the *personal* nature of conversion. Both Butler and Smither rightly noted the importance of catechesis in patristic Christianity. Modern "free church" members may be surprised to learn how early and famous Baptists emphasized catechesis.[61] For instance, Charles Spurgeon, the "Prince of Preachers," set forth his own children's catechism (1855). Yet Spurgeon recognized that the final result of catechesis could be a "catechumen" who was not a "convert."[62] Attempts to counter "easy believism" may falsely

---

58. Hall, "Tradition, Authority, Magisterium," 46.

59. Moreover, I would further accentuate some of his critiques (i.e., of anonymous internet "confessions") and cautions, and I would add that the structure of worship space reflects theology.

60. And one may learn from the courage of certain patristic bishops as they publicly reproved erring individuals (as noted by Matz above, p. 153).

61. As mentioned by Butler, other historic Baptist catechisms include Keach's Catechism of 1677 and the Charleston Catechism of 1813 (above, p. 75 n. 98). Cf. Nettles, "Encouragement to Use Catechisms."

62. Though not a Baptist document, cf. the influential Article 5 of the "Fourteen Point

assume that a process of discipleship will guarantee the authenticity of all "converts."[63]

Much of modern evangelicalism (especially of the "free church" variety) has been affected by Western and American forms of individualism in unwittingly unhealthy ways. Yet I do not conclude that the current disarray will be solved by an abandonment of the priesthood of every believer (as biblically construed) or of the individual's responsibility to study Scripture for himself or herself, as one is personally able to do so. The solution is not the de-emphasis of such doctrines but a complementary re-emphasis upon the communitarian aspects of sound Christianity.[64] Even the plowboy should be able to own and study the Scriptures, but hopefully this same "Berean" plowboy is being formed in faithful community. The "new and living way" inaugurated by the high priestly ministry of Jesus Christ gives each believer "confidence to enter the holy place by the blood of Jesus" and to "draw near with a sincere heart in full assurance of faith" (Heb 10:19–22, NASB). But this personal access to God is immediately tied to the command not to forsake the common assembly but to stimulate one another to love and good works (Heb 10:23–25).

Several contributors to this forum have noted that further scholarship must focus upon the so-called "Constantinian turn" in the early church. Simplistic "free church" models picture a radical historical break with Constantine. While I espouse a Baptistic "separation of church and state," I also know that Constantine did not "force conversion" upon people, as some misleadingly claim. Rather, the so-called Edict of Milan clearly guaranteed "all others" the freedom to observe their personal religious convictions, in accordance with "sound and upright reason." The Edict declared, "Since you see that this has been granted by us to these same Christians, your devotedness understands that to others as well the freedom and full liberty has been granted, in accordance with the peace of our times, to exercise free choice in worshipping as each one has seen

Creed" of the Niagara Bible Conference (also known as the "Niagara Creed").

63. See Houghton, "A Critique of 'Easy Believism.'"

64. At the same time, while I have learned lessons from the communitarian nature of monasticism in Late Antiquity, as a Baptist theologian I also find areas of disagreement with such monasticism, even while admiring the palpable commitment.

fit. This has been done by us so that nothing may seem to be taken away from anyone's honor or from any religion whatsoever."[65] It seems that many laypeople, and not only from a "free church" perspective, anachronistically read the policies of later emperors such as Theodosius I (who reigned 379–395) back into the reign of Constantine (who died in 337). On the other hand, one would be remiss to overlook the role of economic and political incentives in the influx of new members into the post-Constantinian churches. Further research might examine and compare the nature of "personal conversion" in the pre-Constantinian and post-Constantinian eras.[66]

"Activism"

Finally, Bebbington refers to "activism" as a defining quality of historic evangelicalism. He describes "activism" as the stress placed upon evangelism, missions, and other Gospel ministry and service. Edward Smither's essay directly addresses patristic evangelism and discipleship.[67] His concluding "talking points" describe parallels between patristic and contemporary approaches.[68] As noted by Thompson, one should recognize that parallel characteristics do not necessarily entail dependency, of course.[69] The field has already benefited from Smither's investigation of Augustine's development of church leaders.[70] We await further examples of a precisely delineated "learning" from patristic evangelism and dis-

---

65. As found in Novak, *Christianity and the Roman Empire*, 163. See Hartog, "Religious Liberty and the Early Church."

66. See Kreider, *Change of Conversion and the Origin of Christendom*.

67. See also Kreider, "They Alone Know the Right Way to Live," which emphasizes the quality of the church's common life as an evangelistic witness in the early patristic period. "The reason goes to the heart of the early Christian approach to mission. The Christians did not offer the world intellectual formulas; they offered a way of life rooted in Christ" (ibid., 177).

68. Perhaps Smither's essay could benefit from the incorporation of contemporary sociological insights into the nature of "public" and "private" in the ancient world.

69. Above, pp. 189–90.

70. See Smither, *Augustine as Mentor*.

cipleship, and Smither's graduate work in both missiology and patristic history nicely positions him to take up the mantle in his future work.[71]

Another promising young scholar, Brian Matz, has provided a study from his academic forte, patristic social ethics. Matz carefully narrowed his focus to one account of Scripture (Luke 16:19–31), as examined through the sermons of two patristic preachers.[72] These early church leaders remind us that "Pure and undefiled religion in the sight of *our* God and Father is this: to visit orphans and widows in their distress, *and* to keep oneself unstained by the world" (NASB). I felt myself squirm under the impassioned preaching of Jerome and Asterius, and such uncomfortability is good for my soul, surrounded as I am by the comforts of my American (and even ecclesiological) culture.[73] At the same time, an approach to Christian compassion that borrows from the wisdom of the entirety of church history reminds us that churches have sometimes veered from a *Gospel-centered* concern for the less fortunate.[74] In doing so, they have ceased to be truly "evangelical."[75] One may not dismiss

---

71. One acknowledges the broad scope of assigned topics in this forum, as well as the necessary word limits.

72. See also Kalantzis, "Crumbs from the Table."

73. Sometimes the materials in our forum seem to be based upon an implied equivalency between "contemporary evangelicalism" and "contemporary American evangelicalism." Matz avers, "If only the wealthy and powerful would change, life for the rest of us would improve." From a global perspective, even the average American *de facto* is one of the "wealthy and powerful." The correlation of "contemporary evangelicalism" and "contemporary American evangelicalism" is natural, given our contextual location. But we do need to be reminded that "contemporary evangelicalism" is much larger than its American manifestations, and global evangelicalism continues to expand, especially in the southern hemisphere. Moreover, global Christians may learn from the patristic period in very particular, pronounced ways. "Indeed, it has been suggested that there is a critical link between the memory of suffering and the making of a Christian culture, a kind of formation that is presently occurring in the churches of mainland China" (Williams, "*Similis et Dissimilis*," 82).

74. As Litfin has noted, "The Gospel . . . is a proclamation of what Christ has done" (above, p. 96). Explanations of "the Gospel" (or "the whole Gospel" or "the robust Gospel") that mix our deeds of social service with Christ's Gospel work *ex nobis* lead to confusion. See Bauder, "Directions in Evangelicalism: The Gospel According to Scot."

75. To take but one example, the YMCA and the YWCA both resolutely began as overtly "Christian" associations, as reflected in their names. Through time, they have increasingly veered from their original purposes, while still accomplishing social good.

such dangers, even as one boldly calls Christians to repent of their lack of sacrificial compassion.[76] There are forms of "activism" that abandon "crucicentrism," so that the Gospel seems to fade away behind acts of charity not accompanied by the preaching of Christ and him crucified. Only the crucified and risen Savior can ultimately save from the torments described in Luke 16.

Matz further critiques the patristic failure to address systemic economic inequality in the Roman world. Thompson has already observed the difficulty of foisting modern democratic aspirations upon the fathers living in an imperial world.[77] One might also caution that, even in the contemporary world, good intentions must be wedded to sound economic policies that sustain the long-term elevation of the poor in a free society (including the maintenance of private property).[78] Christian stewardship marries sacrificial charity to economic prudence.[79] Even so, Matz insightfully targets the lack of preaching pointed at sacrificial charity in our contemporary context.

"Activism" also relates to the church's apologetic work in the world, as well as its interaction with wider culture. Brian Shelton has painstakingly discussed the varying patristic approaches as analyzed through the rubric of H. Richard Niebuhr's *Christ and Culture*. Shelton rightfully avoids boxing "the" early church into one of the models, judiciously re-

---

76. In a footnote, Matz mentions the Latin American Theological Fraternity. My own grandfather, Emilio Antonio Nuñez, helped found that fraternity, and his theological assessment of liberation theology is still worth reading (see Nuñez, *Liberation Theology*).

77. Matz recognizes that "There are some interesting features in these homilies that make clear they are from a different time and place. For example, they accept slavery as a fact of life." D. H. Williams declares, "Without laboring the point, we may observe that the same architects who contributed toward our doctrines of Christology and trinitarianism simply assumed the acceptability of slave holding" (Williams, "*Similis et Dissimilis*," 74).

78. See Gregg, *Economic Thinking for the Theologically Minded*; Corbett and Fikkert, *When Helping Hurts*.

79. Moreover, to be *fully* virtuous, charity must be voluntary, flowing from a *habitus* of compassion. Interestingly, as Oden describes his journey to "the recovery of Patristic wisdom," he mentions his shift "politically away from trust in regulatory power and rationalistic planning to historical reasoning and a relatively greater critical trust in the responsible free interplay of interests in the marketplace of goods and ideas" (Oden, "Then and Now," 1164–65).

fusing to follow the imprudent lead of others.[80] Shelton's rather openended description of the sundry models of cultural engagement in the early church calls us back to the main point of the introductory essay.[81] The patristic period was complex and diverse, and we therefore expect to find both complexity and diversity in early Christian engagements with culture.[82] Varying patristic authors enjoyed varying educational training and faced varying intellectual and social contexts, and so we find varying approaches to culture within their writings. As Shelton himself recognizes, Niebuhr's plotting of models is overly-simplified, yet I believe Shelton's own correspondence of "culture" with "the world" in Johannine literature may need to be nuanced as well.[83] Nevertheless, Niebuhr's rubric remains a helpful heuristic device, and its use allows Shelton to describe the variety of patristic approaches to culture in fascinating ways. Although his multifaceted essay is mostly descriptive, he rightly uses the patristic evidence to encourage a contextualized "strategic response" to cultural opposition (rather than a "cookie-cutter" approach).[84]

Many of the so-called "Baptist distinctives" center upon ecclesiology, with a defined sense of the nature, functioning, and mission of the local church.[85] It is no wonder, then, that Baptists tend to see the local church (rather than "parachurch" organizations) as the center of biblical activism. Baptists have espoused a "believers' church" model.

80. Cf. the generalization of the entire pre-Constantinian church as espousing a "withdrawal" from any involvement in culture in Eckman, *Christian Ethics in a Postmodern World*, 15–16.

81. As Shelton states, his essay "did not critically evaluate the patristic engagement with culture in an exhaustive manner" but rather "described the diverse approaches" with the aim of prompting contemporary "strategic response" (above, pp. 128–29).

82. Shelton might engage recent, varying definitions of culture beyond Niebuhr's (above, pp. 101–2).

83. See Bauder, "Prelude to a Christian Theology of Culture," 233: "But suppose one assumes that culture is what the New Testament means when it talks about *the world*. The Bible clearly condemns the world as a center of opposition to God. If culture is, or is part of, the world, then it is basically evil and it must be shunned.... Therefore, to find out what the Bible has to say about the problem of Christianity and culture, one must begin with a clear idea of what culture is." One might also clarify the exact relationship between an "anti-gnostic" approach and a *contra* cultural approach.

84. See also Shelton's scholarship in *Martyrdom from Exegesis*.

85. See Garrett, "Major Emphases in Baptist Theology." Some have referred to Baptist "principles" or "characteristics."

The local *ecclesia* is the "called out," voluntarily covenanted community.[86] Concurrently, most Baptists have also held a doctrine of the "universal church" against which the gates of hell shall not prevail.[87] The Reformers obviously faced the question of where this "church" was during the Middle Ages, and they often spoke of the "invisible church" of true believers, which was not to be simplistically equated with any structure or organized group (including medieval Roman Catholicism or the Hussites or the Waldensians, etc.).[88]

Baptists highlight the ministerial role of all members of the congregation, nicely complementing Smither's emphasis upon the ministry of "anonymous" Christians, not just the leaders.[89] The local church, as a believing community, corporately engages in worship, exhortation, instruction, discipleship, fellowship, and service. These essays have highlighted what may be called a "holistic" understanding of the spiritual formation that takes place in such community. Doctrine may not be divorced from practice, nor theology from worship, nor the internal spirit from the external form. In general, Baptists need to appreciate more fully how form carries meaning, as well as the roles of habit and pattern in the modeling and "traditioning" of virtues and character.[90] As John Witvliet insists,

86. The "believers' church" model of the Baptist (and Anabaptist) traditions differs from the "mixed" church model of Callistus (as mentioned in Butler's essay above, p. 67) and, more famously, of Augustine.

87. Some "Landmark" Baptists have denied the existence of the "universal church." One might mention here that the view that Peter is "the rock" of Matt 16 is not unique to Roman Catholicism. Protestant interpreters who agree with this view do not tie it into apostolic successionism. Cf. Gumerlock above, p. 155.

88. As Thompson explains, the Reformers recognized that "their denominations did not consist of *all* the saved; nor did they believe that all within their particular denominations were saved" (above, p. 196). It is not as simple as Gumerlock's assertion that "medieval Catholicism was the church" (above, p. 162).

89. See Kreider, "They Alone Know the Right Way to Live."

90. We must insist that "traditioning" goes beyond the passing on of propositions. "It is a way of being educated, trained and formed in the virtues necessary for Christian life and good theologizing. Along with these virtues come various skills, patterns of experience and habits of perception as well as pieces of knowledge. It's like learning to be a musician or scientist; you don't just learn a bunch of theories; you learn to become a kind of practitioner; as a result you perceive the world differently, make different kinds of judgments and live differently from someone who is unmusical or scientifically illiterate"

"... matters of form are not only inevitable; they are also significant, both theologically and pastorally."[91] At the same time, these essays have repeatedly critiqued facets of "emerging" churches, especially a seemingly grab-bag adaptation of forms without concern for the theological meanings in the traditions.[92] "Contemporary ecclesial practice" must be examined "in the light of a preceding tradition."[93]

Conclusion

So what might a "Baptist *ressourcement*" of the church fathers concretely look like? Let me first tackle this difficult question with an analogical illustration using a theological cousin, Anabaptism. Let us suppose that a Mennonite scholar wished to learn lessons from the patristic period in order to refine and enhance her own theology. Let us suppose that this Mennonite scholar initially decides to study the life and work of Augustine. She picks up the *Confessions* and is mesmerized by Augustine's description of memory, time, and eternity in books ten and eleven. With neophyte wonder, she incorporates new insights into her own personal theology, and she moves on to Augustine's wider corpus with renewed energy. In the process, she learns to admire the bishop of Hippo with such intensity that she eventually agrees with Augustine's understanding of infant baptism and his defense of the use of justified force. This Mennonite scholar has certainly learned from the *Doctor gratiae*, but would the final result be an *Anabaptist* appropriation? Could not one argue that, along the way, the Mennonite scholar has morphed into a scholar who was formerly a Mennonite? So then, what keeps Mennonite scholars who study Augustine and appreciate his thought from adopting all of his views? One assumes that those who are Mennonite "by conviction" honestly believe that non-violence and

---

(Phillip Cary in a private e-mail, as found in Hall, "Tradition, Authority, Magisterium," 33–34).

91. Witvliet, "Embodying the Wisdom of Ancient Liturgical Practices," 191. I also have my own misgivings about facets of "The Call to an Ancient-Evangelical Future" (and Webber's models) while acknowledging that the "Call" was intended for further conversation, not for full agreement in all matters.

92. See also Byassee, "Emerging from What, Going Where?"

93. Husbands, "Introduction," 23.

believer's baptism are scriptural doctrines. And the Good Book trumps the good bishop every time.

Lutheran and Reformed scholars who represent the general, historic consensus of their respective systems will not see eye-to-eye with a convinced Mennonite, of course. They will argue that infant baptism is biblically mandated and "just wars" are scripturally permissible. Nevertheless, we should not assume that our Mennonite friend alone faces a tension. Would we not acknowledge that Lutheran and Reformed scholars who seek to "learn" from Augustine do not fully follow Augustine either? Although a simplistic generalization, there is some truth to the old adage that the sixteenth-century Reformers emphasized Augustinian soteriology while their Roman Catholic opponents underscored Augustinian ecclesiology. We simply cannot dodge such historical complexities.[94]

Let us now suppose that some ambitious soul wishes to become Augustinian to a fault. He is determined to copy Augustine to the last jot and tittle. The pesky nuisance of history will reveal that our Augustinian disciple may at times be forced to ask "which Augustine?" For instance, it is known that Augustine wavered on some issues (such as the origin of the soul) and he simply altered his views on others (such as the advisability of religious coercion). But diachronic questions of an "early Augustine" or "late Augustine" are small hurdles, for our friend's fiery fervor cannot be quenched, and he moves forward by appeal to Augustine's final *Retractiones*.[95] Let us suppose that he comes to rest comfortably upon his critically appropriated Augustinianism.

Now if our Augustinian clone later decided to learn from the entirety of the patristic period, what would he encounter? Would he not awake from his dogmatic slumber? He would discover, of course, that while Augustine held wide facets of theology in common with all of the major authors of the patristic period, Augustine also had his idio-

---

94. Would any knowledgeable scholar actually propose that the church of Jerusalem on the Day of Pentecost fully believed the Augsburg Confession, the Thirty-Nine Articles, the Westminster Confession, or the Baptist Faith and Message? At least in this sense, the *Ur-Form* of the church did not resemble the fully developed nature of any modern system. Therefore, the complexities of diachronic development are patently not peculiar to any one system.

95. Augustine wrote his *Retractiones*, a compendium of reconsiderations of his earlier works, near the end of his life.

syncrasies. Let us imagine that our friend, like a swinging pendulum, now determines that he must learn from *all* the patristic authors.⁹⁶ He becomes an accomplished linguist, and he heeds the call to learn Coptic (both Sahidic and Bohairic), Syriac (both eastern and western dialects), Ethiopic, Armenian, Georgian, and Arabic.⁹⁷ He now becomes even more aware that the early church was not completely unified in all matters of faith and practice.⁹⁸ He quickly realizes that citing one patristic author (or a handful of them) does not mean he has found "the" patristic view. He may indeed find views that are "allowed" by the patristic evidence, although they do not represent a patristic consensus.⁹⁹ As our friend's historiographical skills become further honed, he may come to realize that even if he were to amass all of the *literary* evidence, the *material* evidence demonstrates that the "common" members of the early churches

---

96. I appreciate the critical approach of Thompson, above, p. 191: "... we must learn to listen to all the voices.... Not that all voices are of equal value; nor will we listen uncritically; but we must know all the voices if we are going to understand the context of the fathers and be able to hear their message accurately." Thompson thus supports an approach that is "inclusive in its use of the sources" while still "brutally honest" (p. 199).

97. I do concur with the repeated call in these essays to reach beyond the Greek and Latin fathers.

98. I believe that Butler's statement on the unity of the patristic church could perhaps give a wrong impression ("First, at this point in Christian history, the catholic, or universal, church was unified in a way that has not been seen since"), and therefore could be historically nuanced (above, p. 69). As Matz notes, historians also find "much particularity" in early Christianity (above, p. 131).

99. For example, Gumerlock cites an interpretation of "all" in 2 Tim 2:4 in pseudo-Primasius which supports "all" kinds without distinction rather than "all" individuals without exception. Gumerlock's published scholarship on this issue extends to Fulgentius of Ruspe as well (Gumerlock, *Fulgentius of Ruspe on the Saving Will of God*). His ground-breaking scholarship demonstrates that the view was held in the patristic period but does not establish that it was the patristic consensus (and this, of course, was not Gumerlock's intent). As a fair generalization, the pre-Augustinian fathers tended to view related matters in a manner varying from Augustine, and the "Vincentian canon" could be used against Augustinian theology. "Even within the context of the mid-fifth century, Vincent's approach was rather idealistic. This is most apparent by the fact that the *Commonitory* was in part a refutation of Augustine's theology of grace" (Williams, *Retrieving the Tradition*, 34 n. 50). I agree with Gumerlock that "the mere presence of a teaching in church history does not make it true" (above, p. 178). Nor, one might add, does the minority status of an interpretation in the patristic period necessarily render it false. See also Williams, "*Similis et Dissimilis*," 80.

Evangelicals and the Tensions of Ressourcement—A Baptist Response

sometimes differed from their more literate leaders, leading us to further consider what we mean by "the early church."[100]

How shall we move forward then? I will not draw a detailed map. Rather, I urge us to pull off at the nearest rest area and engage in unhurried reflection. It seems to me that an underlying question lies just below the surface in much of our discussion, ready to spring forth into broad daylight. All these essays claim to "learn from the early church." But is there a method to the menagerie? How do we come to an *objective methodology* as we seek to "learn" from "the early church"?[101] How do we learn from what may seem (at times) like a cacophony of voices?[102] How do we sort between the more developed theologies of the later periods and the decades closer to the biblical authors themselves?[103] Do we hierarchicalize the conclusions of church councils over specific authors, even the "revered doctors of the church"? If so, do we emphasize the "ecumenical councils" into the eighth century?[104] If not, where do we stop chronologi-

---

100. See the fascinating study by MacMullen, *Second Church*.

101. All the while, I would maintain, insisting upon the regnant authority of Scripture.

102. I would add that the role of Scripture is integral to the doctrine of pneumatological "illumination" (1 Cor 2:6–16), which must be remembered when we speak of figures from church history being "illuminated" by the same Spirit who indwells believers today. "The tradition does not lead us away from the Scripture; in its best moments it leads us into the Scripture's depth and riches" (Hall, "Tradition, Authority, Magisterium," 51). Therefore, "one cannot claim the Tradition in support of a teaching that is denied or not supported in Scripture" (Williams, *Retrieving the Tradition*, 95). As but one example, I find things in Gregory the Great that are "denied or not supported in Scripture," even though he is a "revered doctor of the church." Moreover, a "cafeteria approach" to the Fathers (although by no means ideal because of its non-reflective simplicity) does not carry the same culpability as a "cafeteria approach" to the Scriptures, due to the Holy Spirit's inspiration of the Scriptures (and an accompanying unity amidst the diversity of biblical authors, genres, etc.).

103. The essays in this forum praise the anti-monothelite and anti-subordinationist conclusions of later fathers. Yet they also praise the work of Justin Martyr, who espoused a subordinationist theology. How does one respect the second-century authors and their chronological proximity to the New Testament while also incorporating the insights of developed Trinitarianism and Christology? A historically informed view of the diachronic development of theology must assist us.

104. Protestants have traditionally rejected the Second Council of Nicaea (787), which supported the veneration of icons in the "iconoclastic" battles.

cally and why? Do we seek geographical consensus across the Greek East and the Latin West—and beyond? Are we to think of "consensus" more as a general "spirit" of the early church?[105]

We would all acknowledge that the early church councils represent a wide ecclesiastical consensus. How, then, are we to approach the "conclusions" of those same "ecumenical councils" which are represented in their canons? Should bishops (or pastors) be ordained only with the consent of the Metropolitan (canon 6 of the Council of Nicaea)? Shall lapsed Christians who wish to rejoin the church spend a dozen years in various stages of public repentance before being brought back into full communion (canon 11)? Should we insist that bishops and presbyters partake of Communion before deacons, and prohibit deacons from sitting among the elders "contrary to canon and order" (canon 12)? Shall we prohibit clergy and deacons from transferring from one city to another (canon 15)? Shall we prohibit kneeling during Sunday liturgies (canon 20)? Do we treat the creeds and the canons in the same manner, due to their "ecumenical" consensus? If not, what objective methodology do we employ that warrants our conclusions? Will not rigorous historical examinations of the period help us in our theological understanding of the documents? Rather than relaying a "romantic version of the church fathers," our work "must be established on an honest and true assessment of the period."[106]

After we have consciously and conscientiously formed such an objective, rigorous method, let us apply it to test cases in the refining and nuancing of our faith and practice. I propose that we shall *still* find that each of us will (or at least should) do so in a manner that insightfully learns from the fathers with great profit yet ultimately appeals to the final authority of Scripture. We shall take heart, however. For as students of the entirety of church history, we know that we are both children of the fathers and heirs of the Reformation.[107] If it were not so, one would not be

---

105. See Wilken, *Spirit of Early Christian Thought*.

106. Husbands, "Introduction," 13–14.

107. See Wells, *Courage to Be Protestant*. Cf. the differences between John Jewel (1522–1571) and John Daillé (1594–1670) concerning the proper appropriation of the patristic authors. Jewel tended toward a more optimistic appropriation, while Daillé espoused a more pessimistic approach. On November 26, 1557, John Jewel preached his

Evangelicals and the Tensions of Ressourcement—A Baptist Response

an evangelical scholar learning from the early church, but a scholar learning from the early church who was formerly evangelical. Nevertheless, we listen with ears open to the fathers even as our hearts are resolutely bound to Scripture. In other words, we really do learn and yet retain our distinctive theologies.

Let me present one simple example. Most Baptist churches celebrate communion every quarter (three months) or, at most, every month. My study of the patristic period encourages me to consider the possibility of a more frequent celebration of the Lord's Table. A common "free church" rejoinder is that such frequency would lead to thoughtless participation or even boredom (and it seems that the most feared criticism that can be laid upon a contemporary American service is that it is "boring"!). But if the Lord's Supper points us toward the Gospel, are we willing to concede that we would become bored with the Gospel itself? Such openness to more frequent Communion respects Baptist emphases upon the "New Testament church" (cf. the regularity of the Lord's Supper in Acts), learns from the patristic period (cf. the known consensus from Justin's *First Apology* onward), concurs with the Reformers (not only Luther but also Calvin recommended frequent celebration), and highlights the Gospel-centeredness of the label "evangelical" (since Communion is a "Gospel" ordinance).[108]

Perhaps throughout my response I have sounded like a Socratic gadfly. Such characterization may simply accentuate enduring tensions and complexities. I have highlighted the tension between the "one, holy, apostolic" faith and the diversities we find in the extant fathers. The Greek thinkers would remind us that the tension between "the one and the many" is not new. I have emphasized diachronic developments within the patristic period. The Greek philosophers would point us toward the tension between "being" and "becoming," the unchangeable "essence" of an entity and the constant change we always seem to witness. Gadflies

---

"Challenge Sermon" at St. Paul's Cross. "The First five hundred years of the church," he argued, "are worth more than the whole thousand that followed." Contrast Daillé, *Treatise Concerning the Right Use of the Fathers*.

108. 1 Cor 11:26 simply mentions "as often" as you eat this bread and drink this cup. Paul seems to assume a practice of regular communion without delineating that regularity.

may not be well-liked in the *polis*, but their enduring questions have an uncanny ability to survive long after the hemlock has been administered. Each new generation must wrestle with the same difficulties in a faithful yet critical manner.

The enduring nature of these questions simply reminds us that we find ourselves situated in a Tradition that is bigger than us personally or even our contemporary generation collectively. There is wisdom in the ages. "Truly, we stand on the shoulders of giants and we honor them by knowing more about them, learning what they have taught, and seeking to apply insights from them, in the light of Scripture, for us today."[109] May historically-grounded and well-reasoned forays into the complex patristic past continue, and may they return bearing milk, honey, and clustered fruit. The contemporary church will be nourished by the rich harvest that is to come.

---

109. Wellum, "Standing on the Shoulders," 3.

Bibliography

Adams, Mark. "The Significance of Pentecost." Online: http://www.redlandbaptist.org/sermons/sermon20040222.php.
Alcañiz, Florentino. *Ecclesia Patristica et Millenarismus Expositio Historica*. Grenada, Spain: Méndez Caro, 1933.
Alexander, David C. *Augustine's Early Theology of the Church: Emergence and Implications, 386–391*. Patristic Studies 9. New York: Peter Lang, 2008.
Ammundsen, Valdemar. "The Rule of Truth in Irenaeus." *Journal of Theological Studies* 13 (1912) 574–80.
Anderson, Galusha, and Edgar J. Goodspeed, translators. *Ancient Sermons for Modern Times by Asterius, Bishop of Amasia*. New York: Pilgrim, 1904.
Anderson, H. George, T. Austin Murphy, and Joseph A. Burgess, editors. *Justification by Faith*. Lutherans and Catholics in Dialogue 7. Minneapolis: Augsburg, 1985.
Armstrong, Chris. "The Future Lies in the Past." *Christianity Today* 52:2 (2008) 22–29.
Arnold, Clinton E. "Early Church Catechesis and New Christians' Classes in Contemporary Evangelicalism." *Journal of the Evangelical Theology Society* 47 (2004) 39–54.
Associated Press. "Young Christians Ditch Glitz, Reach for Roots." *St. Petersburg Times*, October 11, 2003.
"Athanasian Creed." Online: http://www.ccel.org/creeds/athanasian.creed.html.
Aune, David E. *Revelation 6–16*. Word Biblical Commentary 52B. Nashville: T. Nelson, 1998.
Backus, Irena, editor. *The Reception of the Church Fathers in the West: From the Carolingians to the Maurists*. 2 vols. Leiden: Brill, 1997.
Bader-Saye, Scott. "The Emergent Matrix: A New Kind of Church?" *Christian Century* 121:24 (November 30, 2004) 20–27.
Bain, Andrew C. "Robert Reymond's Attack on the Eternal Generation." Online: http://www.baptistboard.com/showthread.php?t=19471.
Bardy, Gustave. "La Règle de Foi d'Origène." *Recherches de science religieuse* 9 (1919) 162–96.
Barnard, Leslie William, translator. *The First and Second Apologies* (Justin Martyr). ACW 56. Mahway, NJ: Paulist, 1997.

Bibliography

Barnes, Michel R., and Daniel H. Williams, editors. *Arianism after Arius: Essays on the Development of the Fourth Century Trinitarian Conflicts.* Edinburgh: T. & T. Clark, 1994.

Bartlett, Alan. "Redemption." In *The New Westminster Dictionary of Christian Spirituality,* edited by Philip Sheldrake, 528–29. Louisville: Westminster John Knox, 2005.

Bauder, Kevin. "Directions in Evangelicalism: The Gospel According to Scot." Online: http://www.centralseminary.edu/publications/Nick/Nick199.html.

———. "A Prelude to a Christian Theology of Culture." In *Missions in a New Millennium: Change and Challenges in World Missions,* edited by W. Edward Glenny and William H. Smallman, 231–44. Grand Rapids: Kregel, 2000.

———. "Thinking about the Gospel: The Gospel and Christian Fellowship." Online: http://www.centralseminary.edu/publications/Nick/Nick125.html.

———. "Those Pesky Premillennialists." Online: http://www.centralseminary.edu/publications/Nick/Nick228.html.

———. "Understanding Conservative Christianity: A Digression." Online: http://www.centralseminary.edu/publications/20090327Print.pdf.

———. "Understanding Conservative Christianity: Another Digression." Online: http://www.centralseminary.edu/publications/Nick/Nick211.html.

Bauer, Walter. *Orthodoxy and Heresy in Earliest Christianity,* edited by Robert A. Kraft and Gerhard Krodel. Philadelphia: Fortress, 1971. Originally published as *Rechtgläubigkeit und Ketzerei im ältesten Christentum* (Tübingen: Mohr, 1934).

Bebbington, D. W. *Evangelicalism in Modern Britain: A History from the 1730s to the 1980s.* London: Allen & Unwin, 1989.

Benne, Robert. *Quality with Soul: How Six Premier Christian Colleges and Universities Keep Faith with Their Religious Traditions.* Grand Rapids: Eerdmans, 2001.

Bercot, David W., editor. *A Dictionary of Early Christian Beliefs: A Reference Guide to More Than 700 Topics Discussed by the Early Church Fathers.* Peabody, MA: Hendrickson, 1998.

———. *The Kingdom that Turned the World Upside Down.* Tyler, TX: Scroll, 2003.

———. *Will the Real Heretics Please Stand Up: A New Look at Today's Evangelical Church in the Light of Early Christianity.* Henderson, TX: Scroll, 1989.

Bettenson, Henry, editor and translator. *The Early Christian Fathers: A Selection from the Writings of the Fathers from St. Clement of Rome to St. Athanasius.* New York: Oxford University Press, 1969.

Bevans, Stephen B., and Roger P. Schroeder. *Constants in Context: A Theology of Mission for Today.* American Society of Missiology 30. Maryknoll, NY: Orbis, 2004.

Bingham, D. Jeffrey. "Response." Unpublished paper, presented at the 2008 ETS annual meeting, November 2008.

Blowers, Paul M. "The *regula fidei* and the Narrative Character of Early Christian Faith." *Pro Ecclesia* 6 (1997) 199–228.

Boosahda, Wayne, and Randy Sly. "The Convergent Movement." *The Coracle,* July 30, 2004.

Booth, Alan D. "The Date of Jerome's Birth." *Phoenix* 33 (1971) 346–53.

Bosch, David J. *Transforming Mission: Paradigm Shifts in Theology of Mission.* American Society of Missiology 16. Maryknoll, NY: Orbis, 1990.

Bibliography

Boulding, Maria, translator. *St. Augustine's Confessions.* Hyde Park, NY: New City, 1997.

———, translator. *Expositions of the Psalms* (Augustine). 6 vols. WSA, pt. 3, vols. 15–20. Hyde Park, NY: New City, 2000–.

Bradley, Ian. *Celtic Christianity: Making Myths and Chasing Dreams.* New York: St. Martin's, 1999.

Bradshaw, Paul F. *The Search for the Origins of Christian Worship: Sources and Methods for the Study of Early Liturgy.* Oxford: Oxford University Press, 1992.

Bradshaw, Paul F., Maxwell E. Johnson, and L. Edward Phillips. *The Apostolic Tradition: A Commentary,* edited by Harold W. Attridge. Hermeneia. Minneapolis: Fortress, 2002.

Braun, Jon. "A Call to Church Authority." In *The Orthodox Evangelicals: Who They Are and What They Are Saying,* edited by Robert E. Webber and Donald Bloesch, 166–89. Nashville: T. Nelson, 1978.

Bromiley, Geoffrey W. "Promise of Patristic Studies." In *Toward a Theology for the Future,* edited by David F. Wells and Clark H. Pinnock, 125–56. Carol Stream, IL: Creation House, 1971.

Brown, Dan. *The Da Vinci Code.* New York: Doubleday, 2003.

Brown, Peter. *Poverty and Leadership in the Later Roman Empire.* Menahem Stern Jerusalem Lectures. Hanover, NH: University Press of New England, 2002.

Brown, Robert McAfee. "Oral Roberts and the 900-Foot Jesus." *Christian Century* 98:14 (April 22, 1981) 450–52.

———. "The Oral Tradition Strikes Again." *Christian Century* 101:9 (March 14, 1984) 278–79.

Burge, Gary M. *John.* NIV Application Commentary. Grand Rapids: Zondervan, 2000.

Burridge, Richard A. *Imitating Jesus: An Inclusive Approach to New Testament Ethics.* Grand Rapids: Eerdmans, 2007.

Butterworth, G. W., translator. *On First Principles* (Origen). Gloucester, MA: P. Smith, 1973.

Butterworth, Robert, editor and translator. *Contra Noetum* (Hippolytus of Rome). Heythrop Monographs 2. London: Sheed & Ward, 1977.

Byassee, Jason. "Emerging from What, Going Where?: Emerging Churches and Ancient Christianity." In *Ancient Faith for the Church's Future,* edited by Mark Husbands and Jeffrey P. Greenman, 249–63. Downers Grove, IL: InterVarsity, 2008.

Cabié, Robert. "Christian Initiation." In *The Church at Prayer: An Introduction to the Liturgy,* edited by Aimé Georges Mortimort, translated by Matthew J. O'Connell, 3:11–100. New ed. Collegeville, MN: Liturgical, 1987.

———. *The Church at Prayer: An Introduction to the Liturgy,* vol. 2: *The Eucharist.* Edited by Aimé Georges Mortimort, translated by Matthew J. O'Connell. New ed. Collegeville, MN: Liturgical, 1986.

Calvin, John. *Institutes of the Christian Religion.* edited by John McNeill. Philadelphia: Westminster, 1977.

Campbell, Colleen Carroll. *The New Faithful: Why Young Adults Are Embracing Christian Orthodoxy.* Chicago: Loyola, 2002.

Carey, G. L. "Justin Martyr." In *The New International Dictionary of the Christian Church,* edited by J. D. Douglas, 558. Grand Rapids: Zondervan, 1978.

Carroll, J. M. *The Trail of Blood.* Lexington, KY: Ashland Avenue Baptist Church, 1931.

Bibliography

Carson, D. A. *Becoming Conversant with the Emerging Church: Understanding a Movement and Its Implications*. Grand Rapids: Zondervan, 2005.

———. *Christ and Culture Revisited*. Grand Rapids: Eerdmans, 2008.

Carter, Craig A. *Rethinking Christ and Culture: A Post-Christendom Perspective*. Grand Rapids: Brazos, 2006.

Cavallera, Ferdinand. *Saint Jérôme: sa vie et son oeuvre*, 2 vols. Louvain: Spicilegium sacrum Lovaniense, 1922.

"Chicago Call of 1977." Online: http://www.growcenter.org/ChicagoCall.htm.

Clapp, Rodney. *Border Crossings: Christian Trespasses on Popular Culture and Public Affairs*. Grand Rapids: Brazos, 2000.

———. *A Peculiar People: The Church as Culture in a Post-Christian Society*. Downers Grove, IL: InterVarsity, 1996.

Clarkson, John F., et al. *The Church Teaches: Documents of the Church in English Translation*. Saint Louis: Herder, 1955.

Cocchini, Francesca. "Dalla regula fidei riflessioni origeniane sullo Spirito Santo." In *Origeniana octava*, edited by L. Perrone et al., 1:593–603. Leuven, Belgium: Leuven University Press, 2003.

Collins, John J. "Apocalyptic Literature." In *EEC* 1:73–74.

Connolly, R. Hugh, translator. *Didascalia Apostolorum: The Syriac Version Translated and Accompanied by the Verona Latin Fragments*. Oxford: Clarendon, 1929.

Copeland, Kenneth. *The Power of the Tongue*. Fort Worth: Kenneth Copeland Ministries, 1980.

Corbett, Steve, and Brian Fikkert. *When Helping Hurts: How to Alleviate Poverty without Hurting the Poor . . . and Yourself*. Chicago: Moody, 2009.

Countryman, L. William. "Tertullian and the *regula fidei*." *Second Century* 2 (1982) 208–27.

Crehan, Joseph. *Early Christian Baptism and the Creed: A Study in Anti-Nicene Theology*. Bellarmine Series 13. London: Burns, Oates & Washbourne, 1950.

Crenshaw, Curtis I. *Man as God: The Word of Faith Movement*. Memphis: Footstool, 1994.

Cross, Anthony R., and Philip E. Thompson, editors. *Baptist Sacramentalism*. Studies in Baptist History and Thought 5. Eugene, OR: Wipf & Stock, 2007.

Crouch, Andy. "The Emergent Mystique." *Christianity Today* 48:11 (November 2004) 37–41.

Crutchfield, Larry V. "Rudiments of Dispensationalism in the Ante-Nicene Period." *Bibliotheca Sacra* 144 (1987) 254–77, 377–402.

Cutsinger, James S., editor. *Reclaiming the Great Tradition: Evangelicals, Catholics & Orthodox in Dialogue*. Downers Grove, IL: InterVarsity, 1997.

Daillé, Jean. *A Treatise Concerning the Right Use of the Fathers in the Decision of the Controversies that Are at This Day in Religion*. London: J. Martin, 1651.

Daley, Brian. *The Hope of the Early Church: A Handbook of Patristic Eschatology*. Cambridge: Cambridge University Press, 1991.

Daly, Cahal B. *Tertullian: The Puritan and His Influence; An Essay in Historical Theology*. Dublin: Four Courts, 1993.

Daniel, Curt. *The History and Theology of Calvinism*. Dallas: Scholarly Reprints, 1993.

Datema, Cornelius, editor. *Homilies I–XIV* (Asterius of Amasea). Leiden: Brill, 1970.

Bibliography

Davies, J. G. *The Early Christian Church*. History of Religion. New York: Holt, Rinehart and Winston, 1965.
Dayton, Donald W. "Some Doubts about the Usefulness of the Category 'Evangelical.'" In *The Variety of American Evangelicalism*, edited by Donald W. Dayton and Robert K. Johnston, 245–51. Knoxville: University of Tennessee Press, 1991.
Decret, François. *Early Christianity in North Africa*. Translated by Edward Smither. Eugene, OR: Cascade, 2009.
———. *Le christianisme en Afrique du Nord Ancienne*. Paris: Seuil, 1996.
Dehandschutter, Boudewijn. "The Meaning of Witness in the Apocalypse." In *Polycarpiana: Studies on Martyrdom and Persecution in Early Christianity*, edited by Johan Leemans, 181–87. Bibliotheca Ephemeridum theologicarum Lovaniensium 205. Leuven, Belgium: Leuven University Press, 2007.
Demacopoulos, George E. *Five Models of Spiritual Direction in the Early Church*. Notre Dame: University of Notre Dame Press, 2007.
Dennison, James T. "Remarks on the Current Rejection of the Eternal Generation of the Son of God." Paper presented at the 2007 *Kerux* conference, Lynnwood, WA, May 2007.
Denzinger, Heinrich. *The Sources of Catholic Dogma*. Translated by Roy J. Deferrari. Saint Louis: Herder, 1957.
DeSimone, Russell J., translator. *Novatian: The Trinity, The Spectacles, Jewish Foods, In Praise of Purity, Letters*. FC 67. Washington, DC: Catholic University of America Press, 1974.
Di Berardino, Angelo, and Basil Studer, editors. *History of Theology*. Vol. 1: *The Patristic Period*. Translated by Matthew J. O'Connell. Collegeville, MN: Liturgical, 1997.
Dix, Gregory. *The Shape of the Liturgy*. Westminster: Dacre, 1945.
Dix, Gregory, and Henry Chadwick, editors. *The Treatise on the Apostolic Tradition of St. Hippolytus of Rome, Bishop and Martyr*. London: SPCK, 1968.
Dodd, C. H. *The Apostolic Preaching and Its Developments, Three Lectures*. New York: Harper, 1936.
Donna, Rose Bernard, translator. *Letters* (Cyprian). FC 51. Washington, DC: Catholic University of America Press, 1992.
Donovan, Mary Ann. *One Right Reading?: A Guide to Irenaeus*. Collegeville, MN: Liturgical, 1997.
Dorner, I. A. *History of the Development of the Doctrine of the Person of Christ*. Vol. 1. Edinburgh: T. & T. Clark, 1865.
Döpp, Siegmar, and Wilhelm Geerlings editors. *Dictionary of Early Christian Literature*. New York: Crossroad, 2000.
Draguet, René. *Julien d'Halicarnasse et sa controverse avec Sévère d'Antioche sur l'incorruptibilité du corps du Christ*. Leuven, Belgium: Smeesters, 1924.
Dronsfield, W. R. *The Eternal Son of the Father*. London: Bible Truth Depot, 1987.
Easton, Burton Scott, translator. *The Apostolic Tradition of Hippolytus*. Hamden, CT: Archon, 1962.
Eckman, James P. *Christian Ethics in a Postmodern World*. Wheaton, IL: Evangelical Training Association, 1999.

Bibliography

Ehrman, Bart D., and Andrew S. Jacobs, editors. *Christianity in Late Antiquity, 300–450 C.E.: A Reader*. New York: Oxford University Press, 2004.

Elert, Werner. *The Structure of Lutheranism*. Translated by Walter A. Hansen. St. Louis: Concordia, 1962.

Esbroek, Michel van. "The Aphthartodocetic Edict of Justinian and its Armenian Background." *Studia Patristica* 33 (1997) 578–85.

Escobar, Samuel. *Changing Tides: Latin America and World Mission Today*. American Society of Missiology 31. Maryknoll, NY: Orbis, 2002.

"Eternal Generation of the Son." Online: http://www.theopedia.com/Eternal_generation_of_the_Son.

Eusebius. *The Church History*. Translated by Paul L. Maier. Grand Rapids: Kregel, 2007.

"An Evangelical Manifesto: A Declaration of Evangelical Identity and Public Commitment." Online: http://www.anevangelicalmanifesto.com.

Everts, W. W., Jr. *The Church in the Wilderness, or, The Baptists before the Reformation*. Nappanee, IN: Baptist Bookshelf, 1986.

Ewald, Marie Liguori, translator. *The Homilies of Saint Jerome*. 2 vols. FC 48, 57. Washington, DC: Catholic University of America Press, 1966.

———, translator. *Treatises on Marriage and Other Subjects* (Augustine). FC 27. Washington, DC: Catholic University of America Press, 1955.

Eynde, Damien van den. *Les Normes de l'Enseignement Chrétien dans la littérature patristique des trois premiers siècles*. Paris: 1933.

Fairburn, Donald Fairburn. "Contemporary Millennial/Tribulational Debates: Whose Side Was the Early Church On?" In *The Case for Historic Premillennialism: An Alternative to "Left Behind" Eschatology*, edited by Craig L. Blomberg and Sung Wook Chung, 105–32. Grand Rapids: Baker Academic, 2009.

Fellowes, Audrey, translator. *Life of Saint Augustine* (Possidius of Calama). Edited by John E. Rotelle. Villanova, PA: Augustinian Press, 1988.

Feltoe, Charles Lett, editor. *Saint Dionysius of Alexandria: Letters and Treatises*. London: SPCK, 1918.

Ferguson, Everett. "Baptism." In *EEC* 1:160–64.

———. *Baptism in the Early Church: History, Theology, and Liturgy in the First Five Centuries*. Grand Rapids: Eerdmans, 2009.

———. "Catechesis, Catechumenate." In *EEC* 1:223–25.

———. *Church History*. Vol. 1: *From Christ to Pre-Reformation*. Grand Rapids: Zondervan, 2005.

———. "The 'Congregationalism' of the Early Church." In *The Free Church and the Early Church: Bridging the Historical and Theological Divide*, edited by D. H. Williams, 129–40. Grand Rapids: Eerdmans, 2002.

———. *Early Christians Speak: Faith and Life in the First Three Centuries*, vol. 2. 3rd ed. Abilene, TX: ACU, 2002.

———. "How We Christians Worship." *Christian History* 37 (Nov. 1, 1993) 10–15.

———. "Hymns." In *EEC* 1:548–51.

———. "A New Journal." *Second Century* 1 (1981) 3–4.

Finn, Nathan. Review of *Towards Baptist Catholicity* by Steven Harmon. Online: http://www.nathanfinn.wordpress.com.

Bibliography

Flesseman-Van Leer, Ellen. *Tradition and Scripture in the Early Church*. Assen, Neth.: Van Gorcum, 1954.

Folkemer, D. "A Study of the Catechumenate." In *Conversion, Catechumenate, and Baptism in the Early Church*, edited by Everett F. Ferguson, 244–65. Studies in Early Christianity 11. New York: Garland, 1993.

Fortman, Edmund J. *The Triune God: A Historical Study of the Doctrine of the Trinity*. Philadelphia: Westminster, 1972. Reprint: Eugene, OR: Wipf & Stock, 1999.

Foster, Richard J. *Celebration of Discipline: The Path to Spiritual Growth*. San Francisco: Harper & Row, 1978.

Fraenkel, Peter. *Testimonia Patrum: The Function of Patristic Argument in the Theology of Philip Melanchthon*. Travaux d'humanisme et renaissance 46. Geneva: Droz, 1961.

Fraipont, J., editor. *Sancti Fulgentii episcope Ruspensis opera* (Fulgentius of Ruspe). 2 vols. CCSL 91, 91A. Turnhout, Belgium: Brepols, 1968.

Frend, W. H. C. *Martyrdom and Persecution in the Early Church: A Study of a Conflict from the Maccabees to Donatus*. Oxford: Blackwell, 1965.

———. *The Rise of Christianity*. Philadelphia: Fortress, 1984.

Funk, Robert W., Roy W. Hoover, and the Jesus Seminar. *The Five Gospels: The Search for the Authentic Words of Jesus; New Translation and Commentary*. San Francisco: Harper, 1997.

Garrett, James Leo, Jr., "Major Emphases in Baptist Theology." *Southwestern Journal of Theology* 37 (1995) 36–46.

Gibbon, Edward. *The History of the Decline and Fall of the Roman Empire*. 1776–88. Reprint: Norwalk, CT: Easton, 1974.

Gillquist, Peter E. *Becoming Orthodox: A Journey to the Ancient Christian Faith*. Ben Lomond, CA: Conciliar, 1992.

Glorie, Franciscus, editor. *Maxentii aliorumque Scytharum monachorum necnon Ioannis Tomitanae urbis Episcopi Opuscula* (Maxentius). CCSL 85A. Turnhout, Belgium: Brepols, 1978.

Goehring, James. "Monasticism in Byzantine Egypt: Continuity and Memory." In *Egypt in the Byzantine World, 300–700*, edited by Roger S. Bagnall, 390–407. Cambridge: Cambridge University Press, 2007.

González, Justo L. *The Story of Christianity*. Vol. 1: *The Early Church to the Dawn of the Reformation*. San Francisco: Harper, 1984.

Green, Michael. *Evangelism in the Early Church*. Grand Rapids: Eerdmans, 1970.

Grant, Michael, translator. *Tacitus: The Annals of Imperial Rome*. New York: Dorset, 1971.

Grant, Robert M. *Irenaeus of Lyons*. Early Church Fathers. New York: Routledge, 1997.

Grech, Prosper S. "The *Regula Fidei* as a Hermeneutical Principle in Patristic Exegesis." In *The Interpretation of the Bible: The International Symposium in Slovenia*, edited by Jože Krašovec, 589–604. JSOTSup 289. Sheffield, UK: Sheffield Academic, 1998.

Greenslade, S. L. *Early Latin Theology: Selections from Tertullian, Cyprian, Ambrose, and Jerome*. Library of Christian Classics 5. Louisville: Westminster, 1956.

Gregg, Robert C., editor. *Arianism: Historical and Theological Reassessments*. Patristic Monograph Series 11. Cambridge, MA: Philadelphia Patristic Foundation, 1985. Reprint: Eugene, OR: Wipf & Stock, 2006.

Bibliography

Gregg, Robert C., and Dennis E. Groh. *Early Arianism—A View of Salvation*. Philadelphia: Fortress, 1981.

Gregg, Samuel. *Economic Thinking for the Theologically Minded*. Lanham, MD: University Press of America, 2001.

Grudem, Wayne A. *Systematic Theology*. Grand Rapids: Zondervan, 1994.

Grutzmacher, Georg. *Hieronymus: eine biographische Studie zur alten Kirchen Geschichte*. 3 vols. Studien zur Geschichte der Theologie und der Kirche. Leipzig: Dietrich, 1901–8.

Gumerlock, Francis X. "Amillennialism in the Early Church." Paper presented at the New Covenant Theology Seminar, Colorado Springs, CO, September 2005.

———. *Fulgentius of Ruspe on the Saving Will of God: The Development of a Sixth-Century African Bishop's Interpretation of 1 Timothy 2:4 during the Semi-Pelagian Controversy*. Lewiston, NY: Mellen, 2009.

———. "The Interpretation of Tongues in the Middle Ages." *Antiphon* 10 (2006) 160–68.

———. "Mark 13:32 and Christ's Supposed Ignorance: Four Patristic Solutions." *Trinity Journal* 28 (2007) 205–13.

———. "Millennialism and the Early Church Councils: Was Chiliasm Condemned at Constantinople?" *Fides et Historia* 36 (2004) 83–95.

———. "Nero Antichrist: Patristic Evidence for the Use of Nero's Name in Calculating the Number of the Beast (Rev 13:18)." *Westminster Theological Journal* 68 (2006) 347–60.

———. "Olivet Discourse," In *The Early Church and the End of the World*, by Gary DeMar and Francis X. Gumerlock, 79–123. Powder Springs, GA: American Vision, 2006.

———. "A Rapture Citation in the Fourteenth Century." *Bibliotheca Sacra* 159 (2002) 349–62.

———. "The Rapture in the *Apocalypse of Elijah*." Paper delivered at the 2002 Southeastern Regional Meeting of the Evangelical Theological Society, Germantown, TN, March 2002.

———. "Tongues in the Church Fathers." *Reformation & Revival* 13 (2004) 123–38.

Guy, Laurie. *Introducing Early Christianity: A Topical Survey of Its Life, Beliefs and Practices*. Downers Grove, IL: InterVarsity, 2004.

———. "'Naked' Baptism in the Early Church: The Rhetoric and the Reality." *Journal of Religious History* 27 (2003) 133–42.

Haas, Christopher. "Where Did Christians Worship?" *Christian History* 37:12 (1993) 32–35.

Hagin, Kenneth E. *The Present Day Ministry of Jesus Christ*. 2nd ed. Tulsa: RHEMA Bible Church, 1983.

Hahn, August. *Bibliothek der Symbole und Glaubensregeln der Alten Kirche*. Breslau: Morgenstern, 1897.

Hall, Christopher A. "Back to the Fathers." *Christianity Today* 34:13 (September 24, 1990) 28–31.

———. "Introduction." In *Ancient & Postmodern Christianity: Paleo-orthodoxy in the 21st Century; Essays in Honor of Thomas C. Oden*, edited by Kenneth Tanner and Christopher A. Hall, 7–12. Downers Grove, IL: InterVarsity, 2002.

———. *Learning Theology with the Church Fathers*. Downers Grove, IL: InterVarsity, 2002.

———. *Reading Scripture with the Church Fathers*. Downers Grove, IL: InterVarsity, 1998.

———. "Tradition, Authority, Magisterium." In *Ancient Faith for the Church's Future*, edited by Mark Husbands and Jeffrey P. Greenman, 27–52. Downers Grove, IL: InterVarsity, 2008.

Hammerstaedt, Jürgen and Peri Terbuyken. "Improvisation." In *RAC* 17:1202–84.

Hanson, R. P. C. *Origen's Doctrine of Tradition*. London: SPCK, 1954.

———. *The Search for the Christian Doctrine of God: The Arian Controversy, 318–381*. Edinburgh: T. & T. Clark, 1988.

———. *Tradition in the Early Church*. Library of History and Doctrine. London: SCM, 1962.

Harmless, William. "Baptism." In *Augustine through the Ages: An Encyclopedia*, edited by Allan D. Fitzgerald, 84–91. Grand Rapids: Eerdmans, 1999.

———. "Catechumens, Catechumenate." In *Augustine through the Ages: An Encyclopedia*, edited by Allan D. Fitzgerald, 147–48. Grand Rapids: Eerdmans, 1999.

Harmon, Steven R. "'All of Church History as the History of Us All': E. Glenn Hinson, Patristic Christianity, and Baptist Catholicity." *Review and Expositor* 101 (2004) 573–74.

———. *Towards Baptist Catholicity: Essays on Tradition and the Baptist Vision*. Studies in Baptist History and Thought 27. Eugene, OR: Wipf & Stock, 2006.

Harnack, Adolf von. *Mission and Expansion of Christianity in the First Three Centuries*. Translated and edited by James Moffatt. 2 vols. Theological Translation Library 19–20. London: Williams and Northgate, 1908. Online: http://www.ccel.org/ccel/harnack/mission.html.

Harp, Gillis. "Antiquity & Absence." *Touchstone* 19:9 (Nov. 2006) 29.

Harper, Michael. *The True Light: An Evangelical's Journey to Orthodoxy*. London: Hodder & Stoughton, 1997.

Harris, William, translator. "Pliny, *Epistulae*." Online: http://community.middlebury.edu/~harris/Classics/plinytrajan.html.

Hart, Addison H. "Evangelical *Ressourcement*." *Touchstone* 14:3 (April 2001) 38–41.

Hart, D. G. "Born Again Free." *Touchstone* 19:9 (2006) 27–28.

———. *Deconstructing Evangelicalism: Conservative Protestantism in the Age of Billy Graham*. Grand Rapids: Baker Academic, 2004.

Hartley, L. P. *The Go-between*. London: Hamilton, 1953.

Hartog, Paul. "Greco-Roman Understanding of Christianity." In *The Routledge Companion to Early Christian Thought*, edited by D. Jeffrey Bringham, 49–65. London: Routledge, 2009.

———. *Polycarp and the New Testament: The Occasion, Rhetoric, Theme, and Unity of the Epistle to the Philippians and Its Allusions to New Testament Literature*. Wissenschaftliche Untersuchungen zum Neuen Testament 2.134. Tübingen: Mohr Siebeck, 2002.

———. "Polycarp, Ephesians, and 'Scripture.'" *Westminster Theological Journal* 70 (2008) 255–75.

———. "Religious Liberty and the Early Church." *Southwestern Journal of Theology*, forthcoming.

Bibliography

———. "The 'Rule of Faith' and Patristic Biblical Exegesis." *Trinity Journal* 28 (2007) 65–86.

Hatch, Nathan O. "Response to Carl F. H. Henry." In *Evangelical Affirmations*, edited by Kenneth S. Kantzer and Carl F. H. Henry, 95–102. Grand Rapids: Zondervan, 1990.

Hauerwas, Stanley. *After Christendom?: How the Church Is to Behave if Freedom, Justice, and a Christian Nation Are Bad Ideas.* Nashville: Abingdon, 1991.

Hauerwas, Stanley, and William H. Willimon. *Resident Aliens: Life in the Christian Colony.* Nashville: Abingdon, 1989.

Haykin, Michael A. G. "Recovering Ancient Practices." *Southern Baptist Journal of Theology* 12 (2008) 62–67.

———. "Why Study the Fathers?" Reformation 21. Online: http://www.reformation21.org/Content/324.

Haykin, Michael A. G., and Kenneth J. Stewart, editors. *The Emergence of Evangelicalism: Exploring Historical Continuities.* Leicester: InterVarsity, 2008.

Hefner, Philip J. "Saint Irenaeus and the Hypothesis of Faith." *Dialog* 2 (1963) 300–306.

———. "Theological Methodology and St. Irenaeus." *Journal of Religion* 44 (1964) 294–309.

Hellerman, Joe. "Ancient-Future Community: A Lesson from the Early Church." *Sundoulos* (Summer 2006) no pages. Online: http://www.talbot.edu/faculty/sundoulos/archive06summer/leadarticle.

Henry, Carl F. H. *The Christian Mindset in a Secular Society: Promoting Evangelical Renewal & National Righteousness.* Portland: Multnomah, 1984.

Hex, Clete. "Is He 'Another Jesus'? The 'Born Again' Jesus of the Word Faith Movement." *Watchman Expositor* 10:8 (1993) 16–17.

Hill, Charles E. *Regnum Caelorum: Patterns of Millenial Thought in Early Christianity.* 2nd ed. Grand Rapids: Eerdmans, 2001.

Hill, Edmund, translator. *Sermons (51–94) on the New Testament* (Augustine). Edited by John E. Rotelle. WSA pt. 3, vol. 3. Hyde Park, NY: New City, 1994.

Hill, Robert Charles, translator. *St. John Chrysostom: Old Testament Homilies*, vol. 2: *Homilies on Isaiah and Jeremiah.* Brookline, MA: Holy Cross Orthodox, 2003.

Hinson, E. Glenn. "Some Things I've Learned from the Study of Early Christian History." *Review and Expositor* 101 (2004) 729–44.

———. "A Word from . . ." *Review and Expositor* 101 (2004) 577–81.

Hocking, W. J. *The Son of His Love: Papers on Eternal Sonship.* Sunbury, PA: Believers Bookshelf, 1970.

Hodges, Sam. "Prominent Evangelical Returns to Catholic Roots." *The Dallas Morning News*, May 8, 2007.

Hollenweger, Walter J. *The Pentecostals.* Translated by R. W. Wilson. Minneapolis: Augsburg, 1972.

Holmes, Michael W., editor and translator. *The Apostolic Fathers: Greek Texts and English Translations.* 3rd ed. Grand Rapids: Baker, 2007.

Houghton, Myron. "A Critique of 'Easy Believism.'" *Faith Pulpit* (March/April 2008) 1–4.

Howard, Thomas. *Evangelical Is Not Enough.* Nashville: T. Nelson, 1984.

———. "A Call to Sacramental Integrity." In *The Orthodox Evangelicals: Who They Are and What They Are Saying*, edited by Robert E. Webber and Donald Bloesch, 118–45. Nashville: T. Nelson, 1978.

———. *Lead, Kindly Light: My Journey to Rome*. Steubenville, OH: Franciscan University Press, 1994.

Huebner, R. A. *F. E. Raven's Evil Doctrines on the Person of Christ and Their Present Bearing*. Morganville, NJ: Present Truth, 1980.

Hughes, R. Kent. *Disciplines of a Godly Man*. Wheaton: Crossway, 1991.

Husbands, Mark. "Introduction." In *Ancient Faith for the Church's Future*, edited by Mark Husbands and Jeffrey P. Greenman, 9–23. Downers Grove, IL: InterVarsity, 2008.

Husbands, Mark, and Jeffrey P. Greenman, editors. *Ancient Faith for the Church's Future*. Downers Grove, IL: InterVarsity, 2008.

Irvin, Dale T., and Scott W. Sunquist. *History of the World Christian Movement*. Maryknoll, NY: Orbis, 2001–.

Jarrel, W. A. *Baptist Church Perpetuity, or, The Continuous Existence of Baptist Churches from the Apostolic to the Present Day*. Dallas: Jarrel, 1894.

Johnston, Robert K. "Introduction: Unity and Diversity in Evangelical Theology." In *The Use of the Bible in Theology: Evangelical Options*, edited by Robert K. Johnston, 1–17. Atlanta: John Knox, 1985.

Lutheran World Federation and the Roman Catholic Church. *Joint Declaration on the Doctrine of Justification*. Grand Rapids: Eerdmans, 1999.

Jones, Andrew. "Deep Church." Online: http://tallskinnykiwi.typepad.com/tallskinnykiwi/2007/06/deep_church.html.

Jones, Tony. *The Sacred Way: Spiritual Practices for Everyday Life*. El Cajon, CA: Youth Specialties, 2005.

Kalantzis, George. "Crumbs from the Table: Lazarus, the Eucharist and the Banquet of the Poor in the Homilies of John Chrysostom." In *Ancient Faith for the Church's Future*, edited by Mark Husbands and Jeffrey P. Greenman, 156–68. Downers Grove, IL: InterVarsity, 2008.

Kelly, J. N. D. *Early Christian Creeds*. 2nd ed. London: Longmans, 1960.

———. *Early Christian Doctrines*. Rev. ed. San Francisco: Harper & Row, 1978.

———. *Jerome: His Life, Writings, and Controversies*. London: Duckworth, 1975.

Kistemaker, Simon J. "Atonement in Hebrews: A Merciful and Faithful High Priest." In *The Glory of the Atonement: Biblical, Historical & Practical Perspectives; Essays in Honor of Roger Nicole*, edited by Charles E. Hill and Frank A. James III, 163–75. Downers Grove, IL: InterVarsity, 2004.

Kopecek, Thomas A. *A History of Neo-Arianism*. 2 vols. Patristic Monograph Series 8. Cambridge, MA: Philadelphia Patristic Foundation, 1979.

Kreider, Alan. *The Change of Conversion and the Origin of Christendom*. Harrisburg, PA: Trinity, 1999. Reprint: Eugene, OR: Wipf & Stock, 2007.

———. "'They Alone Known the Right Way to Live': The Early Church and Evangelism." In *Ancient Faith for the Church's Future*, edited by Mark Husbands and Jeffrey P. Greenman, 167–76. Downers Grove, IL: InterVarsity, 2008.

Kretschmar, Georg. "The Early Church and Hellenistic Culture." *International Review of Mission* 84 (1995) 33–46.

Bibliography

Ladner, Gerhart B. *The Idea of Reform: Its Impact on Christian Thought and Action in the Age of the Fathers.* New York: Harper & Row, 1967.

Lane, Anthony N. S. *John Calvin: Student of the Church Fathers.* Edinburgh: T. & T. Clark, 1999.

———. "*Sola Scriptura*? Making Sense of a Post-Reformation Slogan." In *A Pathway into the Holy Scripture*, edited by Philip E. Satterthwaite and David F. Wright, 297–327. Grand Rapids: Eerdmans, 1994.

Lane, Belden C. *The Solace of Fierce Landscapes: Exploring Desert and Mountain Spirituality.* Oxford: Oxford University Press, 1998.

Lane Fox, Robin. *Pagans and Christians.* New York: Harper Collins, 1988.

Lanne, Emmanuel. "La Règle de la Vérité Aux sources d'une expression de saint Irénée." In *Lex orandi lex credendi: miscellanea in onore di p. Cipriano Vagaggine*, edited by Gerardo J. Békés and Giustino Farnedi, 57–70. Studia Anselmiana 79. Rome: Anselmiana, 1980.

Latourette, Kenneth Scott. *A History of the Expansion of Christianity.* Vol. 1: *The First Five Centuries.* New York: Harper & Bros., 1937. Reprint: Grand Rapids: Zondervan, 1966.

Lawless, George. "Augustine's First Monastery: Thagaste or Hippo." *Augustinianum* 25 (1985) 65–78.

Leemans, Johan, et al., editors. "*Let Us Die that We May Live*": *Greek Homilies on Christian Martyrs from Asia Minor, Palestine, and Syria (c. AD 350–AD 450).* London: Routledge, 2003.

Leith, John H., editor. *Creeds of the Churches: A Reader in Christian Doctrine, from the Bible to the Present.* Rev. ed. Atlanta: John Knox, 1973.

Lesbaupin, Ivo. *Blessed Are the Persecuted: Christian Life in the Roman Empire, A.D. 64–313.* Translated by Robert R. Barr. Maryknoll, NY: Orbis, 1987.

"The Letter of the Synod in Nicaea to the Egyptians." Online: http://mb-soft.com/believe/txc/nicaea.htm#4.

Lewis, C. S. "Introduction." In *St. Athanasius: On the Incarnation* (Athananius), 3–10. 1944. Reprint: Crestwood, NY: St. Vladimir's Seminary Press, 1993.

———. *Mere Christianity.* London: Macmillan, 1943.

Lightfoot, J. B. *The Apostolic Fathers: A Revised Text with Introductions, Notes, Dissertations, and Translations.* 2 vols. 2nd ed. London: MacMillan, 1889–1890. Reprint: Grand Rapids: Baker, 1981.

Litfin, Bryan M. *Getting to Know the Church Fathers: An Evangelical Introduction.* Grand Rapids: Brazos, 2007.

———. "The Rule of Faith in Augustine." *Pro Ecclesia* 14 (2005) 85–101.

Lovelace, Richard. "The Three Streams, One River?" *Charisma* 10:2 (September 1984) 8.

Lubac, Henri de. *Exégèse médiévale: les quatre sens de L'Ecriture.* Paris: Aubier-Montaigne, 1959–1964.

———. *Medieval Exegesis: The Four Senses of Scripture.* Vol. 1. Translated by Mark Sebanc. Ressourcement. Grand Rapids: Eerdmans, 1998.

Lucas, Sean Michael. "A Call to an Ancient Evangelical Future." Online: http://seanmichaellucas.blogspot.com.

Luce, A. A. *Monophysitism, Past and Present: A Study in Christology.* London: SPCK, 1920.

Bibliography

MacArthur, John, Jr. *Hebrews*. MacArthur New Testament Commentary. Chicago: Moody, 1983.

———. "Reexamining the Eternal Sonship of Christ." Panorama City, CA: Grace to You Ministries, 1999.

———. "The Sonship of Christ." Unpublished paper, November 1991.

MacMullen, Ramsay. *The Second Church: Popular Christianity, A.D. 200–400*. Writings from the Greco-Roman World Supplement Series 1. Atlanta: SBL, 2009.

Maier, Paul L., translator. *Eusebius—The Church History: A New Translation with Commentary*. 4th ed. Grand Rapids: Kregel, 1999.

Mammana, Richard J. "Orthodox Twenty-Somethings." *Touchstone* 16:5 (June 2003) 49–51.

Mandouze, André. *Saint Augustine, l'aventure de la raison et la grâce*. Paris: Études Augustiniennes, 1968.

Marshall, I. Howard. *Acts*. Tyndale New Testament Commentaries. Grand Rapids: Eerdmans, 1991.

Mayer, Wendy. "The Audience(s) for Patristic Social Teaching: A Case Study." In *Reading Patristic Texts on Social Ethics: Issues and Challenges for 21st Century Christian Social Thought*, edited by Johan Leemans, Brian Matz, and Johan Verstraeten. CUA Studies in Early Christianity. Washington, DC: CUA Press, forthcoming.

McClain, Alva J. *The Greatness of the Kingdom: An Inductive Study of the Kingdom of God as Set Forth in Scripture*. Winona Lake, IN: BMH, 1959.

McClay, Wilfrid M. "What Lies Behind." *Touchstone* 19:9 (November 2006) 23–24.

McConnell, D. R. *A Different Gospel: A Historical and Biblical Analysis of the Modern Faith Movement*. Peabody, MA: Hendrickson, 1988.

McGinn, Bernard. *Antichrist: Two Thousand Years of the Human Fascination with Evil*. New York: Columbia University Press, 2000.

McGoldrick, James Edward. *Baptist Successionism: A Crucial Question in Baptist History*. ATLA Monograph 32. Lanham, MD: Scarecrow, 1994.

McGowan, Andrew. "Eating People: Accusations of Cannibalism against Christians in the Second Century." *Journal of Early Christian Studies* 2 (1994) 413–42.

McGrath, Alister E. *Reformation Thought: An Introduction*. 3rd ed. Malden, MA: Blackwell, 1999.

McGuire, Brian Patrick. *Friendship and Community: The Monastic Experience, 350–1250*. Cistercian Studies 95. Kalamazoo, MI: Cistercian, 1988.

McKechnie, Paul. *The First Christian Centuries: Perspectives on the Early Church*. Downers Grove, IL: InterVarsity, 2001.

McKinnon, James W., editor. *Music in Early Christian Literature*. Cambridge Readings in the Literature of Music. Cambridge: Cambridge University Press, 1989.

McKnight, Scot. "From Wheaton to Rome: Why Evangelicals Become Roman Catholic." *Journal of the Evangelical Theological Society* 45 (2002) 451–72.

McLaren Brian D. *Finding Our Way Again: The Return of the Ancient Practices*. Ancient Practices. Nashville: T. Nelson, 2008.

———. *A Generous Orthodoxy*. Grand Rapids: Zondervan, 2004.

———. *A New Kind of Christian: A Tale of Two Friends on a Spiritual Journey*. San Francisco: Jossey-Bass, 2001.

Bibliography

Meer, Frederik van der. *Augustine the Bishop: The Life and Work of a Father of the Church.* Translated by Brian Battershaw and G. R. Lamb. New York: Harper & Row, 1961.

Meier, John. *A Marginal Jew: Rethinking the Historical Jesus*, vol. 3: *Companions and Competitors.* Anchor Bible Reference Library. New York: Doubleday, 2001.

Mendoza, Gerald J. "Why do Catholics Become Evangelicals." *Homiletic and Pastoral Review.* No date. Online: http://www.hprweb.com.

Merdinger, Jane. "Do You Renounce Satan and All his Works? Success and Failure amongst the Catechumenate in Late Roman Africa." Online: http://people.vanderbilt.edu/~james.p.burns/chroma/baptism/merdbapt.html.

Metzger, Bruce M., and Bart D. Ehrman. *The Text of the New Testament: Its Transmission, Corruption, and Restoration.* 4th ed. Oxford: Oxford University Press, 2005.

Meyendorff, John. *Christ in Eastern Christian Thought.* Crestwood, NY: St. Vladimir's Seminary Press, 1975.

Mills, David. "Necessary Doctrines: Why Dogma Is Needed & Why Substitutes Fail." In *Ancient & Postmodern Christianity: Paleo-orthodoxy in the 21st Century; Essays in Honor of Thomas C. Oden*, edited by Kenneth Tanner and Christopher A. Hall, 106–19. Downers Grove, IL: InterVarsity, 2002.

Moll, Rob. "The New Monasticism: A Fresh Crop of Christian Communities is Blossoming in Blighted Urban Settings All Over America." *Christianity Today* 49:9 (September 2005) 38–46.

Moore, Russell D. "Listen Closely." *Touchstone* 19:9 (November 2006) 24–26.

Moorhead, John, translator. *History of the Vandal Persecution* (Victor of Vita). Translated Texts for Historians 10. Liverpool: Liverpool University Press, 1992.

Moreland, J. P. *Love Your God with All Your Mind: The Role of Reason in the Life of the Soul.* Colorado Springs: NavPress, 1997.

Morin, Germain, editor. *S. Hieronymi presbyteri opera, pars II: Opera homiletica.* CCSL 78. Turnhout, Belgium: Brepols, 1958.

———. "Les monuments de la prédication de saint Jérôme." *Revue d'histoire et de littérature religieuses* 1 (1896) 393–434.

Muck, Terry. "God and Oral." *Christianity Today* 31:5 (March 20, 1987) 17.

Mueller, Samuel J. T. "Molanus, Lutheran Irenicist (1633–1722)." *Church History* 22:3 (September 1953) 197–218.

Murray, Stuart. *Church after Christendom.* Carlisle: Paternoster, 2005.

———. *Post-Christendom: Church and Mission in a Strange New World.* Carlisle: Paternoster, 2004.

Musurillo, Herbert, editor and translator. *The Acts of the Christian Martyrs.* OECT. Oxford: Clarendon, 1972.

Neander, August. *General History of the Christian Religion and Church.* Translated by Joseph Torrey. 5 vols. Edinburgh: T. & T. Clark, 1853.

Need, Stephen W. *Truly Divine and Truly Human: The Story of Christ and the Seven Ecumenical Councils.* Peabody, MA: Hendrickson, 2008.

Neill, Stephen W. *A History of Christian Missions.* London: Penguin, 1991.

Nettles, Tom J. "An Encouragement to Use Catechisms." *Founders Journal* 12/13 (1993) no pages. Online: http://www.founders.org/journal/fj10/article3.html.

Nettleton, David. "A Limited Message or a Limited Fellowship." *Baptist Bulletin* 21:7 (December 1955) 11–12.
Neuner, J., and J. Dupuis, editors. *The Christian Faith in the Doctrinal Development of the Catholic Church.* Rev. ed. New York: Alba House, 1982.
Newbigin, Lesslie. *The Gospel in a Pluralist Society.* Grand Rapids: Eerdmans, 1989.
Nicholls, Bruce J. "Towards a Theology of Gospel and Culture." *Gospel & Culture*, edited by John Stott and Robert T. Coote, 69–82. Pasadena, CA: William Carey Library, 1979.
Nichols, Stephen J. *For Us and For Our Salvation: The Doctrine of Christ in the Early Church.* Wheaton, IL: Crossway, 2007.
Niebuhr, H. Richard. *Christ and Culture.* New York: Harper & Row, 1951.
Noll, Mark A. *The Scandal of the Evangelical Mind.* Grand Rapids: Eerdmans, 1994.
Norris, Richard A. "Theology and Language in Irenaeus of Lyon." *Anglican Theological Review* 76 (1994) 285–95.
Novak, Ralph Martin, Jr., editor. *Christianity and the Roman Empire: Background Texts.* Harrisburg, PA: Trinity, 2001.
Nuñez, Emilio Antonio. *Liberation Theology.* Translated by Paul E. Sywulka. Chicago: Moody, 1985.
Oberhelman, Steven M. *Rhetoric and Homiletics in Fourth-Century Christian Literature: Prose Rhythm, Oratorical Style, and Preaching in the Works of Ambrose, Jerome, and Augustine.* American Classical Studies 26. Atlanta: Scholars, 1991.
Ochagavía, Juan. *Visibile Patris Filius: A Study of Irenaeus' Teaching on Revelation and Tradition.* OrChrAn 171. Rome: Pontifical Institute of Oriental Studies, 1964.
Oden, Thomas C. *After Modernity—What?* Grand Rapids: Zondervan, 1990.
———. "Fighting about the Fathers." *First Things* 94 (June/July 1999) 2–7.
———. *How Africa Shaped the Christian Mind: Rediscovering the African Seedbed of Western Christianity.* Downers Grove, IL: InterVarsity, 2007.
———. *Life in the Spirit.* Systematic Theology 3. San Francisco: Harper & Row, 1992.
———. *The Living God.* Systematic Theology 1. San Francisco: Harper & Row, 1987.
———. *The Rebirth of Orthodoxy: Signs of New Life in Christianity.* San Francisco: HarperCollins, 2002.
———. *Requiem: A Lament in Three Movements.* Nashville: Abingdon, 1995.
———. "Then and Now: The Recovery of Patristic Wisdom." *Christian Century* 107:36 (December 12, 1990) 1164–68.
———. *The Word of Life.* Systematic Theology 2. San Francisco: Harper & Row, 1989.
O'Keefe, John J., and R. R. Reno. *Sanctified Vision: An Introduction to Early Christian Interpretation of the Bible.* Baltimore: Johns Hopkins University Press, 2005.
Olson, Roger E. *Pocket History of Evangelical Theology.* Downers Grove, IL: InterVarsity, 2007.
Osborn, Eric. "Was Tertullian a Philosopher?" *Studia Patristica* 31 (1997) 322–34.
Outler, Albert C. "Origen and the *Regulae Fidei.*" *Second Century* 4 (Fall 1985) 133–41.
Ouweneel, W. J. *What Is the Sonship of Christ?* Sunbury, PA: Believers Bookshelf, 1976.
Packer, J. I. "A Stunted Ecclesiology?" In *Ancient & Postmodern Christianity: Paleo-orthodoxy in the 21st Century; Essays in Honor of Thomas C. Oden*, edited by Kenneth Tanner and Christopher A. Hall, 120–27. Downers Grove, IL: InterVarsity, 2002.

Bibliography

Pagels, Elaine H. *Beyond Belief: The Secret Gospel of Thomas*. New York: Random House, 2003.

Patterson, W. Morgan. *Baptist Successionism: A Critical View*. Valley Forge, PA: Judson, 1969.

Pearson, Birger Albert. *Gnosticism, Judaism, and Egyptian Christianity*. Studies in Antiquity and Christianity. Minneapolis: Fortress, 1990.

Pelikan, Jaroslav, editor. *Luther's Works*. Vol. 1. St. Louis: Concordia, 1958.

Pelikan, Jaroslav, and Valerie Hotchkiss, editors. *Creeds & Confessions of Faith in the Christian Tradition*. Vol. 1. New Haven, CT: Yale University Press, 2003.

Perrin, Nicholas. *Thomas: The Other Gospel*. London: SPCK, 2007.

Philpot, J. C. *The True, Proper, and Eternal Sonship of the Lord Jesus Christ, the Only Begotten Son of God*. 1926. Reprint: Grand Rapids: Sovereign Grace, 1971.

Photius. *Bibliotheca*. Translator unknown. Online: http://www.tertullian.org/fathers/photius_03bibliotheca.htm.

Piepkorn, Arthur C. "Calixt(us), George." In *Lutheran Cyclopedia*, edited by Erwin L. Lueker, 349–50. St. Louis: Concordia, 1954.

Poe, Gary. "E. Glenn Hinson: The Baptist Patristics Scholar." *Review and Expositor* 101 (2004) 589–614.

Porter, Stanley. "Contemporary Church Music." *ChristianWeek*. http://www.christianweek.org/stories/vol21/no06/sacred.html.

Preus, Robert D. *The Theology of Post-Reformation Lutheranism; A Study of Theological Prolegomena*. 2 vols. St. Louis: Concordia, 1970–72.

Rebenich, Stefan. *Jerome*. ECF. London: Routledge, 2002.

Renard, John. "Comparative Theology: Definition and Method." *Religious Studies and Theology* 17 (1998) 3–18.

Reymond, Robert Y. *A New Systematic Theology of the Christian Faith*. Nashville: T. Nelson, 1998.

Ricoeur, Paul. *Time and Narrative*. Vol. 1. Translated by Kathleen McLaughlin and David Pellauer. Chicago: University of Chicago Press, 1983.

Ritchie, Daniel F. N. *The Regulative Principle of Worship*. Longwood, FL: Xulon, 2007.

Robeck, C. M., Jr. "Schaepe, John G." In *Dictionary of Pentecostal and Charismatic Movements*, edited by Stanley M. Burgess and Gary B. McGee, 768–69. Grand Rapids: Zondervan, 1988.

Roberts, Oral. *How to Get Through Your Struggles*. Tulsa: Oral Roberts Evangelistic Association, 1977.

———. *The Miracles of Christ*. Tulsa: Pinoak, 1975.

———. "The Gifts of the Spirit." In *What the Spirit Is Saying to the Churches*, edited by Theodore Runyon, 29–61. New York: Hawthorne, 1975.

Robinson, J. Armitage, editor. *Clement of Alexandria: Quis dives salvetur*. Cambridge, 1897. Reprint: Eugene, OR: Wipf & Stock, 2004.

Robinson, Jeff. "Whitney: Worship Should Be God-Centered and Biblical." *Baptist Press*, November 11, 2003. Online: http://www.bpnews.net/BPnews.asp?ID=17059.

Roll, Susan K. *Toward the Origins of Christmas*. Liturgia Condenda 5. Kampen, Neth.: Kok Pharos, 1995.

Rosenbladt, Rod. "Who Do Televangelists Say That I Am?" In *The Agony of Deceit*, edited by Michael Horton, 107–20. Chicago: Moody, 1990.

Ross, Bob L. *Old Landmarkism and the Baptists*. Pasadena, TX: Pilgrim, 1979.

———. *The Trinity and the Eternal Sonship of Christ*. Pasadena, TX: Pilgrim, 1993.

Rousseau, Philip. *Basil of Caesarea*. Transformation of the Classical Heritage 20. Berkeley, CA: University of California Press, 1994.

———. "The Spiritual Authority of the 'Monk-Bishop': Elements in Some Western Hagiography of the Fourth and Fifth Centuries." *Journal of Theological Studies* 23 (1971) 380–419.

Routh, Martin Joseph. *Reliquiae sacrae, sive, Auctorum fere jam perditorum: secundi Tertiique saeculi post Christum natum quae supersunt*. 5 vols. 2nd ed. Oxford: E Typographeo Academico, 1846–48.

Sahas, Daniel J. "Lent." In *EEC* 2:673–74.

Salmon, Jacqueline L. "Feeling Renewed by Ancient Traditions." *Washington Post*, March 8, 2008. Online: http://www.washingtonpost.com/wp-dyn/content/article/ 2008/03/07/ AR2008030702925_pf.html.

Sample, Robert L. "The Christology of the Council of Antioch (268 CE) Reconsidered." *Church History* 48 (1979) 18–26.

Sandy, D. Brent. *Plowshares & Pruning Hooks: Rethinking the Language of Biblical Prophecy and Apocalyptic*. Downers Grove, IL: InterVarsity, 2002.

Sauer, Val J., Jr. *The Eschatology Handbook: The Bible Speaks to Us Today about End Times*. Atlanta: John Knox, 1981.

Scandrett, Joel. "The Trouble with Tradition: Caveats to Evangelical *Ressourcement*." Unpublished paper presented at the Wheaton Theological Conference, Wheaton, IL, April 2007.

Schaff, Philip. *History of the Christian Church*. Vol. 2: *Ante-Nicene Christianity, A.D. 100–325*. 1884. Reprint: Grand Rapids: Eerdmans, 1966.

Schnabel, Eckhard. *Early Christian Mission: Paul and the Early Church*. Vol 2: *Paul & the Early Church*. Downers Grove, IL: InterVarsity, 2004.

Schüssler, Hermann. *Georg Calixt: Theologie und Kirchenpolitik; eine Studie zur Ökumenizität des Luthertums*. Veröffentlichungen des Instituts für Europäische Geschichte Mainz 25. Wiesbaden: F. Steiner, 1961.

Sennott, Thomas M. *On Exonerating Pelagius*. Winchester, NH: Crusade of Saint Benedict Center, 1991.

Serfass, Adam. "Wine for Widows: Papyrological Evidence for Christian Charity in Late Antique Egypt." In *Wealth and Poverty in Early Church and Society*, edited by Susan R. Holman, 88–102. Holy Cross Studies in Patristic Theology and History. Grand Rapids: Baker, 2008.

Seventh-Day Adventists Believe: A Biblical Exposition of 27 Fundamental Doctrines. Washington, DC: General Conference of Seventh-Day Adventists, 1988.

Shelton, W. Brian. *Martyrdom from Exegesis in Hippolytus: An Early Church Presbyter's Commentary on Daniel*. Studies in Christian History and Thought. Milton Keynes, UK: Paternoster, 2008.

———. "Resounding the Chicago Call: A Plea to Restore Evangelicalism's Theological and Historical Foundation." *Reformation & Revival* 13 (2004) 43–47.

Bibliography

Sider, Ron. *The Scandal of the Evangelical Conscience: Why Are Christians Living Just Like the Rest of the World?* Grand Rapids: Baker, 2005.

Simonetti, Manlio. "Arius–Arians–Arianism." In *EEC* 1:76–78.

Sire, James W. *Habits of the Mind: Intellectual Life as a Christian Calling.* Downers Grove, IL: InterVarsity, 2000.

Sloan, Karen. *Flirting with Monasticism: Finding God on Ancient Paths.* Downers Grove, IL: InterVarsity, 2006.

Smith, Joseph P., editor and translator. *Proof of the Apostolic Preaching* (Irenaeus). ACW 16. Westminster, MD: Newman, 1952.

Smither, Edward L. *Augustine as Mentor: A Model for Preparing Spiritual Leaders.* Nashville: B & H Academic, 2008.

Snyder, Graydon F. *Ante Pacem: Archaeological Evidence of Church Life before Constantine.* Macon, GA: Mercer University Press, 1985.

Sordi, Marta. *The Christians and the Roman Empire.* Translated by Annabel Bedini. London: Routledge, 1994.

Souter, Alexander, editor. *Pseudo-Augustini quaestiones veteris et novi testamenti CXXVII.* Vienna: Tempsky, 1908.

Spener, Philipp Jacob. *Pia Desideria.* Edited and translated by Theodore G. Tappert. Philadelphia: Fortress, 1964.

Spurgeon, C. H. *Lectures to My Students.* 2nd ed. 1885. Reprint: Grand Rapids: Zondervan, 1979.

Stark, Rodney. *The Rise of Christianity: A Sociologist Reconsiders History.* Princeton: Princeton University Press, 1997.

Steinhauser, Kenneth B. "The Aesthetics of Paradise: Images of Women in Christian Antiquity." In *Equal at the Creation: Sexism, Society, and Christian Thought,* edited by Joseph Martos and Pierre Hégy, 49–66. Toronto: University of Toronto Press, 1998.

Sterk, Andrea. *Renouncing the World Yet Leading the Church: The Monk-Bishop in Late Antiquity.* Cambridge, MA: Harvard University Press, 2004.

Stovall, Charles B. *Baptist History and Succession.* Booneville, KY: Kentucky Mountain Baptist Schools, 1945.

Svigel, Michael J. "The Phantom Heresy: Did the Council of Ephesus (431) Condemn Chiliasm?" *Trinity Journal* 24 (2003) 105–12.

Sweet, Leonard, editor. *The Church in Emerging Culture: Five Perspectives.* Grand Rapids: Zondervan, 2003.

Tabbernee, William. "To Pardon or not to Pardon?: North African Montanism and the Forgiveness of Sins." *Studia Patristica* 36 (2001) 375–86.

Teske, Roland, translator. *Letters 100–155* (Augustine). Edited by Boniface Ramsey. WSA pt. 2, vol. 2. Hyde Park, NY: New City, 2004.

Tighe, William J. "Calculating Christmas." *Touchstone* 16:10 (December 2003). Online: http://touchstonemag.com/archives/article.php?id=16-10-012-v.

Tollinton, R. B., translator. *Selections from the Commentaries and Homilies of Origen.* New York: Macmillan, 1929.

Tolson, Jay. "A Return to Tradition." *U.S. News & World Report,* December 24, 2007, 42–48.

Toon, Peter. "English Strict Baptists." *Baptist Quarterly* 21 (1965) 30–36.

———. *Yesterday, Today and Forever: Jesus Christ and the Holy Trinity in the Teaching of the Seven Ecumenical Councils*. Swedesboro, NJ: Preservation, 1996.

Torrance, T. F. *Theology in Reconciliation: Essays towards Evangelical and Catholic Unity in East and West*. Grand Rapids: Eardmans, 1975. Reprint: Eugene, OR: Wipf & Stock, 1996.

Toussaint, Stanley D. *Behold the King: A Study of Matthew*. Portland: Multnomah, 1980.

Trebilco, Paul R. "Christian Communities in Western Asia Minor into the Early Second Century: Ignatius and Others as Witnesses against Bauer." *Journal of the Evangelical Theological Society* 49 (2006) 17–44.

Trevijano Etcheverría, Ramón M. "Orígenes y la 'regula fidei.'" In *Origeniana: Premier Colloque International des Etudes Origéniennes*, edited by Henri Crouzel, Gennaro Lomiento, and Josep Rius-Camps, 327–38. Quaderni di "Vetera Christianorum" 12. Bari, Italy: Istituto di Letteratura Christiana Antica, 1975.

"2000 Baptist Faith and Message." Online: http://www.sbc.net/bfm/ bfm2000.asp.

Vaggione, Richard Paul, editor. *The Extant Works* (Eunomius). Oxford Early Christian Texts. Oxford: Clarendon, 1987.

Vailhé, S. "Corrupticoles." In *Dictionnaire de théologie catholique: contenant l'exposé des doctrines de la théologie catholique*, edited by A. Vacant, E. Mangenot, and É. Amman, vol. 3, pt. 2, pp. 1911–13. Paris: Librairie Letouzey et Ané, 1938.

Vallée, Gérard. *A Study in Anti-Gnostic Polemics: Irenaeus, Hippolytus, and Epiphanius*. Studies in Christianity and Judaism 1. Waterloo, ON: Wilfrid Laurier University Press, 1981.

Van Slyke, Daniel G. "The Changing Meanings of *sacramentum*: Historical Sketches." *Antiphon* 11 (2007) 245–79.

Veith, Gene Edward, Jr. *Postmodern Times: A Christian Guide to Contemporary Thought and Culture*. Turning Point Christian Worldview. Wheaton, IL: Crossway, 1994.

Viola, Frank, and George Barna. *Pagan Christianity? Exploring the Roots of Our Church Practices*. Rev. ed. Wheaton, IL: Tyndale, 2008.

Walker, Andrew, and Luke Bretherton, editors. *Remembering Our Future: Explorations in Deep Church*. Carlisle, UK: Paternoster, 2007.

Walvoord, John F. *Jesus Christ Our Lord*. Chicago: Moody, 1969.

Ward, Karen. "The Emerging Church and Communal Theology." In *Listening to the Beliefs of Emerging Churches: Five Perspectives*, edited by Robert Webber, 159–182. Grand Rapids: Zondervan, 2007.

Watkins, Oscar D. *A History of Penance*. Vol. 1: *The Whole Church to A.D. 450*. New York: B. Franklin, 1961.

Wax, Trevin. "Evangelicalism's Blast from the Past." Online: http://trevinwax.com/2008/ 02/12/evangelicalisms-blast-from-the-past.

Webb, William J. *Slaves, Women & Homosexuals: Exploring the Hermeneutics of Cultural Analysis*. Downers Grove, IL: InterVarsity, 2001.

Webber, Robert. *Ancient-Future Evangelism: Making Your Church a Faith-Forming Community*. Ancient-Future Faith. Grand Rapids: Baker, 2003.

———. *Ancient-Future Faith: Rethinking Evangelicalism for a Postmodern Word*. Ancient-Future Faith. Grand Rapids: Baker, 2008.

Bibliography

———. *Ancient-Future Worship: Proclaiming and Enacting God's Narrative.* Ancient-Future Faith. Grand Rapids: Baker, 2008.
———. "The Call to an Ancient-Evangelical Future." Online: http://www.aefcenter.org/read.html.
———. *Common Roots: A Call to Evangelical Maturity.* Grand Rapids: Zondervan, 1978.
———, editor. *Listening to the Beliefs of Emerging Churches: Five Perspectives.* Grand Rapids: Zondervan, 2007.
———. *Signs of Wonder: The Phenomenon of Convergence in the Modern Liturgical and Charismatic Churches.* Nashville: Star Song, 1994.
———. *Worship Old & New: A Biblical, Historical, and Practical Introduction.* Rev. ed. Grand Rapids: Zondervan, 1994.
———. *The Younger Evangelicals: Facing the Challenges of the New World.* Grand Rapids: Baker, 2002.
Webber, Robert, and Donald G. Bloesch, editors. *The Orthodox Evangelicals: Who They Are and What They Are Saying.* Nashville: T. Nelson, 1978.
Weinrich, William C. "Death and Martyrdom: An Important Aspect of Early Christian Eschatology." *Concordia Theological Quarterly* 66 (2002) 327–38.
———, editor. *Revelation.* ACCS, New Testament 12. Downers Grove, IL: InterVarsity, 2005.
Wells, David F. *The Courage to Be Protestant: Truth-Lovers, Marketers, and Emergents in the Postmodern World.* Grand Rapids: Eerdmans, 2008.
———. "The Nature and Function of Theology." In *The Use of the Bible in Theology: Evangelical Options*, edited by Robert K. Johnston, 175–99. Atlanta: John Knox, 1985.
———. "Reservations about Catholic Renewal in Evangelicalism." In *The Orthodox Evangelicals: Who They Are and What They Are Saying*, edited by Robert Webber and Donald G. Bloesch, 213–24. Nashville: T. Nelson, 1978.
Wellum, Stephen J. "Standing on the Shoulders of Giants." *Southern Baptist Journal of Theology* 12 (2008) 2–3.
White, Barrington R. "Why Bother with History?" *Baptist History and Heritage* 4 (1969) 85.
White, L. Michael. *The Social Origins of Christian Architecture.* Vol 1: *Texts and Monuments for the Christian Domus Ecclesiae in Its Environment.* Valley Forge, PA: Trinity, 1990.
Wigram, W. A. *The Separation of the Monophysites.* London: Faith, 1923.
Wilhite, David E. *Tertullian the African: An Anthropological Reading of Tertullian's Context and Identities.* Millennium-Studien 14. Berlin: de Gruyter, 2007.
Wilken, Robert L. *Remembering the Christian Past.* Grand Rapids: Eerdmans, 1995.
———. *The Spirit of Early Christian Thought: Seeking the Face of God.* New Haven, CT: Yale University Press, 2003.
Willard, Dallas. *The Spirit of the Disciplines: Understanding How God Changes Lives.* San Francisco: HarperCollins, 1988.
Williams, D. H. *Evangelicals and Tradition: The Formative Influence of the Early Church.* Evangelical Ressourcement. Grand Rapids: Baker Academic, 2005.
———, editor. *The Free Church and the Early Church: Bridging the Historical and Theological Divide.* Grand Rapids: Eerdmans, 2002.

———, editor. *Tradition, Scripture, and Interpretation: A Sourcebook of the Ancient Church*. Evangelical Ressourcement. Grand Rapids: Baker Academic, 2006.

———. *Retrieving the Tradition and Renewing Evangelicalism: A Primer for Suspicious Protestants*. Grand Rapids: Eerdmans, 1999.

———. "*Similis et Dissimilis*." In *Ancient Faith for the Church's Future*, edited by Mark Husbands and Jeffrey P. Greenman, 69–89. Downers Grove, IL: InterVarsity, 2008.

Williams, Rowan. "Arianism." In *EEC* 1:107–11.

———. *Arius: Heresy and Tradition*. Rev. ed. Grand Rapids: Eerdmans, 2002.

———. *Why Study the Past? The Quest for the Historical Church*. Grand Rapids: Eerdmans, 2005.

Winter, Bruce W. "Gallio's Ruling on the Status of Early Christianity (Acts 18:14–15)." *Tyndale Bulletin* 50 (1999) 213–24.

Wipszycka, Ewa. "Diaconia." In *The Coptic Encyclopedia*, edited by Azis S. Atiya, 3:895–97. New York: Macmillan, 1991.

Witvliet, John D. "Embodying the Wisdom of Ancient Liturgical Practices: Some Old-Fashioned Rudimentary Euchology for the Contemporary Church." In *Ancient Faith for the Church's Future*, edited by Mark Husbands and Jeffrey P. Greenman, 189–215. Downers Grove, IL: InterVarsity, 2008.

Yarnold, Edward. *The Awe-Inspiring Rites of Initiation: The Origins of the RCIA*. 2nd ed. Collegeville, MN: Liturgical, 1994.

Young, Robin Darling. "Texts Have Consequences." *First Things* 91 (March 1999) 41.

Zeller, George W. "A Critique of John MacArthur's Booklet 'The Sonship of Christ.'" Unpublished paper presented to the National Executive Committee of the Independent Fundamental Churches of America, November 1991.

———. "A Doctrinal Crisis: The IFCA and Doctrinal Integrity." Middletown, CT: Middletown Bible Church, 1992.

Zeller, George W., and Renald E. Showers. *The Eternal Sonship of Christ*. Neptune, NJ: Loizeaux Brothers, 1993.

Zuck, Roy B. *Basic Bible Interpretation*. Wheaton, IL: Victor, 1991.

Zumkeller, Adolar. *Augustine's Ideal of the Religious Life*. Translated by Edmund Colledge. New York: Fordham University Press, 1986.

www.ingramcontent.com/pod-product-compliance
Lightning Source LLC
Chambersburg PA
CBHW050438240426
43661CB00055B/2431